Littoral of the Letter

The Bucknell Studies in Latin American Literature and Theory Series Editor: Aníbal González, Pennsylvania State University

Dealing with far-reaching questions of history and modernity, language and selfhood, and power and ethics, Latin American literature sheds light on the multi-faceted nature of Latin American life, as well as on the human condition as a whole. This series of books provides a forum for some of the best criticism on Latin American literature in a wide range of critical approaches, with an emphasis on works that productively combine scholarship with theory. Acknowledging the historical links and cultural affinities between Latin American and Iberian literatures, the series welcomes consideration of Spanish and Portuguese texts and topics, while also providing a space of convergence for scholars working in Romance studies, comparative literature, cultural studies, and literary theory.

Titles in Series

Littoral of the Letter

Saer's Art of Narration

Gabriel Riera

Lewisburg
Bucknell University Presses

Associated University Presses
2010 Eastpark Boulevard
Cranbury, NJ 08512

The paper used in this publication meets the requirements of the American National Standard for Permanence of Paper for Printed Library Materials Z39.48-1984.

Library of Congress Cataloging-in-Publication Data

Riera, Gabriel.
    Littoral of the letter : Saer's art of narration / Gabriel Riera.
        p. cm.
    Includes bibliographical references and index.
    ISBN-10: 0-8387-5665-4 (alk. paper)
    ISBN-13: 978-0-8387-5665-2 (alk. paper)
    1. Saer, Juan José, 1937—Criticism and interpretation. 2. Narration (Rhetoric)
I. Title.

PQ7797.S22435Z85 2006
863'.64—dc22

                                    2006008746

PRINTED IN THE UNITED STATES OF AMERICA

A Silvia

Contents

Acknowledgments

THE RESEARCH FOR THIS BOOK WAS MADE POSSIBLE BY THE GENEROUS support of two Princeton University research grants.

Versions of this work are forthcoming in *Revista Iberoamericana* (2006); others have appeared in the *Encyclopædia of the French Atlantic*, edited by Bill Marshall, Oxford, ABC-Clio (2005): *Revista de Crítica Literaria Latinoamericana*, 57 (November 2003): 91–106; and *MLN*, 111, no. 2 (1986), 368–90. I thank the editors for authorizing me to reproduce these materials.

List of Abbreviations

EZ	*En la zona*
R	*Responso*
PH	*Palo y hueso*
VC	*La vuelta completa*
UL	*Unidad de lugar*
LR	*El limonero real*
M	*La mayor*
NNN	*Nadie nada nunca*
EE	*El entenado*
JJS	*Juan José Saer por Juan José Saer*
G	*Glosa*
RO	*El río sin orillas*
P	*La pesquisa*
CF	*El concepto de ficción*
NO	*La narración-objeto*
CC	*Cuentos completos* (1957–2000)
W	*The Witness*
I	*The Investigation*
NN	*Nobody Nothing Never*

Littoral of the Letter

Introduction: A Literature
without Attributes or
For an Ethics of Writing

CHARACTERIZED BY AN UNCOMMON COHERENCE AND RIGOR, JUAN JOSÉ Saer's writing defies simple categories. In both his fictional and essayistic writing Saer defamiliarizes the reader by questioning some of his most cherished certainties, especially those having to do with the role ascribed to Latin American literature, the uses of prose and poetry in the present, and the relation between language and the mass media. In the 1970s European critics saw the novel's future in the Latin American literature then being produced.[1] This was a future epitomized by the novel of the Boom and magical realism, where novelistic intrigue still played a central role and there was an unproblematic contiguity between reality and language. To this view Saer responded by declaring that the novel is a historically finished genre.[2] And if Latin American intellectuals enthusiastically endorsed the baroque as a way of characterizing the continent's permanent modernity, constructed out of the cultural debris from the centers of power,[3] Saer posited a "literature without attributes."[4] Critics have hardly begun to assess the implications of a project like Saer's that places itself against the grain of dominant cultural discourses and refuses to subordinate literary writing to any preexisting agenda.

Neither "Latin American" à la Boom, nor "baroque" nor even "regional," Saer's literature is precisely "without attributes" and it is also because of its "eccentricity" with respect to the Argentine literary canon. It therefore cannot be considered the expression of a particular personality trait or the endorsement of a reactive ideology, but rather the mark of literature's loyalty to its own post-artistic condition. Saer's is not an idealistic gesture that seeks to preserve the purity of the literary against the invasive threat of more popular cultural manifestations that are, perhaps, better equipped to survive in a neo-liberal market economy. A literature without attributes speaks of the *anomaly* literary writing has become and, in this sense, it is also an affirmation of fidelity to a historical mutation that, by a movement that is both internal and external, has deprived literature of any certainty, of any essence able to justify its right to exist. This is a complex process through which literature, stripped of its classical attributes, exposes itself to an absence of norm—what here we will call *anomaly*.[5]

Illegitimate, orphan, and bastard (*entenada*): Saer's literary writing is loyal to its own historical regime; it is the survivor of a double disaster that put an end to the notion of writing as a social endeavor guided by an essence or regulative Idea ("Art," "Revolution") and whose legacy has been a multiplicity without figure, law, model, or canon. Without subject or object, this survivor Saer aptly calls "writing without attributes" arranges the ruins of traditions (the center/periphery hierarchy) and genres (novel, story, poem) without covering up the void that is precisely its impossible condition of possibility (anomaly or lack of norm).[6] According to its own means and procedures, it also resists the ravages of a new regulative Idea that critical discourse wishes to install in that very void: the Market.

Saer's anomalous characteristics also find parallels in his intellectual trajectory; in the late 1960s he went directly from Santa Fé province (the region known as the Littoral), his place of birth, to Paris without stopping in Buenos Aires, the center of cultural and literary legitimacy at the time. Although he settled in Paris and produced most of his work there, he has not viewed this experience as a cultural initiation, as was the case with many Argentine writers during the nineteenth century and well into the first half of the twentieth century; he has also not produced nostalgic aesthetic myths of Paris, as in Julio Cortazar's *Hopscotch* (1963). Saer's relation to European and French cultures is complex. Saer does not revere European ideas per se but questions the unity of so-called European culture. For him the most significant writers of European modernity (Hölderlin, Flaubert, Mallarmé, Rimbaud, Lautréamont, Kafka, Celan, and Beckett) are not the representatives of cultural greatness or superiority, but evince a permanent conflict with the culture of their time, which often causes isolation, madness, and even suicide.[7] This critique of a monolithic, monumental, peaceful, and progressive vision of European culture affects how Saer conceives his own literary production. Unlike many highly publicized postcolonial writers who nevertheless tend to reaffirm a Eurocentric reading of non-European literatures (Rushdie, Dongala), Saer questions all forms of "Latin Americanism" that privilege an exoticist view (magical and marvelous realisms) and thus assert a European gaze on the Americas, as well as any form of the baroque which is subservient to this gaze. His poetics combines the formal rigor of modern narration with the perceptive intensity of poetic language.[8]

His first texts appeared in the cultural supplement of the newspaper *El Litoral*, where he was editor during 1956 and 1957. During that time, Saer took part in several local literary groups, the most famous of which was *Adverbio,* and through his acquaintance with the poet Juan L. Ortíz collaborated in *Poesía Buenos Aires,* a literary magazine that was influential in the renewal of postmodernist poetic language. Saer also taught film at the Instituto de Cinematografía de Rosario, and before leaving for Europe in 1968 to study film he published several collections of short stories and novels: *En la zona* (1960), *Responso* (1964), *Palo y hueso* (1965), *La vuelta completa* (1966), *Unidad de lugar* (1967), and *Cicatrices* (1969). This is a period dominated by a desire to represent a fragment of reality and is thus influenced by realist aesthetics.

His work will progressively abandon this modality and produce a terse and exact prose, rhythmically arranged according to expressive needs that draw from the poets of the "alchemie du verbe," as in "Sombras sobre vidrio esmerilado" and "La mayor." These two stories are written in "pure prose" and anticipate a long reflection on language and an intense experimentation with the function of narrative prose. It also marks a break with the texts written during the period 1960 to 1968.

In *Cicatrices*, *El limonero real* (1974), *La mayor* (1977), and *Nobody Nothing Never* (*Nadie nada nunca,* 1980), Saer employs narrative procedures that bear similarities to those of the French *nouveau roman*, but which he also finds in the objectivist writing of the Argentine Antonio Di Benedetto. Saer claims that the theories of the novel that some *nouveaux romanciers* proposed are incompatible with their own literary and technical insights. Yet the ways in which his own texts explore a link between objectivism and subjectivism, his questioning of any mimetic form of realism, as well as the permanent tension between representation and what exceeds it, allow us to situate Saer's narrative prose in the context of the narrative avant-garde of the last century. He not only engages it in a productive dialogue, but also solves some of its most pressing technical problems. *The Witness* (*El entenado,* 1983), a text that converses with the *Chronicles of the Indies* and other anthropological accounts, marks a turning point in Saer's conception of narrative fiction. In this text, an account of a sixteenth-century survivor who lives among cannibals for decades, becomes a fable of both the primal scene of the River Plate area and of Saer's own narrative project.

Cicatrices, *Nobody Nothing Never, Glosa* (1986), and *Lo imborrable* (1993) contain elements of the political novel. The first one is set during the historical period that marked a whole generation of Argentine writers, the Peronist government of 1946–55. However, because its formal principles and constructive procedures exceeded the horizon of social realism prevalent at that time, it went almost unnoticed by critics. The other three texts are set during the "dirty war" and propose explorations of the horror and death drive that underlie Argentine society. *The Investigation* (*La pesquisa*, 1995) revisits some of these issues by combining elements of the hard-boiled and the political novel and for the first time brings together Paris and the "zone," the recurring setting of the area around the Paraná River characteristic of Saer's fictional universe. After *The Event* (*La ocasión*, 1988), which earned him Spain's Nadal Prize, and *Las nubes* (1997), Saer published *Lugar* (2000), a collection of stories. His posthumous and unfinished *La grande* has just been published in 2005.

Saer has also published a collection of poems with the suggestive title *El arte de narrar* (1977) and three collections of essays on literature: *El concepto de ficción* (1997), *Una literatua sin atributos* (1988), and *La narración-objeto* (1999). *El río sin orillas* (1991) revisits the narratives of nineteenth-century French and British travelers to the River Plate area, as well as the genre known as the essay of national interpretation. It presents a personal account of Argentine culture that at times intersects with Saer's own fictional prose and must therefore be considered an auto-fiction.

Saer's place within the Argentine literary canon has been fraught with misunderstandings. At times, he was perceived as a "provincial" writer,[9] at others as an "Argentine writer living in France;" Saer's place has always been eccentric.[10] Some of his early experimental works found little reception in Argentina except for a small group of specialized literary journals. It was not until the late 1980s that Saer was legitimized and became a central figure in the Argentine literary system.[11] Since then major publishing houses have constantly reedited his works and translated them into several languages.

My approach to the ensemble of Saer's texts aims neither to look for an internal dialectic nor to develop an exhaustive monographic study, but rather to examine how his texts question their own generic protocols and exhibit their *anomalous* condition: a writing "without attributes." By focusing on a reduced corpus of texts, my goal is to elucidate a series of issues that touch the core of the interpretation of certain fundamental tendencies in contemporary literature. My work takes as its point of departure a precise and well-delimited frame, whose main coordinates are what Saer calls a writing "without attributes," understood as an intraliterary historical sign, but also as a maxim for an ethics of writing; the status of narrative prose and in particular its relation with the poem; the status of the "object-narration" and finally the possibility of producing "encounters" with the real in an age dominated by the image and the products of the culture industry.

The question that guides my reading is how writing can encounter the *real*. Let me state from the outset that the prospects seem to be disheartening: the novel genre (the most regressive forms of detective fiction, of the historical novel, of the family romance, and of autobiographical texts), as well as the movies of the big studios and TV (the products of the "culture industry"), provide the schemas that shape our thoughts and emotions. These schemas respond to only two criteria: gratification and rentability, thus their need for "happy endings," since they tend to affirm a general feeling of nothing really happens here. In the era of televised simulacra (embedded journalism and its symmetrical twin, reality TV), "reality" is a byproduct whose veracity is simply affirmed by marketing techniques and by the debris of novelistic discourses still shaped by nineteenth-century conventions, as if the achievements of the avant-gardes and neo–avant-gardes had no currency whatsoever. "Reality" is the novels and discourses shaped on nineteenth-century novelistic "realist" codes; they not only condition the stereotypical roles we play in our lives, but also their low affective level of investment. If we adapt one of Lacan's formulations, it is possible to claim that "reality" is structured like a fiction.

This fiction is held together by language and by a particular mode of speech, prose, which according to Saer is "the instrument of the State."[12] However, Saer's position consists in implementing narrative prose in opposition to the state's use, against the "reign of the communicable" and against the reductive assimilation of prose theory and that of the novel with which:

> se busca siempre cuando se la interroga . . . la coincidencia de texto y referente. En música, en artes plásticas, en poesía, la ausencia de referente es, por distintas, razones toleradas. La novela no goza de ese beneplácito: *está condenada a arrastrar la cruz del realismo.* A decir verdad, nadie de un modo claro sabe qué es el realismo, pero se exige de la novela que sea realista por la simple razón de que está escrita en prosa. Casi que me atrevería a definir el realismo como el procedimiento que encarna las funciones pragmáticas generalmente atribuidas a la prosa. (NO 58, emphasis mine)

[The theory of prose and the theory of the novel are confused together: what is being sought through it is the correspondence between text and referent. In music, in the plastic arts, in poetry, the absence of the referent is tolerated. The novel does not enjoy that benefit; it is condemned to carry the cross of realism. To be honest, no one really knows for sure what realism is, but it is demanded that the novel be realist for the simple reason that it is written in prose. I would even venture to define realism as the procedure that embodies the pragmatic functions generally attributed to prose.][13]

If realism is threatened by a double colonization (the state and the market) that transforms the historical critical force of this procedure into a dead weight able to fit in within a pragmatic economy, how can the conditions for encountering the real be created? This is the recurring question that each of Saer's texts puts into play. As one of my basic hypotheses I posit that Saer's texts compose the "fiction" *of* this fiction ("reality") and that through this splitting they "soften" their solidified imaginary formations. This softening makes it possible to touch a point of the real in which the sense of *experience* (death, finitude, desire, joy) keeps "speaking" at a time in which nobody wants to hear or know anything of the real. The impossible and unsayable *real*, the unerasable remainder, is what maintains Saer's writing in permanent tension.

The latent poem allows Saer's writing to subtract prose from the instrumental role that the state assigns it and to change its *function*. He does so by treating the language of prose with a series of *poetic* procedures (the rectification or isolation of certain words; the intensifying expansion of a recollection; the lengthening of the phrase or the phrasing of variations; the comic's sudden outburst) in an attempt to say what exempts itself from the instrumental realism of the state and the market: the unsayable. Two additional procedures must also be added: a limited and recurring repertoire of characters and a highly circumscribed setting (the "zone," the Paraná River's coastline, but also the *pampas*).[14] Saer's writing gives density to what subtracts itself and he does so in the realm of the prose poem. By introducing the term "unsayable" my aim is not to make Saer a mystic or a romantic. What matters here is to signal Saer's relation to a modernity for which language's power of presentation folds itself around an enigma whose "mystery is precisely that all poetics have at their center what cannot be represented."[15]

Saer's "art of narration" (*arte de narrar*) refers to realist prose's very *limit*; a limit that the poets of the "alchemie du verbe" (Rimbaud, Mallarmé, Lautréamont, but also Vallejo, Darío, Juan L. Ortíz) had to confront:

"*the unsayable* is what has neither been thought nor said before the advent of the poem; it is also not the product of an intellectual and logical discovery."[16] The poem's *unsayable* becomes the point of resistance of a prose that aims to subtract itself from the prosaism of the state and the market. If the destiny of the modern poem occurs in its *becoming prose*, for Saer the destiny of prose is played out in the proximity of the prose poem, of the becoming poem of prose.[17] This explains why Saer's writing (its rhythm, syntax, and connections) resembles more the modern poet's inhumanity than the *vraisemblance* of the "realist" novelist.

A strange poet, it is true, since his subjects do not come from the "great" lyric tradition; in Saer horror, death, terror, madness, orgies, and the menace of the feminine body are all prevalent. However, his way of implementing a set of neuter directives ("neither *melancholic* nor *nostalgic*")[18] on the current situation of a writing that has left behind the "time of the promise" and knows that "here nothing is promised but the power to be faithful to what is to come"[19] allows us to speak of Saer as a (post)-modern poet. Consequently, Saer's writing must be placed within the lineage of great modern literature, since in a world deprived of the promise of the Other, it consists of a descent into the very foundations of the symbolic universe. *The Witness* is a good example of how fictional writing draws the fragile frontiers of the speaking subject and touches the scene of primary repression, the bottomless point of the real. In this experience "subject" and "object" reject and confront each other so as to delve into the limit of what can be thought and said.

There is an ethics of writing in Saer since the change in the function of narrative prose shows that the writer "does not give up on his desire," to quote Lacan's famous phrase, but that on the contrary it operates under the maxim "Da lugar a tu deseo" (Make room for your desire).[20] His loyalty to the event called "literary writing" (a writing "without attributes") is a wager against both the deadly simplifications of mediatic pragmatism and the realism that seeks to please the taste of the mass public (recall the aesthetics of the theater troop in *The Witness*). Also, his texts not only "soften" the imaginary formations of "reality," but also shape a series of scenarios that narrate the (impossible) encounters with the real. And although the subject matters Saer chooses may not seem conducive to an "elevated" aesthetic feeling, his poetic prose composes momentary clusters of beauty that render the intensity of existence's inprescriptive fragments. He achieves this through a work of negation (whose main figures are death, exile, and narcissistic blows) but *always* in view of an affirmation. This work of negation is more prevalent and visible in *El limonero real* (1974),

La mayor (1976), and *Nobody Nothing Never*, while the affirmative gesture becomes dominant in *The Witness* due, in part, to the more linear reorganization of the narrative. However, this more streamline pattern is much more problematic than at first seems since the apparent development of the plot in the foreground of the story goes hand in hand with a complex articulation of narration itself: a modulation of its tones and times that César Aira has called Saer's "constructive *savoir faire*."[21]

This constructive know-how supposes a way of treating language that destabilizes its relationship with a referent and therefore exceeds the scope of knowledge (remember the closing lines of *The Witness*: "but knowing is not enough . . . "), as well as of perception. When dealing with Saer we must handle the latter with care.[22] The so-called "school of the gaze" provides a crucial element in the organization of narrative economy: the idea that there is no qualitative difference between subject and object. The gaze's constitutive duplicity plays an active role here; it is a gaze no longer limited to the object's illusory appearance on the side of the observer, which suggests that the object results from the interdependence of the gaze and what is seen. As a consequence of this interdependence, a "realist" aesthetic based upon a binary system and belief in the existence of an autonomous, solid, and well-defined preexisting world loses ground, thus compelling writers to develop alternative models. In the *nouveau roman* and in Saer's texts, there is no such thing as an absolute point of view. Always implicated in the body of the observer, the point of view necessarily evinces a fracture of knowledge in whose fault-line arises the constitutive enigma of the partial apprehension of things. The relation body-world is not exhaustive because it is experienced as an escape of the inner core to the outside, an "extimate" space that covers no objective virtual outside.[23]

Therein lies the need to replace perception with the term *percepts*,[24] since the former tends to suggest an object-subject binary relation while the "extimate" real is the only dimension accessible to a fragmentary consciousness. *Percepts* also allow us to separate the residues of a "natural" pre-comprehension of the referent still implicit in perception. Saer is quite clear regarding this last point: "a Reality Prior to the Text gives us the impression of being similar to a First Cause with respect to the appearance of the world."[25] Saer's texts expose perception to a methodical doubt and operate its reduction or bracketing. This explains the persistence of repetition in both *El limonero real* and *Nobody Nothing Never* (in which objectivist and hyperrealist procedures prevail) ,[26] as well as a rhetoric of *rectification* that in *Glosa*, for example, is characteristically signaled by expressions like "so to speak," "to put it that way," "right?," "although there's no sense saying it," "what we call . . ." (*por así decir, como quien dice, ¿no?, aunque no tenga sentido decirlo, de eso que llamamos . . .*). Here we are not simply dealing with signs of an oral dialect[27] but with the markers of a permanent adjustment between the narration's constative and performative dimensions.[28]

Saer's texts come face to face with what interrupts perception. Interruption belongs to the event, the real: it is what *forces* language to produce an image or a name in excess of the laws of communication. What rectification produces is the dissolution of the natural attitude and of the not so natural codes that tend to reaffirm it: realisms, empiricisms, as well as the pregnancy and value that some positive forms of knowledge (sociologisms, historicisms, statistical polls) assert about the real. This is evident in *The Witness* where Father Quesada's and the narrator-protagonist's positions in relation to writing are distributed along two different "slopes of language."[29] While for the former writing "was like pliers for handling the incandescence of the sensible,"[30] an ideal instrument that makes it possible to represent the unknown (the cannibal) according to knowledge validated by ethnographic discourse (the "encyclopedia"), for the latter writing "was like going out to hunt the beast that had already devoured me." In this second slope, writing is characterized by fascination ("for me, fascinated as I was by the force of contingency . . ."),[31] a term that signals the encounter with the real, short-circuits finality, and subtracts writing from the instrumental order validated by the father figure.

We must also not forget that in Saer perception always has a hallucinatory quality and that a *forcing* of perception must occur[32] if the trace of the real, the event, or the unknown ("what persists and remains beyond the fleeting gift of the empirical")[33] is to take place. If writing transgresses the order of knowledge, it is because it responds to the order of truth: "the way in which a truth manifests itself is secondary. What is important is that the truth be discerned."[34] Understood as *speculative anthropology*, fiction thus engages truth: a dimension that exceeds knowledge.[35]

While perception deals with phenomena, the unknown belongs to the enigma. Here I understand enigma in a slightly different sense than what is found in traditional detective fiction; by enigma I mean what installs itself at the very limits of language.[36] This *forcing* of the phenomenon and of perception into enigma is an eminently poetic operation that consists in the production of an image or name (a figure) that, before disappearing, produces a subjective supplement that allows a fidelity to its passage. Saer's ethics of writing lies in the indiscernible character of this fidelity to the event: "we are in agreement that all this belongs to the realm of the conjectural. The evidence comes off and on nearer and farther from words."[37] To say that the event is indiscernible means that it subtracts itself from any type of marking and cannot be treated like an object. The event's indiscernible character demands the production of a poetic image or name; in this production the very possibility of encountering the real occurs as an ethical instance.

Saer's prose isolates and highlights elements through which narrative fiction can be envisioned as an affirmative practice. These are:

1. Movement: displacement from one place to another, exile, errancy, the return;
2. Being or what interrupts the "nothing" there is at the beginning: "the zone," the place, or Place; time and the nature of the present; memory; appearances, perceptions, and sensations that are transfigured into *percepts*; drives, the dreams, and phantasms; the precarious nature of representation;
3. Language;
4. The same and the other.

These elements both determine and are determined by the different procedures in Saer's fictions. These fictions are themselves a thinking of fiction: of its scope and of the nature of its procedures.

In this book, I do not study Saer's work in order to highlight its potential coherence or define the thematic or analytic universe of the author. I focus rather on a series of recurrent questions that involve the status of the subject of writing and language. The singular adventure of a narrative voice that encounters the real reaches a remarkable complexity and heightened intensity in Saer's texts. Inasmuch as it constitutes the (atopic) "center" of each of his texts, it compels us to read both the effects of enunciation (frame, framed narratives, "object-narration") and of writing (the rapport prose-poem, *percepts* or the production of a name/image that interrupts the order of perception and, finally, their ensuing *affects*). And due to the remarkable rigor and thoroughness with which Saer treats this constellation of issues, it also sheds light on that larger spectrum of contemporary literature for which, according to Blanchot, writing begins when it becomes a "question of writing."[38] My approach seeks to make Saer's main narrative procedures explicit, to elucidate the thread that weaves together prose and the poem, percepts and affects, and to bring to the forefront the main features of his ethics of writing: what desire do their texts produce? What is at stake in the act of reading them? My reading differs from other critical assessments of Saer's work that have sought to convert his texts into a more stable and well-defined object by unfolding its inner dialectic in terms of a unique, albeit debatable, structural pattern.

"Littoral of the Letter" is conceived as a cartography of a fluvial "landscape" in which sensations become *percepts,* and the passage to the "other scene" liberates *affects.* "Littoral," because Saer's "zone" is not simply the imaginary contiguous equivalent to the homonymous geopolitical region, but rather an inner image ("Lugar") that occurs when literature is written in the regime called "without attributes." Without subject or object, the text is a block of sensations carved by the chisel of the letter; it is the effigy of the writer's impersonal face and the sensible monument to his world. The "littoral" marks a border between the two domains or territories in which knowledge and joy are placed and, for this reason, the letter that draws this littoral has two sides, a signifying one and a joyous one.[39]

Chapter 1, Saer Before Saer: From "Zone" to "Place," deals with the fundamental coordinates of Saer's fictional universe: the zone, the place, and Place; these are all terms that at first function as operators of literary ideologies crucial for the formulation of a new poetics, but that gradually transform themselves into metafictional signs or signifiers of the "object-narration." Although it is evident that certain biographical elements must be considered, the experience of exile, common to Saer's generation, is more than a biographeme: it acts as the hinge between Saer's relation to Argentine literature (the regional and the more cosmopolitan varieties) and the broader series of European and North American texts with which he entertains a dialogical rapport. This tension inscribes an "external perspective"[40] as well as an experience with language whose outcome is a fundamental reshaping of the traditional binary oppositions and hierarchies that have characterized the Argentine literary system. As an experience of writing, the phrase "literature without attributes" becomes synonymous with exile. This expression ciphers the anomaly of Saer's writing and, at the same time, its ethical maxim. The latter consists of a change in the function of narrative prose by grafting the affective intensity of the poem with the combinatory rigor of narration (whose characteristics borrow much from the narrative neo-avant-gardes of the 1950s and 1960s).

Chapter 2, Littoral, Literal: The Joys of the Letter, focuses on Saer's grafting of poetic language onto narration, on the objectivist and hyperrealist narrative procedures he employs in order to redefine the function of narrative prose, and on how he situates his poetics with regard to the narrative experiments of the neo-avant-garde of the 1950s and 1960s. Finally, the chapter traces how Saer's "zone," the littoral, becomes a topological figure in which to read a passage to the "other scene" of perception and representation (the working of dreams and the primary process). This passage also makes it possible to establish a typology of the encounters with the real.

The status of fiction becomes the main focus of chapter 3, where I read *The Witness* in light of Saer's maxim "fiction as speculative anthropology."[41] *The Witness* stages a fable of perception in which percepts and affects weave the "primal scene of the River Plate" and of Saer's own fiction. This text also allows us to formalize the *anomalous* (absence of law) condition of a text that stages the law of narration (paternal, Oedipal) and, at the same time, its transgression. *Anomaly* (the story's "lack of attributes") occurs as an interruption of the order of discourse (of knowledge) and the paternal law (the *Relación de Abandonado* by Father Quesada) and as an excess with respect to the intertextual matrix (the *Chronicles of Indies* and classical European ethnological discourse). The text thus inscribes a margin, a space of writing that unfolds between the *fading* of the subject (the narrator protagonist's, who gives up his own identity before writing the text we read) and the object's loss ("the true men" that vanished in part due to the narrator and whose memory he strives to preserve).

Chapter 4, Voices and Tones: History, Memory, and Trauma, is devoted to Saer's treatment of most recent Argentine history, to the status of the historical past in his poetics and, particularly, to how it differs from other literary projects whose main goal has been to render a novelistic revision of the past. If Saer's texts produce encounters with the real, what role does the historical past play? Let's remember that although Saer's fiction traces an epistemological frame, the two dimensions on which it operates are the real and truth and these always exceed or interrupt the order of knowledge. Also, since representation is only one of the threads which Saer uses in order to weave his texts, his main goal cannot be to provide a representation of the past, a "re-writing of history" that seeks to denounce the "official" history and replace it with a more accurate version of the past. For these reasons, the trauma is the temporal trope which subtracts the condition of a dispersed community (due to the repression of the state and ensuing exile) from the schemas of a "novelistic version of Argentine history." Although often claiming a moral and epistemological superiority, these approaches have not necessarily been exempt from simplifications, shortsightedness and, at times, of deadly heroism. Saer's reconfiguration of the literary representation of the past evinces a passage from a tragic paradigm to comedy, from death as the possibility of finitude to finitude as impossibility. This is a painful passage that compels the writer to sustain the inerasable (*lo imborrable*) as the adventure of language. A "literature without qualities" thus reveals its ethical side since it is no longer a question of covering up this void with imaginary formations seeking to reconcile the irreconcilable, but rather to endure this barren real in order to avoid perpetuating the disaster.

Chapter 5, *"Regia victoria"*: Affects and Percepts, brings together insights from chapters 4 and 5 in order to make the function of Saer's desiring machines explicit. Within the framework of narrative representations, pain, sorrow, and horror are themes that bear witness to a series of affects. However, they come from strata older than symbolization or narrative representation. For this reason, I claim that *The Investigation* inscribes a series of residual formations that precede the symbolic order and yet survive its law; consequently, the Oedipal metanarrative that this fiction stages fails to fully subsume them in its own economy. I call these formations a "writing of the affects" and claim that this is the crucial dimension of Saer's desiring machines. For this reason, in *The Investigation* I read a *"regia* (albeit fragile) *victoria"* on this side of the phantasm: the singular affirmation of an encounter with the real. While the order of language and the Oedipal metanarrative regulate the working of the phantasm (therein its transubjective nature), the affects and the vision that is its figure (the *victoria regia*) exceed them and are, therefore, singular.

1

Saer Before Saer:
From "Zone" to "Place"

"In the Zone":
A Place For Saer's Fiction

Saer's literary production can be divided into different phases where important displacements in the constructive principles and shift in dominant materials of his work are discovered. These displacements are crucial for understanding not only the work's development, but also the invariants of his poetics.

The first phase of Saer's literary production includes *En la zona* (1960), a collection of short stories, the nouvelle *Responso* (1964), *Palo y hueso* (1965), short stories, and the novel *La vuelta completa* (1966). This is the period in which Saer gives shape to the main components of his fictional universe: a well-delimited space and a limited and recurring set of characters. Saer calls the space of his literary fictions the "zone" and it includes the city of Santa Fé, Rincón, Colastiné, and the adjacent Paraná River with its islands. In the programmatic short story "Algo se aproxima," Barco, one of the characters, introduces a traditional *topos* in Latin American literature, the city surrounded by nature (el *desierto*) and devoid of a solid cultural tradition, as only the European supposedly possesses; this *topos* is part of the well-known dichotomy civilization/barbarism:

> Por eso me gusta América: una ciudad en medio del desierto es mucho más real que una sólida tradición en el espacio . . . Yo escribiría la historia de una ciudad. No de un país, ni de una provincia: de una región a lo sumo. (CC 517)

> [That's why I like America: a city in the middle of the desert is much more real than a solid tradition in space . . . I would write the history of a city. Not of a country, nor even of a province—of a region at the most.]

28

Like Joyce's Dublin, Saer's zone functions as the repository of experiences and memories. However, one cannot fully assimilate this space to the aesthetics of realism, nor to the spaces of the new emerging poetics of Borges and Cortázar.[1] We can define a zone as the minimal spatial device where encounters among people that express different views on literature and, therefore, encounters with other stories and literary traditions takes place. Although at this stage it functions as a producer of plots, its scope is constantly under scrutiny and revision. "Discusión sobre el término *zona*" (1976), one of *La mayor*'s "Argumentos," questions the demarcating value of the term[2]; from then on "zone" will be transmuted into "lugar" (*place*): the site where narration can encounter the real ("the thick forest of the real")[3] and thus approach universal themes according to the singular nature of the Argentine writer. Finally, in texts written in the 1990s the imagined legitimacy of a "birth place" is done away with and "Lugar" (*Place*) is now capitalized, indicating that the term has acquired an ontological dimension that exceeds the frame of an imaginary region traced over a geographical one.[4]

Going back to the main components of Saer's first published works, there is a limited set of characters that reappear in different works with similar functions. Although this set of characters has some biographical ground, it shapes a recurring procedure dominant in this first phase: a scene that gathers several characters, often a group of friends or colleagues (a barbecue, a party, a reunion at a cafe or bar) in which dialogue is the catalyst of the story (there are multiple subjects of enunciation and at least one of them reflects on literature).[5] A realist representation of a fragment of reality with its peculiar characteristics and its situational determinants dominates these texts.

An important shift takes place in the second phase—*Unidad de lugar* (1967), short stories; *Cicatrices* (1969), a nouvelle; *El limonero real* (1974), a novel; *La mayor* (1976), short stories and the novel *Nobody Nothing Never* (*Nadie nada nunca*, 1980).[6] The texts' constructive principles now come to the forefront. In this reorganization of textual space dialogue is not as frequent and central a procedure and instead a single narrative voice, a narrator in the first person, takes charge of the story (*Cicatrices* being the exception). The problematic nature of a subjective consciousness that perceives a world; the complex co-implication of perception, sensation, and memories play a central role in shaping the stories, as well as the no less difficult status of temporality and, in particular, of the present. This last element plays an important structuring function not only at the level of the text's form but also at the level of enunciation; here it is not only a question of finding formal correlates for the dense fabric of time, but of accounting for the aporia proper to the internal perception of time.

It is possible to consider this second period as a rewriting of the first, as changes in the titles make evident: *En la zona* becomes *Unidad de lugar*. Rewriting is a central device in Saer's work that operates not only at the level of discursive materials, but fundamentally at the level of procedures. The stories of this second period tend to elaborate and complicate some of the most traditional realist procedures of the first period. An important shift in the overall organization of the stories is that metanarrative or the reflective segments dealing with literary issues detach themselves from the history or plot line and begin to operate on the materials and procedures that are, in themselves, enactments of the issues being explored.

The dissolution of the story's intrigue or plot characterizes this phase. In *La mayor* (1976), especially in the stories "La mayor" and "A medio borrar," this dissolution occurs at the level of the phrase. The former employs a new phrastic syntax based upon the hyperbaton, the anaphora, and the use of punctuation marks that tend to break down the statement into smaller cells whose rhythm is more akin to the poem: "Antes, ellos, podían. Mojaban, despacio, en la cocina, en el atardecer, en invierno, la galletita, sopando, y subían . . . (M 11) [Before, they, could. They dunked, slowly, in the kitchen, at dusk, in winter, the cookie, dipping, and raised . . .].[7]

This new phrastic syntax undermines the thetic function of language and is the basic operation of a text whose main goal is to question representation. "A medio borrar" produces a rearrangement of the connotative vector that characterizes the realist descriptive statement, equating the process of perception with the composition of a text:

> Una columna oblícua de luz que entra, férrea, por la ventana, y que deposita, sobre el piso de madera, un círculo amarillo, y en su interior un millón de partículas que rotan, blancas, mientras el humo de mi cigarillo, subiendo desde la cama, entra en ella y se disgrega despacio, en esta mañana de mayo, de la que puedo ver por los vidrios, el cielo azul: la vigilia. (M 55)[8]

> [An oblique column of light that comes, solid, from the window and that leaves, on the wood floor, a yellow circle, and inside a million white rotating particles, while the smoke of my cigarette, rising from the bed, gets inside it and disintegrates slowly, in this morning in May, of which I can see from the window, the blue sky: the vigil.]

In order to assess Saer's aesthetics we need to place it within the intellectual scene of the late 1950s and 1960s, a time when the poetics of writers linked to the *Sur* journal is still in force: Eduardo Mallea and Ernesto Sábato have a central place at this time and their novels revolve around individual psychological conflicts that reach a metaphysical tragic dimension.[9] But there are other poetics that not only take a stand against the psychological novel, but also against realist literature: Jorge Luis Borges's short stories and Adolfo Bioy Casares's novel *Morel's Invention*, as well as Julio Cortázar's *Bestiary* and José Bianco's *La pérdida del reino*. If the psychological novel employs more "elevated" forms of narration, these marginal alternative poetics take their constructive principles and procedures from less prestigious forms: detective fiction and fantastic literature.

The 1960s see the emergence of the journals *Contorno* and *Primera Plana*. While the former produces a major revision of the Argentine literary canon, the second promotes the *Boom*.[10] This is the time of the polemic on realism begun by Georg Lukács whose work is translated by one of *Contorno*'s members: Juan José Sebreli, and of the translations of works by T. W. Adorno and W. Benjamin, which are of crucial importance for Saer's generation. David Viñas's novel best expresses *Contorno*'s idea of literature. However, an important literary event occurs in 1963: the publication of Cortazar's *Hopscotch,* which opens up a new horizon of reading and creates the conditions for engaging in a serious reevaluation of nonrealist literature, such as Borges's. This type of literature was relegated to a marginal place by the ideology of the Sartrean commitment to which most of the realist writers subscribed, although Saer's group seems to be an exception.[11] These are also the years of the *Boom* of Latin American literature, when Borges shares an important international literary price with Samuel Beckett.

Saer's work develops in this context.[12] While *Sur*'s critical discourse authorizes Mallea and Borges's production, *Contorno* authorizes Viñas's. Saer remains on the margin of these critical discourses and finds no legitimacy in the literary sphere. His texts must therefore create their own conditions of reading. But it is not until the 1970s that these conditions find critical resonance. At first critics tend to affiliate him to the regional literary canon, but in 1976 Saer explicitly states that he does not subscribe to its principles and that, like in Borges, the region or zone is a pretext to write about the universe. In his *Literatura y subdesarrollo*, Adolfo Prieto situates Saer's work, especially *Responso*, within the debate on realism and relates some of the novel's techniques to those of film. Prieto however does not mention Borges's influence on Saer's conception of a literary space that, although grounded in a highly clearly demarcated "local" space, is open to universal themes. The idea of grounding a literary project on the foundation of an imaginary space, which also recalls Borges's early writing, is central in the first Saer and is never fully abandoned by him.[13]

This explains why space then becomes an organizing formal element in *En la zona* (1960), a book that is divided in two different parts separated by a poem called "Paso de baile." Space defines characters and histories, but also demarcates distinct spheres: the city, the coast, and the islands that serve to differentiate histories and classes of characters. The first part is set in the port (*orilla* or *margin*), an underworld of criminals and prostitutes. Although this "orilla" is Saer's response to Borges's world of marginal urban characters, in *En la zona* Borges's presence is clear, especially in the conjectural style of "Un caso de ignorancia" and "Bravo"; in the stories that are citations of other stories ("Bruto"); and in characters that are the specular doubles of others ("Los amigos"). These procedures and operations are a clear indication that when defining his narrative poetics Saer makes a conscious choice and, against a realist tradition imbued with social contents, opts for Borges's innovative techniques and conception of literature. However, Saer combines this Borgean *topos* with the narrative techniques of the American hard-boiled novel, which Borges had earlier repudiated.[14]

In the second part of *En la zona*, "Más al centro," Saer's typical characters appear: young writers and intellectuals not fully integrated into the cultural mainstream (Tomatis, Barco, Angel Leto, Marcos, Pichón y el Gato, the Garay twins, Washington Noriega, and so on) These characters recur not only in Saer's narrative prose, but also in his poems. The poetic principle of repetition that Saer applies to both narrative contents and to materials and procedures begins to unfold here.

"Algo se aproxima," the last story in the book, deals with literature's problematic character. The story revolves around a central scene, a get-together that quickly turns sour and that justifies the story's main procedure: dialogue. In this story (but also in the other texts that make up this collection of stories) the narrator's discourse describes objects, behaviors, and gestures, while the character's discourses are of a more reflexive nature and tend to transmit ideas about literature. These scenes of get-togethers, celebrations, and reunions condense biographical elements (the literary groups in which the young Saer used to take part)[15] but, given Saer's marginal place, they must be read as representations of the imaginary place of the writer.

"Algo se aproxima" explicitly posits the question of literature's possibility: how can one create literature in a country devoid of long and enduring traditions? This is a question whose main precedent is Borges's essay

"The Argentine Writer and Tradition," but here Saer raises a series of issues about literature (possible literary models; the writer's situation; the use, value, and richness of the Spanish language; the debate on nationalism vs. Europeanism) as materials for fictional texts that also shape the stories' procedures (a story within the story).[16]

PERCEPTION, MEMORIES AND THE POEM
(FABLES OF DESIRE)

> La aparición del poema en prosa tuvo consecuencias de primera magnitud en la evolución de las formas literarias al liquidar la antigua división retórica entre prosa y poesía.
>
> —Saer, JJS 15

> [The appearance of the prose poem had consequences of the first magnitude in the evolution of literary forms because it did away with the old rhetorical division between prose and poetry.]

Unidad de lugar marks the beginning of Saer's second period. Although all the texts that belong to this period are clearly anchored in the "zone," an important reorganization of narrative space takes place. First, the characters no longer take charge of the stories' metanarrative level (the reflections on literature), which instead becomes autonomous and begins to function directly upon the story's own constructive devices and materials. If in the first period many conventional realist elements were still present, a break becomes evident now. The focal point of the stories is no longer the representation of a given fragment of reality, but their own process of composition. However, it would be a mistake to conclude that Saer's stories are just allegories of their own process of writing. "Sombra sobre vidrio esmerilado," the story that opens *Unidad de lugar*, is a good example of this shift.

"¡Qué complejo es el tiempo, y sin embargo qué sencillo!" (How complex time is and yet how simple!) This opening sentence of the story poses an antithesis that is indicative of the text's function: "Ahora estoy sentada en el sillón de Viena, en el living, y puedo ver la sombra de Leopoldo que se desviste en el cuarto de baño . . . La sombra de Leopoldo se proyecta sobre el vidrio esmerilado (UL 11, 13) (Now I am sitting in the rocking chair in the living room and I can see Leopold's shadow undressing in the bathroom . . . Leopold's shadow projects itself on the frosted glass). We are faced with a reduced set of actions: a first-person narrator, the poet Adeline Flores, sits in a rocking chair in her living room and observes her brother-in-law's shadow projected on frosted glass (*vidrio esmerilado*). This series of actions make up the hypotext or basic story, which is "basic" not only because it is the basis of the story, but also because the set of actions it contains are simple or elementary. The focus of the story is not there, but on a more speculative level that deals precisely with time's complexity, with the dense status of the "now." Adeline Flores's main action consists of reflecting on the mystery of time, while simultaneously she remembers and imagines events of the past and of the immediate present. In the same way that Leopold's actions in the bathroom project a shadow on a treated surface, a glass polished with emery, Adeline's also project a "shadow" (a poem) on the treated surface of the story that, in turns, casts a shadow of desire whose truth is still an open wound. The story, focused on Adeline's reflexive mood, is the history of her internal processes (in fact, the story is narrated as a monologue), as well as the history of how the threads of perception, recollection, and imagination weave a poem. It is possible to schematize the story's overall structure as follows, where the subscript characters mark the process of their transformation:

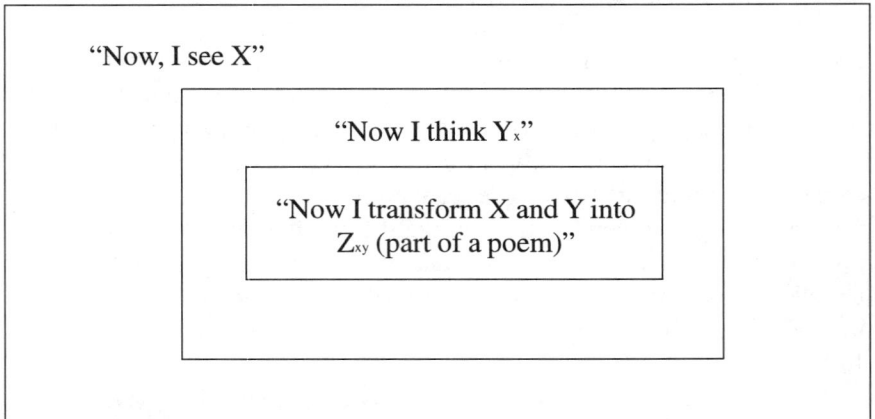

"Now, I see X"

    "Now I think Y_x."

        "Now I transform X and Y into Z_{xy} (part of a poem)"

One can distinguish three different levels in the story: the hypotext or basic story, which focuses on Adeline's mostly visual but also aural perceptions; a second narrative based on Adeline's mental processes, which is narrated as a monologue (this narrative is made up of a family romance, a love story, and episodes of Adeline's public standing as a poet); and, finally, the scene of the poem's composition (what is being written *at the same time* that Adeline sees, thinks, and imagines).

It is tempting to read "Sombras sobre vidrio esmerilado" as a story that simply narrates its own mechanisms of production. This would suppose that the "right" order moves from perception to memory and from memory to the poem, when in fact there are indications that show the process is more complex and that there is an overdetermination of the three threads that weave the story.[17] After all, as soon as the story introduces its focal point, Adeline Flores, in a first-person narrative, a rhetorical question disrupts the space of enunciation. It is not an exaggeration to say that there where Adeline remembers, she does not see, and there where she does not see, she imagines.[18] The waters of reflection are not those of a mirror, but what the text calls " la transparencia del deseo" (the transparency of desire), a more opaque surface than that of "frosted glass."

If the order of reading creates the illusion of a streamline process, the order of writing indicates that the story plays out a scene (the poem's process of composition); it is within this scene that the poem gives the story the "directions" to put a fable of desire into play: a scenario in which the operations of condensation, displacement, and figuration are the main *actants* of the story.[19]

We know that Saer wishes to erase the borders between poetry and prose and that the type of relations these two modalities entertain in this second period are rather complex: the poem not only provides materials for a narrative, but also the structural patterns that defy the linearity of realist storytelling and its syntactical causal connections.[20] This is evident if one takes into account that the poem's "unfolding" at times makes it difficult to read some of the sentences: because it interrupts the story's plot and produces a short-circuit in the reading process. In other words, there where one sees the poem's fragment, one cannot read (the story); there where one reads the story, one cannot see (the poem). In order to imagine what happens between these two series the reader is forced to come up with a paradigmatic and two-faced reading.

The poem contains the story's constructive principle; once written (and nothing bars us from thinking that the poem could have been written beforehand), it is disseminated throughout the story and, in turn, motivates the story to establish a series of connections that "mime" the paradigmatic and associative operations of the poem. The poem both highlights and dissimulates its constructive power. That the poem provides the story's constructive principle becomes evident if we focus on the title of the latter, which is a fragment of the poem. The poem has no title; its first line, which traditionally performs that function, migrates to the story and becomes its title. The story also closes with a brief and separate section with its own title: "Envío" (Envoi), a typical poetic device which here retains one of its traditional and more "narrative" functions: to sum up the poem's theme. So we have a crisscrossing of generic boundaries: the story is structured like a poem and the poetic "conclusion" assumes a narrative form.

What the story wants to capture is the simultaneity (of perceiving, thinking, and imagining) in the process of composing a poem and this is why the "now" is the story's kernel. The interrelation between the three levels displays the complexity of time to which the first line of the story refers: "en este momento, únicamente esa sombra es 'ahora', y el resto del 'ahora' no es más que recuerdo" (at this moment only that shadow is 'now' and the rest of 'now' is no more than memory [UL15]). Adeline's spatial immobility goes hand in hand with the mobility of her thoughts; it is her consciousness that moves back and forth in time. This is a movement that produces a series of temporal imbrications and shifts: "Al hamacarme, yendo para adelante y viniendo para atrás, la sombra da primero la impresión de que avanzara, y después le de retrocediera" (While rocking, going forward and backward, the shadow at first appears to be advancing, and then retreating [UL 21]). The story figures its own proleptic and analeptic shifts.

Adeline's consciousness is at the forefront of the story: a personal discourse told in the first person and presented as an inner monologue organizes the narration. This level of narration recurs regularly through a series of "shifters" ("I," "now," "here"): the text constantly returns to these signifiers each time that the present (Adeline's series of perceptions) appears as the main focus; each of the (re)-turns to this basic level of narration follows an expansion or contraction toward other temporal and spatial dimensions. Since the story is in constant tension between a series of convergences and expansions that tend toward its disintegration, the syntactic level imposes the story's coherence (expressions such as "for that reason" [por eso] and "in this way" [así] that establish connections between sequences are quite common), although at times the parenthetical fragments of the poem transgress the syntactic order of the narrative phrase and disintegrate the sentence. Coherence thus must be secured through "vertical" operations that go well beyond the syntagmatic order of narration: repetitions (anaphors) and associations (metaphors) that are, strictly speaking, operations of the poem.

What does Adeline's consciousness tell us about herself? "Soy la poetisa Adelina Flores. ¿Soy la poetisa Adelina Flores? Tengo cincuenta y seis años y he publicado tres libros: *El camino perdido, Luz a lo lejos* y *La dura oscuridad*" (UL12) [I am the poet Adeline Flores. Am I the poet Adeline Flores? I am fifty-six and I've published three books: *The Lost Path, Light at a Distance* and *Hard Darkness*]. The referential vector of this passage is immediately contaminated by literature (the mention of books, as well as the "narrative," melodramatic pattern that the titles introduce), but also by a syntactical anomaly that touches the very framework of enunciation. An interrogative sentence immediately follows the affirmative one and produces uncertainty as to whom to ascribe the production of meaning: who is the text's subject? The focal point that says, "I am Adeline Flores" refers to the same subject that composes the poem? The text not only renders problematic the level of action, but also the level of enunciation and, as soon as we focus on the central question of temporality through the composition of the poem, the level of the text itself. Let's focus on this last point:

> ¡Qué complejo es el tiempo, y sin embargo qué sencillo! Ahora estoy sentada en el sillón de Viena, en el living, y puedo ver la sombra de Leopoldo que se desviste en el cuarto de baño. Parece muy sencillo al pensar "ahora", pero al descubrir la extension en el espacio de ese "ahora", me doy cuenta enseguida de la pobreza del recuerdo. El recuerdo es una *parte muy chiquita* de cada "ahora" y el resto del "ahora" no hace más que aparecer, y eso muy pocas veces, y de un modo muy fugaz, como recuerdo. La sombra de Leopoldo se proyecta sobre el vidrio esmerilado. (UL 11, my emphasis)

> [How complex time is and yet how simple! Now I am sitting in the rocking chair in the living room and I can see Leopold's shadow undressing in the bathroom. It seems very simple to think of "now," but in discovering the extension in space of that "now," I realize immediately how poor memory is. Memory is only a small part of each "now" and the rest of "now" appears fleetingly, and rarely, as memory. Leopold's shadow projects itself on the frosted glass.]

This passage presents one of Saer's constant preoccupations, which is particularly dominant in the texts of this second phase: the present's complexity. Saer recurs to a Proustian intertext and to a spatial metaphor in order to account for the simultaneity of things that may occur in the present but unfold in different spaces:

> Tomemos el caso de mi seno derecho. En el ahora en que me lo cortaron, ¿cuántos senos crecían lentamente en otros pechos menos gastados por el tiempo que el mío? Y en este ahora que veo la sombra de mi cuñado Leopoldo proyectándose sobre los vidrios de la puerta del cuarto de baño y

llevo la mano hacia el corpiño vacío, relleno de un falso seno de algodón puesto sobre la blanca cicatriz, ¿cuántas manos van hacia cuántos senos verdaderos, con temblor y delicia? Por eso digo que el presente es en gran parte recuerdo y que el tiempo es complejo aunque a la luz del recuerdo parezca de lo más sencillo. (UL 11–12)

[Let's take the case of my right breast. In the now in which they cut it, how many breasts grew in other chests less worn by time than mine? And in this now that I see the shadow of my brother-in-law Leopold projecting itself on the glass of the bathroom door, and I take my hand toward the empty bra, stuffed with a false breast of cotton put over the white scar, how many hands go toward how many real breasts, trembling with pleasure?]

The text sets in motion a network of synecdoches that make up a series of homologies: the now is to the recollection of time what a part is to the whole; in fact it is the visible part of an invisible or only fleeting visible whole. But the breaking down of the whole into parts affects all levels of the story: Adeline's body (that lacks a part, her right breast); Leopold's visible shadow but also his body (whose sexual organ is the only part Adeline has stamped on her memory since the day she saw him having sexual relations with her own sister); what she can now tolerate seeing, the top half of Leopold's body; the poem, which is an array of parts that, at times, disrupt the whole of the story and, finally, the "Envoi," the detached "conclusion" of Adeline's story. "Sombras" presents a fable of desire that revolves around four partial objects: the gaze, the voice, the breast and the phallus, and it is their interplay that tells the truth of Adeline's desire.[21]

Adeline's fable of desire is suspended between two poles: mutability and immutability. Her body bears a mutilation (according to Tomatis) or a scar (according to Adeline):

Advierto que tengo la mano sobre el puñado de algodón que le da forma al corpiño en la parte derecha de mi cuerpo, y bajo la mano. He visto crecer y cambiar ciudades y países como a seres humanos, pero nunca he podido soportar ese cambio en mi cuerpo. Ni tampoco el otro: porque aunque he permanecido intacta, he visto con el tiempo alterarse esa aparente mutabilidad. (UL13)

[I realize that I have my hand over the clump of cotton that gives form to the bra in the right part of my body, and I lower my hand. I have seen cities and countries change and grow like human beings, but I have never been able to tolerate that change in my body. The other one either—because even though I have remained intact I have seen the apparent mutability change with time.]

Even after Tomatis's admonition Adeline's poem barely breaks with the sonnet's straitjacket:

> Veo una sombra sobre un vidrio. Veo
> Algo que amé hecho sombra y proyectado
> Sobre la transparencia del deseo
> Como sobre un cristal esmerilado.
> [I see a shadow on glass. I see
> Something I loved made shadow and projected
> Over the transparency of desire
> Like frosted glass]

> En confusion, súbitamente, apenas,
> Ví la explosion de un cuerpo y de su sombra
> Ahora el silencio teje cantilenas
> Que duran más que el cuerpo y que la sombra
> [In confusion, suddenly, hardly,
> I saw the explosion of a body and its shadow
> Now the silence weaves cantilenas
> That last more than a body and its shadow]

> Ah, si un cuerpo nos diese, aunque no dure,
> Cualquier señal oscura de sentido
> Como un olor salvaje
> Contra las formaciones del olvido

> [Oh, if a body would give us, even if it does not last,
> Any sign, however dark, of sense
> Like a savage smell
> Against forms of forgetting]

> Y que por ese olor reconozcamos
> Cuál es el sitio *de la casa humana*
> Como reconocemos por los ramos
> De luz solar la piel de la mañana.

> [So that by that smell we could recognize
> The site of the human house
> Just like we recognize by its branches
> Of sunlight the skin of the morning]

The poem (which I reconstructed by pasting together its different fragments) consists of four quartets of hendecasyllabic verses, a traditional form related to the sonnet. The poem recognizes the loved lost object as the truth of the speaker's desire and thus becomes the lasting substitute for what still remains, a shadow. The poem laments the absence of clear signs that would be equivalent to the transparency of desire. The kernel of the poem is the traumatic event of Adeline's family romance, as the intertextual mention of Alfonsina Storni's poem makes clear (line 16). One should remember that the day Adeline saw her sister Susan having sexual relations with Leopold she had been reciting Alfonsina Storni's poems "y cuando llegué a donde dice 'Una punta de cielo / rozará *la casa humana*', me separé de ellos y me fui lejos, entre los árboles para ponerme a llorar" (and when I got up to where it says *"A point of the sky / will graze the human house,"* I left them and went far away between the trees so I could cry [UL 22, my emphasis]).

The poem's glass (*vidrio esmerilado* or frosted glass) casts a shadow on Adeline's "transparency of desire," a desire that seeks to refute the mother's desire as well as Tomatis's. But it is also a desire that hopes for "a dark signal of meaning." The sense of the poem is the story, but the story proves that the truth of desire eludes meaning. After returning home from a literary round-table where she is admonished by the irreverent Tomatis to abandon the straitjacket of the sonnet form and "fornicate more often", Adeline states:

La niebla envolvía la ciudad; parecía vapor, y la luz de los focos de las esquinas parecía un polvo *blanco* y húmedo; una miríada de partículas *blancas* girando en lenta rotación . . . Afuera no había más que niebla; pero yo vi tantas cosas en ellas, que ahora no puedo recordar más que unas pocas: unos sauces inclinados sobre el agua, proyectando una sombra transparente; unas manos aferradas—los huesos y los cartílagos *blanquísimos*—a las solapas de mi traje sastre; una mosca entrando a una boca abierta; algunas palabras leídas mil veces, sin acabar nunca de entenderlas; un millón de cigarras cantando monótonamente y al unísono ("del olvido"), en el interior de mi cráneo; una cosa horrible, llena de venas y nervios, apuntando hacia mí, balanceándose pesadamente desde un matorral de pelo oscuro; una imagen borrosa impresa en papel de diario, hecha mil pedazos y arrojada al viento por una mano enloquecida. Todo esto era visible en las paredes mojadas por la niebla, mientras el taxi atravesaba la ciudad. Y era lo único visible. (UL 36–7, my emphasis)

[The fog covered the city; it looked like vapor and the lights in the street corners looked like *white* humid dust; a myriad *white* particles moving in slow rotation . . . Outside there was only the fog, but I saw so many things in it that now I can only remember a few: some willows bending over water projecting a transparent shadow, hands clutching—the bones and cartilage

were extremely *white*—the collar of my jacket, a fly entering an open
mouth, some words read a thousand times, without ever understanding
them completely, a million cicadas singing monotonously and in unison
("of forgetting"), inside my head, a horrible thing, full of veins and nerves,
pointing toward me, suspended heavily in a thicket of dark hair; a blurred
image printed on newspaper, torn in a thousand pieces and thrown to the
wind by a maddened hand. All this was visible on the walls dampened by
the fog while the cab crossed the city. And it was the only thing visible.]

In a scene reminiscent of Borges's "El Aleph," she sees the obscene dimension of her desire, which the text figures as a sperm cloud. This scene
is metonymically connected to the recollection of her nocturnal wanderings throughout the city. "The walls dampened by the fog " become the
white screen in which Adeline sees the "transparency of desire."

The poem is a prosthesis, it fills a void both in the body and in the mind;
it is a montage that cuts through memories and perceptions, condensing
them in a *corpus* that recomposes a *body*: of the day on the beach with her
sister Susan and Leopold, Adeline remembers her sister's white naked
bosom, a whiteness that contrasts with the obscene whiteness of Leopold's
sexual organ, the dead mother's hand and the deadly rictus of her father's
face (UL 37). Adeline juxtaposes the whiteness of this breast to the white
cotton that fills her own missing breast:

> Estaba verdaderamente ("por los ramos" "de luz solar") hermosa esa tarde,
> alrededor de las cinco, cuando Leopoldo se levantó de un salto, volvién-
> dose hacia mí con el traje de baño a la altura de las rodillas—la cosa ba-
> lanceándose pesadamente, apuntando hacia mí—, dejando ver al saltar las
> partes de Susana que no se habían tostado al sol. No era la blancura lisa y
> morbosa de Leopoldo, sino una blancura que deslumbraba. (UL 39)

> [She looked ("by the braches" "of sunlight") truly lovely that afternoon,
> around five o'clock, when Leopold suddenly sprang up, turning towards me
> with his bathing suit to his knees—the thing suspended heavily pointing to-
> wards me—revealing the parts of Susan not tanned by the sun. It wasn't
> Leopold's smooth and morbid whiteness, but a whiteness that dazzled.]

The poem is both mutilation *and* scar. In a clear allusion to Borges's Emma
Zunz, who was able to fulfill her desire with an anonymous sailor in her
nocturnal walks through the city, Adeline does not dare to reach the port in
order to break with the straitjacket of her virginity. In spite of what she
states in the "Envoi," she does not seem to have any reasons to refute her
mother's doubt regarding the meaning of life.

In "Sombras" Saer transgresses the borders between two genres, prose
and poetry; he also weaves a text by tying together materials and procedures in a tight fabric. The poem is not only the product of the narrative
plot, but fundamentally the text's core and the textual matrix that provides
a structuring principle. However, the text is too focalized on consciousness. "La mayor" complicates this structure, making the link between
memory and perception much more problematic.

RIEN N'A EU LIEU QUE LE LIEU (PERCEPTION, MEMORIES, AND THE IMPERATIVE OF SAYING)

> Una narración podría estructurarse mediante una
> simple juxtaposición de recuerdos . . . La nueva
> narración hecha a base de puros recuerdos, no
> tendría ni principio ni fin. Se trataría más bien de una
> narración circular y la posición del narrador sería
> semejante a la del niño que, sobre el caballo de la
> calesita, trata de agarrar a cada vuelta los aros de
> acero de la sortija. Hacen falta suerte, pericia,
> continuas correcciones de posición, y todo eso no
> asegura, sin embargo, que no se vuelva la mayor
> parte de las veces con las manos vacías.
> —Saer, M 189.

> [One could structure a narration in terms of a single
> juxtaposition of memories . . . The new narration
> made up of pure memories would have neither
> beginning nor end. It would be a circular narration
> and the narrator's position would be like that of the
> child mounted on the horse of a merry-go-round who
> at each turn tries to grab the ring. One needs luck, skill
> and a constant repositioning, all of which does not
> guarantee that one will not end up empty-handed.]

A unique paragraph of approximately twenty pages makes up "La
mayor," a story that is also an inner monologue, although this time the
voice has no identity.[22] The action is even more limited than in "Sombras":

> Otros, ellos, antes, podían. Mojaban, despacio, en la cocina, en el atarde-
> cer, en invierno, la galletita, sopando, y subían, después, la mano, de un
> solo movimiento, a la boca, mordían y dejaban, durante un momento la
> pasta azucarada sobre la punta de la lengua, para que subiese desde ella, de
> su disolución, como un relente, el recuerdo, masticaban despacio y esta-

ban, de golpe, ahora fuera de sí, en otro lugar, conservado, mientras hubiese, en primer lugar, la lengua, la galletita, el té que humea, los años: mojaban, en la cocina, en invierno, la galletita en la taza de té, y sabían, in-
mediatamente, al probar, que estaban llenos, dentro de algo y trayendo,
dentro, algo, que habían, en otros años, porque había años, dejado, fuera,
en el mundo, algo, que se podía, de una u otra manera, por decir así, recu-
perar, y que había, por lo tanto, en alguna parte, lo que llamaban o lo que
creían que debía ser, ¿no es cierto?, un mundo. Y yo ahora me llevo a la
boca, por segunda vez, la galletita empapada en el té y no saco, al probarla,
nada, lo que se dice nada. Sopo la galletita en la taza de té, en la cocina, en
invierno, y alzo, rápido, la mano, hacia la boca, dejo la pasta azucarada,
tibia, en la punta de la lengua, por un momento, y empiezo a masticar,
despacio, y ahora que trago, ahora que no queda ni rastro de sabor, sé, de-
cididamente, que no saco nada, pero nada, lo que se dice nada. Ahora no
hay nada, ni rastro, ni recuerdo, de sabor: nada. (M11)

[Before, others, they, could. They dunked, slowly, in the kitchen, at dusk,
in winter, the cookie, dipping and, then, all at once, they raised their hand,
toward their mouth, they bit and left for a while the sugary paste on the tip
of the tongue so that it could rise from it, from its dissolution, as dew, the
memory, they chewed slowly and were, all of the sudden, outside of themselves, in another place, preserved, as long as there was first the tongue, the
cookie, the steaming tea, the years: they dunked, in the kitchen, at dusk, in
winter, the cookie, and they immediately knew, when trying it, that they
were full, inside something, and bringing, something, inside, that they had,
in other years, because there were years, left, out, in the world, something
that it was possible, in a way or other, so to speak, to regain, and that,
therefore, there was, somewhere, what they called, or what they believe
should have been, isn't it so, a world. And now I bring, for a second time,
to my mouth, the cookie soaked in tea and, when tasting it, I get nothing,
what is called nothing. I dunk the cookie in the cup of tea, in the kitchen, in
winter, and raise, quickly, the hand, toward the mouth, I leave the warm
sugary paste, for a moment, on the tip of my tongue, and start to chew,
slowly, and now that I swallow, now that any trace of flavor vanishes, I
know, with certainty, that I get nothing, nothing, what is called nothing.
Now there is nothing, neither trace, nor memory of flavor: nothing.]

The intertext of the story is Proust's famous episode of the *madelaine* in
which "comme dans ce jeu où les Japonais s'amusent à tremper dans un
bol de porcelaine rempli d'eau, des petits morceaux de papier jusque-là in-
distincts qui, à peine y sont-ils plongés s'étirent, se contournent, se co-
lorent, se différentient . . . de même maintenant . . . tout Combray et ses en-
virons, tout cela qui prend forme et solidité, est sorti, villes et jardins, de

ma tasse de thé" (and just as the Japanese amuse themselves by filling a porcelain bowl with water and steeping in it little crumbs of paper which until then are without form, the moment they become wet, stretch themselves and bend, take on color and distinctive shape . . . just now . . . the whole of Combray and of its surroundings, taking their proper shapes and growing solid, sprang into being, town and gardens alike, from my cup of tea).[23] Saer' s story rewrites this episode by focusing on the outcome of tasting the *madelaine*, but it also replicates a literary experiment to see whether the outcome can be duplicated as well.

Let's remember that Proust's *madelaine* is a condensation of what encompasses two moments and two spaces within "the vast structure of recollection" (*l'ediffice immense du souvenir*)[24] and that writing for Proust is a form of transubstantiation. *A la recherche du temps perdu* is the monument to memory that Proust erects at a time when memory was not in good standing. The memory that Proust deals with is not a mnemotechnique, but rather poetic memory, a deeper form of sensibility he calls *involuntary memory*, where reason and perception play no decisive role.

Unlike other texts by Saer where the latent poem has an organizing function and even provides constructive materials, "La mayor" is not ruled by the poem, nor is it a text that, like Proust's, plunges deep into the comparative power of language. It is rather a dry, abstract, "soporiferous" text in which a rhythmic arrangement (anaphora) minimally compensates for its monotony. Repetition invades all levels of the text: it is a repetition of a key episode in modern literature and having to do with one of the decisive "faculties" in Saer's poetics and with its materials, memory, and above all, with the ontological scandal they entail. The "and now . . . " (*y ahora*) syntagm punctuates the non-sequential organization of the text (the story is told from beginning to end without any breaks) and the story's syntactical pattern consists, as in "Sombras sobre vidrio esmerilado," in an expansion of the "now." The generative cell of the story, "Before, they, could" responds (in the musical sense of the term) to the repetition of this minimal phrastic element. The phrase's punctuation in *stacatto* is one of the two concessions the text makes to the latent poem. There are also repetitions with variations of several diegetic segments that once narrated in the present are immediately retold in the continuous present; the differential repetition creates an interval that fills in the void left by the recollection that fails to arise from the deepest recesses of memory ("the swamp," or *el pantano*). These repetitions, in turn, weave a compact text that is arranged like a minimalist and atonal musical score. The story focuses on the inner states of the subject of enunciation and on the mute and gelid facticity of the outside; it unfolds as a permanent readjustment of the inner states and of the enumeration and verification of the things outside the mind.

Although "La mayor" stages the imperative of saying, it also tells us something about being and about "place" (*lugar*): "estoy estando, siempre, ahora, en el mismo, con la taza vacía y las manos cruzadas, . . . *lugar*" (I am being, always, now, in the same, with the empty cup and arms crossed, . . . *place* [M 12]). The text's dryness is the result of a disciplined saying that imposes a rule on itself: a fidelity to perception. Paradoxically, the spring-board for this fidelity is a literary episode; the text thus consists of an experimental literary reduplication in terms of a loyalty to perception.

Although the action referred in the story is rather scant (a subject's comings and goings from the kitchen to his bedroom and to the terrace), an initial break between two situations structures the text: the "before, they, could" and the "now I can't do what before they were able to"; this break blocks the possibility of a passage into "another state" and "another place," but is also quite telling regarding the coordinates of Saer's poetics.

The imperative of saying that commands the text and the production of a recollection appears in relation to what is "there" to be said, the "hay" (there is):

> Hay la habitación fría, titilante . . . , hay en la habitación fría, titilante, la cama, el escritorio verde, la carpeta verde en la que he escrito, con grandes letras rojas, irregulares, rápidas, de imprenta, PARANATELLON, los libros, los papeles apilados atrás, la biblioteca . . . (M18)
> . . . y en la penumbra azul, en la altura, en el cielo, está la luna. (M 12)

> [There is the cold, titillating room . . . There is in the cold, titillating room, the bed, the green desk, the green binder on which I've written, quickly, in big irregular red print letters, PARANATELLON, the books, the piled up papers behind, the bookshelves . . .]
> [. . . And in the bluish half light, above, in the sky, the moon.]

The "there is" (*hay*) has two names throughout the text: "half light" and "darkness." "There is" what appears *in* the "half light" and what it allows appearing in the realm of visibility. But "there is" also what makes the void appear as an interval, in the separation of what appears. The act of (dis)-appearing is the central experiment of the text. Here "penumbra" lacks any autonomy and is thus subordinated to "darkness": the universe is a void infected by obscure formations or shadows (stains, phosphorescence, clouds and spirals of smoke), and the text reaches the point of formulating the equation "all is one." The void is an interval between shadows, a "penumbra," which is also the name of being.

The "half light" contains a series of inscribed terms. One can only account for what is inscribed in being, however, and since the horizon of the imperative of saying is that of the absence of direction, meaning, message, evidence, or certainty, what is inscribed in being is open to constant rectification:

> Porque ellos, antes, otros, *por así decir*, podían: de una cara redonda, mate, con un hoyuelo . . . podían, proyectándose, algún signo, algún mensaje, una evidencia, *o mejor*, una certidumbre, *como por decir así*, un diamante de su ganga, sacar. De un signo a otro, de un mensaje, o de una certidumbre, tiraban, *por decirlo de algún modo*, las líneas, y ponían, en el mundo, como una madre al parir, en el espacio, sólida, a la vista, externa, o como en el aire, volando, imaginariamente, en el vacío, una paloma, irrefutable, una construcción que servía: una medida que por estar, solamente, cortaba, despedazaba, clasificando, dividiendo, adelante, atrás, después, antes, arriba, abajo, ahora, la mancha continua, vaga, errabunda, idéntica a sí misma, en cada punto, sin centro, en cada punto, sin centro, y sin, más oscuro, o menos nítido, arrabal. Ningún mensaje para mí . . . , nada. (M 15, my emphasis)

> [Because they, before, others, *so to speak*, could: from a round face, brown, with a dimple . . . they *could*, projecting themselves, some sign, some message, some evidence, *or better still*, a certainty, *so to speak*, a diamond from its gangue, extract. From one sign to another, from a message or from a certainty, they connected, *in so many words*, the dots and brought, to the world, like a mother that gives birth, in the space, solid, in plain view, external, or like in the air, flying, imaginarily, in the void, a dove, irrefutable, a construction that worked: a measure that simply by being, cut and broke, classifying, dividing, in front of, behind, after, before, up, down, the stain continuous, blurred, wandering, identical to itself, in each point, without a center, and without, darker, or less sharp, satellite. No message for me . . . nothing.]

This passage is an example of the self-reflexive character of the text (it reflects on its own conditions and possibilities and *at the same time* gives clues on how it places itself within its own context of production) and of the process of rectification. The question that subtends this imperative of saying is how to orient oneself in thinking, the main task being to explain why there are simultaneously "visual" configurations of the human (the house, the TV, the city) *and* the imperative of saying. In other words, what can thinking (writing) say about the question of being once a historical abdication of meaning has occurred (witness the lurking presence of the TV as a sign of this historical mutation; a sign that is absent of course in the Proustian intertext):

> A mi alrededor, y concéntrica, apretándose, como anillos, la muchedumbre de casas, en uno de cuyos cuartos, en cada una, la misma imagen titila, azulada, tocando vagamente las caras vacías, sin expresión, cambiando, organizada, dada, en la televisión, racimos de mundos dados, dentro de uno, más arduo, que no se da. (M15–16)

> [Around me and in concentric circles, pressing down, as rings, the block of houses, in one of whose rooms, in each of them, the same image titillates, bluish, touching from afar the expressionless, empty faces, changing, organized, given, in the TV, clusters of given worlds, inside of a more arduous one that does not materialize.]

In the figuration of the text, thinking appears as a body ("the test tube of the body," or *la probeta del cuerpo*) that is progressively reduced to the head and the eyes, the perceptive system or "membrane that separates the infinite from the actual" (M 17). Drowsiness and somnolence follow the dominant state of attention to both the inner and outer changes. The place, the body, and its state are *one*, which means that there is no constitutive duality; this unity always accounts for three: for itself, for others, and the world.

The thematic ensemble of "La mayor" thus encompasses the "there is," which is placed under the imperative of saying; the question of being (the void, the "half light," the silence); the question of the appearing of what is inscribed in the "there is" (shadows, stains; phosphorescence and objects) and the question of thinking. This ensemble forms a minimal device that knots together being, existence, and thinking; it also sets a repetitive orientation on the "now" of saying. Within this configuration, being ("half light") appears under the category of the void; existence ("shadow") under that of the same and the other, while the question of thinking can be approached through the complex interplay between saying and seeing (the *body* reduced to the head and eyes or "membrane that separates the infinite from the actual").

To what exigency does the imperative of saying respond? "Now there is nothing . . . nothing" (M 11): an analysis of lexical frequency would confirm that "nothing" (*nada*) and "neither . . . nor" (*ni . . . ni*, M 22) are the recurring and dominant terms of the text. The imperative of saying takes the figure of a repetition that is experienced as a trial involving effort and labor:

Verdaderamente preguntarse si . . . (M 14) [To really ask oneself if . . .]

. . . interrogar: interrogar, . . . Interrogar, interrogar: todavía . . . (M 18–19)
[. . . Ponder: ponder, . . . Ponder, ponder: still . . .]

Fijar la vista. En algo. (M 21) [Fix the gaze. On something.]

O fijar, la vista, quiero decir, en algo, en otra cosa, y ver, durante un momento, lo que sea necesario, tratando de hacer salir, si fuese posible, por
una vez, aunque más no sea, una, por llamarla de algún modo, señal. (M 23)

[Or to fix, the gaze, I want to say, on some thing, on another thing, and see,
for a moment, whatever is necessary, trying to extract, if possible, for once
at least, just to give it a name, a signal.]

Ver de ver algo, ahora. (M 32) [See of seeing something, now.]

Saying *unsays* the said (the utterance): double negation ("ni . . . ni") and in-
terrogation are the main modalities of this operation; they reduce the referential illusion at the core of words in order to create the conditions for a
recollection to emerge. There is thus a failure in naming that lies in the absence of "measure," "certainty," "evidence," "direction" or "construction,"
all of which have an impact on the correlation between seeing and saying
—to see well is to misname:

Y en la pared, sobre el escritorio, con mucho blanco alrededor, detrás del
vidrio, el *Campo*, ¿pero es verdaderamente un campo?, *de trigo*, ¿pero es
verdaderamente trigo?, *de los cuervos*, y uno podría, verdaderamente, preguntarse, si son verdaderamente cuervos. (M 14)

[And on the wall, on top of the desk, with lots of white around it, behind
the glass, the *Field*, but it is really a field? Of *wheat*, but is it really wheat?
Of *crows*? And one could, really, ask, if they are really crows.]

Language here says more about less and uses more words in order to limit
what is said: the dissolution of the canvas's referential illusion occurs by
inserting an interval between each word in the title, by voiding them of
their referential certainty, and by isolating them as if each were the stains
or layers of colors they are *in fact*:

El cuadro: manchas negras, amarillas, azules, verdes, rojizas, pardas, girando, inmóviles, o en estampida, arremolinándose, trazos aglomerados,
inestables, en suspensión, no de conflagración, ni de ruinas, sino de inminencia, sin nada, pero nada, ni de este lado, ni del otro . . . ¿en estampida?,
¿en suspensión?, ¿aglomerándose?, ¿dispersándose? . . . (M 22)

[The picture: black stains, yellow, blue, green, reddish, brown, turning, motionless, or in a stampede, in a whirlwind, unstable clustered traces, suspended not by conflagration or ruination, but by imminence, with nothing, but nothing, neither on this side nor on the other . . . In a stampede? Suspended? Clustering? Dispersing? (M 22)

Painting motivates the dissolution of words, it triggers freedom of perception but it also introduces a state of "drowsiness" (M 21). Although objects and shadows may disappear—disappearing being one of the key operations of the imperative of saying—, and although movement occurs, there is an inner immobility proper to the imperative of saying:

Estoy parado, pareciera, entonces, inmóvil, en la terraza fría, pareciera, sí, momentáneamente, sin poder sacar, de todo esto, nada. Es un estado que, se diría, no debiese . . . , no debía haber mejor, apareciendo, confundido o fundido. Se diría que, por decir así, de algún modo, fluyendo, y estando, siempre, más bien, en el mismo, nuevamente, lugar, no le queda, como quien dice, para fluir, ningún otro—ningún otro, es decir, en otra parte, donde no esté fluyendo inmóvil, como decía, lugar. (M 39)

[I am standing it seems, thus, motionless, in the cold terrace, it would seem, yes, momentarily, without being able to extract, from all of this, nothing. It is a state that, one would say, shouldn't . . . should not have, better, appearing, be confused or fused. One could say, so to speak, somehow, flowing, and always being rather in the same, once again, place, so to speak, to flow, there is no place left, that is, another place—no other, somewhere else, where it is not flowing motionless, as I was saying, place.]

This means that there is *one* ontological situation: there is only *one place* and no other (being is one in terms of its own localization). Consequently, movement is relative since it does not authorize going outside the unity of being. This thesis regarding the unity of place (another rewriting of *Unidad de lugar*) has important implications for understanding Saer's poetics: it does not give way to a passage from one level of reality to another (there is no "other sky," as in Cortázar), nor the proliferation of possible virtual worlds (as in Borges).[25] In Saer, to quote Mallarmé, whose constellation is never far from his, "rien n'aurai lieu que le lieu" (nothing will have taken place but the place),[26] and this explains why the Proustian episode of the *madelaine* must be rephrased.

After vigilant perception yields to a drowsy state of receptivity, the replication of the literary experiment seems to succeed:

Y ver, ahora, pareciera, *sí*, ver, desde esta nada, si es posible, como antes, como otros, sacar, como en un sueño, por decir así, un recuerdo, algo:

porque ellos, otros, antes, podían: mojaban, despacio, en el atardecer, en la cocina, en invierno, la galletita, la taza de té, la alzaban hasta la boca depositándola en la punta de la lengua, y desde ahí, de golpe, o gradual, desde la lengua, o desde la pasta azucarada, desde alguna parte, como un vapor, de los pantanos, subía, victorioso, nítido, *el recuerdo, el recuerdo* que, aunque no sepa, de ningún modo, de qué es recuerdo, ni si hay algo, fuera, que recordar, podría fundar, sin embargo, en la negrura, algo. (M 32, emphasis mine)

[And I see, now, it seems, *yes*, I see from this nothing, if it were possible, as before, as others did, to extract, as in a dream, so to speak, a memory, something: because, they, others, before, could: they dunked, slowly, at dusk, in the kitchen, in winter, the cookie, the cup of tea, raising it to their mouth, placing it on the tip of the tongue, and from there, suddenly, or gradually, from the tongue, or from the sugary paste, from somewhere, as a vapor, from the swamps, rose, clear and victorious, *the memory, the memory* that, although one does not know, of what it is a memory, nor if there is something, outside, to be remembered, could found, nevertheless, in the darkness, something.]

Their recollection and *his* recollection seem to coincide for once: as the syntactic apposition indicates, there is a confluence. But the coincidence stops here because if the memory of Combray is more real than the real Combray, in Saer there is no such contiguity, no metonymic or metaphoric magic wand that could establish a bridge between the contents of the recollection and those of reality. "There is" recollection: this is the only thing one is authorized to say; recollection is an event. The text presents it as a supplement, in a scene that is placed at a distance from the main scene ("now"): "que fluya, si quiere, constantemente, así . . . Y se levanta ahora, tenaz, como un sol, en el sol, otra vez, el recuerdo" (it should flow, if it wishes, constantly, thus . . . And now, tenaciously, it rises, as a sun, in the sun, once again, the memory [M 33]). This scene (M 34-36) marks a break with regard to the scene of the "now," pushing the subject and the imperative of saying to their own limits: no possible coincidence can occur between the recollected contents (their visual images) and the perception of the objects that are the basis of these visual contents ("no, no hay, en el recuerdo de ese café, ningún café [there is no coffee, in the memory of that coffee, M 36]). Even if the subject's state changes, there is no change of place:

Y estoy estando siempre, ahora, en la negrura, en el mismo, flotando, errabundeando, dentro de algo, o en algo que transcurre, con el recuerdo móvil

que sube, desparece, y vuelve, empecinado, victorioso, a subir, desde el
pantano, incierto, cambiante y en reposo, reducido . . . lugar. (M 34)

[And I am being always, now, in the darkness, in the same, floating, erring,
inside something, or within something that happens, with the mutable
memory that rises, disappears, and stubborn and victorious, rises once
again from the swamp, uncertain, changing and at rest, reduced . . . place.]

y la bufanda amarilla, de la que debiera nacer la mancha amarilla que sube
ahora, sola, del pantano, flota, desintegrándose, ¿en qué mundo, o en qué
mundos? (M 36)

[And the yellow scarf, whose yellow stain that now rises, alone, from the
swamp, should emanate, floats, disintegrating, in which world, or in what
worlds?]

However, no matter how thorough the work of negation (imperative of
saying) is, something remains: the final question concerning the nature of
place is an indication that a recoiling of the subject to the very limits of
being, of what can be said has occurred.[27] "La mayor" is a Proustian variation executed in the minimalist language of a Beckett and with the "starry"
score of Mallarmé's "Un coup de dés."

2

Littoral, Literal:
The Joys of the Letter

Como el sueño para Freud, la escritura se apoya con
un pie en el pasado y con el otro en el presente.
—Saer, JJS 16.

[Like the dream in Freud, writing stands with one
foot in the past and the other in the present.]

Ce qui fait avancer le roman, c'est . . . le désir de
donner la parole au temps.
—Blanchot, *Le livre à venir* 15.

[What enables the novel to progress is the desire to
give a voice to time.]

FIGURES

EL LIMONERO REAL (1974) IS THE CROWNING WORK OF A PERIOD OF
experimentation with narrative forms that sought to displace the certainties
of the realist novel (regional, social, magical, and marvelous). As we saw
in the previous chapter, this experimentation produced "Sombras sobre
vidrio esmerilado," a story that stages a complex interplay between the
poem; narration and desire; and "La mayor," a story that tries to recount
the simultaneity of the present and time itself. Two structuring elements of
these two texts play a decisive role in *El limonero real*. On the one hand,
the poem, whose rhythm and distribution in homologable series finds its
correlate in the hyperrealist descriptive utterance, which is a dominant in
this text. On the other, the question of temporality, which the text not only
thematizes in its overall formal organization but also explores in its deep-

est constitutive layers. *El limonero real* must be placed at the intersection of two series of texts: that of the realist-regional type (the stories of *Palo y hueso* and "Al campo" in *En la zona*), of which it preserves settings, themes, linguistic registers, and that of the "pure" or "abstract" type ("Sombras sobre vidrio esmerilado" and "La mayor"), of which it takes some of its more innovative formal procedures.

Critics have read *El limonero real* as an allegory of its own mechanisms of narrative production, as a metanarration that narrates its own origin and gestation and that, at the same time, unfolds a "universal history of the story" on its diachronic axis.[1] Correct as these observations may be, they run the risk of imposing an absolute notion of the literary that, by understanding beforehand what the enigma of *literariness* is (at a time when the writer has lost most of his traditional certainties) makes the text a triumph, a form of knowledge and the concretion of "good form." Although anchored in a realist thematic and at times simulating an adscription to realist procedures, *El limonero real* transgresses them and radically dislocates the horizon of reading. The second risk amounts to neutralizing the adventure or event at stake in narrating "the story's origin" (supposing that something like a nonwritten margin or "origin" can exist), that descent into hell in search of Eurydice whose figure resembles a corpse.[2] While criticism ties itself to the mast of discourse in order to shield itself from the Sirens' song fatal attraction,[3] *El limonero real* is the story of the *encounter* that can only occur through a descent into the foundations of the symbolic order. *El limonero real* stages another version of the story's "foundation" or "origin"; it is the origin with which it does not and cannot coincide, and the new version it composes sets up a nonverbal other at the heart of narrative discourse.

"Relato de un relatar" (A story of narrating)[4] is a more apt expression to convey what unfolds in *El limonero real*. However, given their complex interpenetration, we should not forget that the line delimiting the action from its end product is difficult to isolate. Here it is a "relatar" (narrating) whose signs are those of a "relato" (story) that in turn refers to a unique sign encompassing both the act and the actor.

If the traditional novel form presupposes a signification that is external to it, for Saer, signification does not preexist the text and therefore not even the "meaning" of what is "literary" can guarantee the completion of a form that transgresses the realist code. Although the text unfolds several stagings of the story's history (which is not the same; the text offers itself as an "archeology of storytelling" since it touches the most primary processes of its constitution), the decisive operation is to present its constitutive matrix.

This matrix is a product of the complex interaction of the primary and secondary processes that underlie the story. The story of a scar, of a process of mourning (the character's, as well as the novelistic form of narration), *El limonero real* ciphers itself as the back and forth movement of that

> *enjambre* de visiones, de recuerdos, de pensamientos, [que vuelve], gradualmente, sin orden, a entrar de nuevo al *panal*, merodeando primero alrededor de la *boca negra*, entrando por grupos que se desprenden de la masa compacta, homogénea, de puntos negros que giran sin decidirse a entrar, hasta que van quedando, en el exterior, cada vez menos dispersos, revoloteando sin orden, entrando y volviendo a salir, caminando, con sus patas frágiles, peludas, sobre el *marco pétreo de la abertura*, indecisos, y cuando queda por fin el espacio vacío, sin nada, hay todavía algo que sale, bruscamente, de la boca negra, sin dirección, y vuelve, con la misma rapidez, a entrar. (LR 226–27, my emphasis)

> [*Swarm* of visions, memories and thoughts [that return], gradually, without order, into the *beehive,* prowling first around the black mouth, entering in groups that detach themselves from the compact mass, from the black points that move around without deciding to enter, until they remain, outside, each time less dispersed, stirring without any order, entering just to once again get out, walking, undecided, with their fragile hairy legs on the *opening rocky hardness*, and when in the end the space is empty, without anything, there is something yet that, without direction, suddenly comes out of the black mouth just to go back inside at the same speed.]

The story focuses on the traces of sensations (*percepts, affects, visions*) that Wenceslao experiences on December 31, a day he spends with his relatives celebrating the end of the year. These are the principal materials that will in turn shape the different types of stories in the narrative. The beehive (*colmena*) is the central figure of these materials, envisioned as a field of intensities and energies that are at times bounded and at others unbounded. In a text whose main trait is the repetition of actions and narrative segments, it is quite significant that the figure of the beehive appears only once. I claim that this is a figure of the subject (of its processes) that must be related to the black and white butterflies (figures of the text) that Wenceslao "sees" in section IV (table p. 65).

The text presents itself as a field of conflictive forces, as a movement of opening and closure that is isomorphic to the drives it sets in motion. The "black mouth" *(boca negra)* of the beehive, receptacle of energies, finds its homology in a plastic figure (non-linguistic): the black square inserted on

the white page that interrupts the thread of the story and marks the passage
to a pre-discursive scene. A regression from language to "lalangue"[5] occurs
when the dimension of the letter comes to the forefront: words break down
into discrete units and acquire the sonority of things—the buzzing of bees
("Zddzzzzzzzzzz," LR 138–39).[6] If the *limonero real* (royal/real lemon-
tree) is a textual figure that orients reading (a structuring metaphor), the
beehive is the figure of the process of writing itself.

Much like the *limonero real*, which is simultaneously full of flowers
and fruits at all seasons and is here an emblematic object of the text, there
is something that surges from "that black mouth," the root of the story. The
"influx of death" (LR 32) at work both in Wenceslao's desire and in the
text is what differentiates these two figures of plenitude. And yet something remains between the nothing of death and the nothing of forgetting
(without ignoring the paragrammatic play with the verb *nada-r*, to swim,
an activity that functions as the hinge between the story and its "other
scene"): an utterance that affirms a desire whose fulfillment cannot take
place. A transgression of desire and a desire of transgression are thus the
two main coordinates of the text.

One can read this process of mourning (persistent and incomplete in the
case of the nameless feminine character, or complete, although not without
the feeling of guilt in Wenceslao-Layo's, the father figure and "permanent
son")[7] as the process or trial that the text itself imposes on realist literature,
on the novel genre, and even on literature itself. The text does what it says,
producing, as Wenceslao-Layo does, a surface that is both legible *and* illegible (what later, in *Lo imborrable*, is called "continous, discontinuous").
This is a text that, as the shirt Wenceslao refuses to wear, has a black band
"embroidered on white fabric."[8] Critics have privileged the circle and circularity as the figures that cipher the text's form and the story's ontogeny
and phylogeny. Without wishing to minimize the important function they
both play, I will align the circle and circularity with the figure of the beehive in an attempt to approach the text's illegible layers, of which the more
legible one is just a fragment.

OBJECTIVISM, HYPERREALISM, THE NEW NOVEL, AND SAER'S "STYLE"

A unity of place (the islands of the littoral, the fragments of the "zone")
structures the story: the events of the day (the unity of time) when Wenceslao gets together with his family to celebrate the end of the year. He leaves

his island and his wife in the morning (she refuses to go to her sister's house because, even though six years have passed since the death of her son, she is still in mourning) and returns at dawn the following day. However, this spatial and temporal unity, overdetermined as it is by the metaphor of concentric circles (of the lemon tree and of the islands), is more tenuous than first appears. The eight sections that comprise the story lack progression and instead make up a series of segments in which description is the central device, thus disintegrating the narration's progressive movement.

Published in Spain in 1974, *El limonero real* went almost unnoticed except for a small number of specialized journals.[9] There are various reasons to explain this silence: the theme, the election of a regional instead of an urban setting, and a repertoire of marginal characters linked Saer's text to the literary form of the regional novel. This form was not favorably looked upon in Buenos Aires, which was the center of cultural legitimacy at the time and where Borges's and Cortázar's cosmopolitan literature was dominant.[10] Perhaps more importantly, *El limonero real* was a formally transgressive text that did not make the "typical" character of regional literature into a paradigmatic representative (the poor, marginal and illiterate islander), but the *figurant* of processes that underlie representation itself. Another consideration should be added to the challenges that this text posited to its readers: Saer incorporated certain objectivist methods that were marginal in the literary scene at the time, as well as those of the French *nouveau roman*, which had been discredited by traditional humanists (Ernesto Sábato being a paradigmatic case), as well as by critics on the Left.[11]

Regarding objectivist precursors in Argentina, it is important to mention the novel *Sin embargo Juan vivía* (1947) by Alberto Vanasco, which some critics considered "objectivist *avant la lettre*."[12] Structurally circular, narrated in the second person and in the future tense (conjectural time), this novel broke with the reigning traditional realism. Another important Argentine precursor, who had much more influence on Saer, was Antonio Di Benedetto, especially *Zama* (1956) and the stories included in *Declinación y Angel* (1958), where the narration lacks plot structure, the details assume singular importance, and description becomes an important device.[13] Finally, we should mention that "objectivist" narrative experimentation found fertile ground not only in the River Plate region, with the work of Juan Carlos Onetti, but also in Mexico with Salvador Elizondo, Vicente Leñero, José Emilio Pacheco, Juan García Ponce, and Juan Vicente Melo, as well as with the Cuban Julieta Campos.[14] Objectivist procedures sought to explore new roads for Latin American literature (or what will be called the New Latin American novel, produced in the shadow of the *Boom*) and to leave behind the ethnological-documentary tendency then dominant, as well as those forms of realism that presupposed a contiguous relation between language and reality.

Saer closely followed the initial projects of the *mouvance*, later called the *nouveau roman*: in 1967 he translated "La playa" by Robbe-Grillet into Spanish for the Santa Fé journal *Setescientosmonos,* and in 1968 his translation of *Tropismes* by Nathalie Sarraute appeared.[15] When he wrote *El limonero real*, Saer expressed the conviction that "the *nouveau roman* is, for me, heir to the grand narrative . . . I think that one cannot write at present without taking into consideration what has been said by Robbe-Grillet, Nathalie Sarraute or Michel Butor."[16] This does not mean, however, that this is simply another case of European influence on a Latin American writer. One should not forget that Saer dedicates *El limonero real* to the Paraguayan writer Augusto Roa Bastos, whose *I, the Supreme* (*Yo el supremo*) rearticulates realism's methods and those of the "new novel" and therefore marks an important turning point in the Latin American novel. However, the "style" in which Saer combines the narrative methods of objectivism and of the *nouveau roman* with certain nuclei of realist literature is singular, and *El limonero real* is an ideal text to make his poetics explicit. Before doing so, however, we will review a series of materials and procedures that define the new novel on both sides of the Atlantic and are therefore essential for elucidating Saer's poetics.

In Saer's aesthetics as well as in those of the *nouveau roman*, formal experimentation is not an epiphenomenon, but rather a necessary operation derived from extreme attention to the real and its mutations. It thus finds its justification in a consciousness which is not only aware of its own historicity, but which also assumes and legitimates it. It is possible to isolate two dominant procedures from among the different and rather diverse attempts at restituting and/or creating the complex relations between man and the real. The first is an objective vision of things, as in the case of Alain Robbe-Grillet and Claude Simon. This procedure aspires to restituting objects to their bare presence, which is prior to any intention to signify. In the second method, there is a subjective vision that seeks to substitute the truths of traditional psychology with deeper truths. An exploration of the imaginary realm, born out of images and phantasms, yields the partial nature of vision (Sarraute's "sous-conversations" and tropisms) that prevails here. Saer combines both objectivist and more subjectivist procedures and devices: detailed descriptions that decompose objects in a multiplicity of planes; as in "La mayor," *El limonero real,* and *Nobody Nothing Never;* and a sustained attention to inner states, to their discrete displacements, but also to the libidinal economy that underlies and traverses the story (as in "Sombras sobre vidrio esmerilado," *Cicatrices, El limonero real*).

The new novel rejects signification as well as the notion that the novel is able to restitute a message that precedes and is external to it. Instead there is rather a legitimating of immanence: the author and the message do not preexist the production of the text; they are its product.[17] This new conception understands the novel as an authentically literary production aware of its own specificity, which implies putting in question the realist illusion. This position explains the frequency and length of metatextual passages whose connotative procedures reflect the utterance in the process of narrative imbrication: therein the innovative character, at first, of devices such as the *mise en abîme* and self-reflexive (specular) sequences.[18]

There is also a reflection on the nature of enunciation within the frame of a discursive imbrication, which is why there are often many denotative metatextual commentaries: passages endowed with a pedagogical function that stress the novel's hyperliterarity and hyperfictional nature and make these traits visible throughout the work. Given that new relations between writer, reader, and work are forged, this experimentation also supposes a radical change in novelistic form: the reader now becomes partners with the writer. Writing implies constructing "corridors of signification" that produce changes in the reading process itself. The writer now demands that the reader assumes a critical stance that will permit him to reject the illusion of realism. At the level of form, this demand translates into the adoption of uncommon narrative structures, whose most remarkable traits are the permanent displacements of points of view, the confusion in the enunciation's origin, the repetition of the same scenes or diegetic segments, the apposition of contradictory versions of a same event, the frequent recourse to narrative modalization, and the dissemination of the story into a plurality of fragments. The reader can only recreate the story as she reads it, adopting a tabular reading instead of a linear one.

The so-called "school of the gaze"[19] is crucial in the organization of narrative economy since it posits that there is no qualitative difference between subject and object. The gaze's constitutive duplicity plays an active role here; the gaze is no longer limited to the object's illusory appearance on the side of the observer, suggesting that the object results from the interdependence of the gaze and what is seen. As a consequence of this interdependence, a "realist" aesthetic based upon a binary system and grounded in the belief in the existence of an autonomous, solid, and well-defined pre-existing world loses its privileges and compels writers to develop alternative models. In the *nouveau roman* and in Saer's texts, there is no such a thing as an absolute point of view. Always implicated in the body of the observer, the point of view evinces a fracture of knowledge in whose fault-line emerges the constitutive enigma of the partial apprehension of things. The relation body-world is not exhaustive because it is experienced as an escape from the inner core to the outside and thus creates a space that is "the outside of the inner core" and that covers no objective virtual outside. To account for this key element of Saer's poetics, critics have coined the expression "narrating perception,"[20] which for us is valid only if it does not suggest a binary object-subject relationship, but rather that "the outside of the inner core" is the only dimension accessible to a fragmentary consciousness.

Made up of partial views or vistas, the new novel's narrative diegesis does not lay out a *continuum*; it organizes a limited set of iterative sequences or arranges the movement of its alternation and variation. As a result of the "perceptive" process that rules narration, it follows that these novels often present themselves as restituting a history (for example, Claude Simon's *Le vent*, whose subtitle is *Tentative de restitution d'un retable baroque*) and, even when they exhibit their blanks or lacunae, as complete and coherent histories. The standard of coherence varies, of course, as in Saer, where his attempt to narrate *simultaneity* imposes forms of coherence that he extrapolates from poetic discourse.

These texts also posit the relationship between reality and fiction in a new way by questioning the traditional idea according to which the latter would elaborate the former's reflection. These novels abolish such a positivistic dichotomy by employing a procedure that brings about a series of decisive consequences. This procedure entails situating the histories they refer to at the level of their narration. In the referential plane, reality by definition appears as an enigma, a kaleidoscope, and an accumulation of diverse and dispersed vistas and contradictory versions. This situation frees the narrative utterance from its narrow obedience to verisimilitude and what is readable: any interpretation is plausible and at the same time open to discussion, a situation that also explains the proliferation of imaginary scenes (dreams, daydreams, and false representations).

At the level of narrative diegesis, therefore, fiction and reality tend to be confused without any regard for common sense logic and the unity of the story. Given that it results from multiple rectifications, the concept of reality tends to disperse itself in a generalized fiction, thus becoming a simple product of human imagination. At the level of writing, the only reality that is declared to exist is the *mise en texte* itself: narrative diegesis reveals itself as the history of creatures of ink and paper and fiction as an effect of writing (a montage). Finally, by exhibiting their internal contradiction, these texts tend to make problematic the very function of fiction and to create the time of narration: that is nothing else than the text's work, a textual materiality. Fictional writing offers itself as what it is, a work of concatenation, distribution, and interpretation.

In Saer there is no description of the world, but rather a series of successive states of the "perceived" world that are mediated by a subjectivity issuing from the text, devoid of any material continuity and of a solid temporal basis. The narrative magma of *El limonero real* produces discrete ruptures in its frame (a unit of time encompassing a day) and in its narrative logic. In a text constructed with minute care, moments of disintegration are not ruled out, indicating that narrative form plays a critical function and is not the expression of frivolous experimentation.

El limonero real is a carefully plotted text that deals with banal themes; it tells a meager history and mixes literary genres and myths (its fragments or mythemes). In this text, woven with the threads of "visions, memories and thoughts," writing seems to be the "mimesis" of a discrete set of signs that "mime" a unique sign, a *homo scriptus*—the voice that configures the story's space: "it is difficult to communicate perception. What is objective is unverifiable. Description is impossible. Experience and memory are inseparable."[21] There does not seem to be any difference between what the writer states regarding his work and what the writer does in his fictional text.

The suspension of narration's normative temporality (beginning, middle, end) makes the univocal chronological placement of narrative events quite difficult; time therefore loses the objectifying, ordering, unifying force it used to have in the traditional novel. Saer develops affective structures devoid of time but rich in *durée*; *El limonero real*'s mnemic cycle feeds on the "repetition with variation" of diegetic sequences that in turn are repetitions of a deeper matrix: the dream and its process of elaboration.[22]

El limonero real's space is, as in a dream, the site of being as "infinitive presence" in which the past returns only to erase itself continuously, while the present is simultaneous to anticipation (memory of the future) and to what happened previously. Uncertainty rules, *durée* disgregates; the time that "is" is a fetal present, a present that links the infinite to eternity: writing is the image of a birth that never ends (as becomes more explicit *El entenado* and *Lo imborrable*), but in *El limonero real* the scene of birth is overdetermined by the son's death.

STRUCTURES, MATERIALS,
AND PROCEDURES

The text consists of a generative cell and eight diegetic segments. "Amanece/y está con los ojos abiertos" (Day breaks / and his eyes are open, LR 9, in bold in the original) is made up of two phrases, an impersonal verbal phrase that describes an objective state or process and a second verbal phrase with an implied singular subject that describes a personal state and its subjective modality. Both phrases appear in the present indicative and establish a link (simultaneity) between a personal and a nonpersonal process. Although it seems to have a descriptive orientation, the generative cell's position at the top of the page, its typographical highlighting (the two lines are in bold letters), and its disposition in two periods likens it a poetic utterance.

By focusing not on the referential function of narrative statements but on its internal functioning instead, semiotic-structuralist theories of description posit a strong homology between poetic and descriptive utterances. Accordingly, the prevalence of the paradigmatic axis of language in the textual economy, the highlighting of one or several "lists" in a text or of the text as (virtual) "list," characterizes the descriptive utterance.[23] This descriptive ordering or focalization of the text along the paradigmatic axis and the "series," or as an explicitly serialized text, authorizes the homology with the poetic utterance, such as Jakobson, Levin, and Ruwet define it.[24] The latter's main traits are parallelism, the original constructions of a matrix with homologous sites that tend to fit in positions (syntactical, prosodic, textual) equivalent to the so-called equivalent units (phonemes, words, phrases).

El limonero real's dominant procedure is descriptive, and even when the narration "progresses" it does so, paradoxically, through description's delaying mechanism: "yo veía adelante el camino blanco y derecho . . . Más avanzábamos más nos costaba avanzar. No va que llega un momento en que casi no avanzo más (LR 156) [. . . ahead I saw the white and straight road . . . The more we advanced the harder it was. Suddenly I can't follow any longer.]. This passage not only sets the rules for reading the procedure, but also that of the whole text. The text is exemplary then of how Saer defines his own project: "[to relate] the poem's intensity with narration's combinatory rigor."[25]

With respect to the function of description in *El limonero real,* two observations must be made. The first sequence of the text is descriptive and consists of a topology of Wenceslao's property to which the descriptor[26] juxtaposes the familiar everyday toponymy that its dwellers employ:

> *Wenceslao se queda un momento* inmóvil . . . es para Wenceslao y para ella, en efecto, así "la mesa"; ahí almuerzan y cenan de octubre a marzo, a no ser que llueva o sople viento del norte. En esos casos comen en "la mesita chica" . . . El patio delantero es "adelante." "Atrás" hay naranjos, mandarinos y limoneros plantados a tresbolillo . . . (LR 11–13, my emphasis)

> [*For a moment Wenceslao remains immobile* . . . the "table" is, in effect, this way for Wenceslao and for her; there they have lunch and dinner from October to March, if it does not rain or a Northern wind blows. In that case they eat at the "small table" . . . The patio is what they call "the front yard." In what they call "the backyard" there are orange, mandarin and lime trees planted in quincunxes.]

The passage that introduces the habitat, its inhabitants, and their habits is shaped according to the conventions of a nineteenth century readerly-realist narration: a narrative pause signals that a change in the horizon of reading is about to occur. What follows, however, is not simply or totally descriptive: there is no staging of a character in a setting, nor the scene's ornamentation, even less the declension of typified knowledge given beforehand about the islanders' habits or social traits. What follows the narrative pause defies the expectations of the realist text since the passage subordinates the referential orientation of the description to its metadescriptive function: what the passage describes is a behavior or linguistic habit—how the inhabitants name their habitat. In the last instance, the passage describes the functioning of a certain type of descriptive regime that will not be dominant in the text: the passage is a re-marking of the realist description's conventions that, consequently, produces a change in function of the descriptive procedure. Such a change in function not only subtracts materials from the subgenre called regional literature, but also sets them within a frame in which description is no longer in charge of propping up "reality" (Barthes' famous "reality effect"). Through the use of hyperrealist procedures, description decomposes the materiality of objects and, as we will see, recomposes the immateriality of sensation.

The hyperrealist description in *El limonero real* distorts the "natural" principles of construction of the thing perceived. With the juxtaposition of multiple and diverse planes and the "zooming out" of details, it composes a figure-image or *percepts* that deconstructs perception and consequently materializes in a differential space. This figure deconstructs the silhouette's contour and transgresses the revealing trace (physiognomy, portrait, sketch, landscape). As in Picasso's drawings or in his paintings of the so-called analytic cubist period, the border gets deconstructed, which is the line that marks the existence of a unique point of view (the interval separating discrete linguistic units, narrative instances, diegetic units, in the case of the textual space):

> El vestido verde de Rosa desaparece en la esquina del rancho cuando Teresa llega a la punta de la mesa. Rogelio la ve doblar la esquina blanca del rancho y desaparecer. Parada junto a la parrilla . . . observando la mitad del cordero que se asa todavía despidiendo una columna de humo oblicua y plácida, Rosa ve venir a Teresa con la otra fuente vacía . . . En la otra punta de la mesa, Wenceslao, que ha seguido con la vista, mientras escuchaba hablar a Rogelio, el trayecto de Teresa . . . alza el tenedor hacia su boca con el primer bocado de cordero . . . Mientras atravieza el patio trasero en dirección al excusado Rosa mira la parra . . . Entra con precaución y deja la puerta entreabierta . . . Se baja los calzones hasta la rodilla y después, acuclillándose, comienza a orinar. Le llegan voces confusas del patio delantero, y por sobre todas ellas la de la Negra, que suena ronca y como furiosa. Sin embargo, la Negra no sabe bien por qué grita: no ha visto más que a Wenceslao toser, con la cara roja, y después pararse bruscamente, lo mismo que Rogelio que le golpeaba la espalda con la mano abierta. La silla de Wenceslao cae hacia atrás. Rosita . . . [y Amelia] miran en dirección a Wenceslao y Rogelio . . . Rosa se para y se levanta los calzones. (LR 191–93)

> [Rosas's green dress disappears in the house's corner when Teresa reaches the end of the table. Rogelio sees how Rosa turns around the house's white corner and disappears. Standing next to the grill . . . looking at half of the lamb that is still cooking . . . Rosa sees that Teresa is approaching with the other empty tray . . . At the opposite end of the table, Wenceslao who, while he listened to what Rogelio was saying, has followed Teresa's trajectory . . . lifts his fork with his first mouthful of lamb . . . While going across the backyard toward the outhouse, Rosa stares at the grapevine. She enters with care and leaves the door ajar . . . She pulls her underwear down to her knees and crouching down, urinates. Mixed up voices reach her from the front yard and from among all of them, Negra's hoarse voice sounds upset. However, it is not clear why Negra cries: she has only seen a red-faced Wenceslao coughing, who all of the sudden stands up, as does Rogelio who is slapping him in the back with his open hand. Wenceslao's chair falls down behind him. Rosita . . . [and Amelia] look toward Wenceslao and Rogelio . . . Rosa stands and pulls her underwear up.]

The coexistence of several "contours" or "planes" in the same passage produces the simultaneity of different points of view. Hyperrealist descriptions thus disturb the nomenclatures of knowledge since their goal is not to decline an object *of* knowledge (a predetermined object by a series of discursive grids, an already known object that the reader's knowledge would come to "confirm" by recomposing the text's virtual paradigms), but rather the immaterial nature of sensation.

Coming back to the generative cell, it is important to stress that the present temporal dominant plays a decisive role in the story. This explains why it does not produce a generative transformation of its initial state ("there was a time when . . . and they lived happily ever after."),[27] but rather expands the present's very "thickness." If "La mayor" dealt with the internal perception of time by means of a recursive expansion of simultaneous series, thus saturating the now's discrete character through the obstinate application of a minimalist-atonal musical scheme, *El limonero real* introduces two procedures: a paradigmatic (descriptive) saturation and a juxtaposition of planes. While the former "stops" the narrative line, the latter decomposes the present's materiality, reducing all actions and processes to light corpuscles and patches of shadow. Finally, the text's descriptive dominant tends to break up the story's causal connectors and to introduce different relations of integration and composition:

> —Viene gente, dice.
> Agustín y Rogelio hacen girar la cabeza y miran. Rogelio se incorpora y entrecierra los ojos, poniéndose la mano como visera sobre los ojos. Ahora ellos también van a ver las manchas verde, azul y colorada, debatiéndose móviles y avanzando por el camino arenoso . . . Después sabrán que son la Negra y Josefa, las hijas de Agustín, que vienen de la ciudad con una amiga que han traído de paseo a conocer la costa [*the sequence in the future tense anticipates what will occur once the women arrive*] . . . Las manchas—azul, verde, colorada—refulgen. Parecen clavadas contra el horizonte de árboles, suspendidas sobre el camino Amarillo, sin siquiera rozarlo, moviéndose sobre él con contorsiones ondulantes y leves, sin avanzar. Después llegarán y serán reconocidas como la Negra, Josefa y su amiga Amelia [*a sequence in the future tense follows that expands the one above and narrates what will occur once the women join the family group*].
> (LR 77–78)

> [—People are coming, she says.
> Agustín and Rogelio turn their head and look. Rogelio stands up and squints, putting his hands over his eyes as a visor. Now they are also going to see the green, blue and red spots moving forward along the sandy path. Later they will know that they are Negra and Josefa, Agustín's daughters, that come from the city with a friend they brought . . . (*the sequence in the*

future tense anticipates what will occur once the women arrive) . . . The
spots—blue, green, read—shine. They seem nailed against the horizon of
trees, suspended above the yellow path, without even brushing it, moving
above it with light and weaving contortions, without progressing. They
will arrive afterwards and will be recognized as Negra, Josefa and her
friend Amelia (*a sequence in the future tense follows that expands the one
above and narrates what will occur once the women join the family group*).

The sequence produces a synchronic "cut" in the present and works its expansion by juxtaposing other temporal planes; at the same time, it breaks
up perception in its most discrete elements (*percepts* and affects).

Finally, the typographic materiality of the generative cell, which initi-
ates a series of nine repetitions (eight appear at the top of the different segments and one leaves the text open after the final segment's full stop, indicating the possibility of additional repetitions), isolates it from the rest of
the narrative utterances, making it hard to know whether they fall under the
enunciator-descriptor's jurisdiction or if they are autonomous. Do these utterances belong to the series of the "swarm of visions, memories and
thoughts" that define the instance Wenceslao-Layo or to the "opening's
rocky hardness"? It is more likely that they point to a unique sign that encompasses both the text and its textual operator.

What matters is that this diptych frames and commands the dual organization of the text's eight sequences, imposing a binary rhythm upon them:

I (5 pages)	VIII (5 pages)
Initial narrative situation narrated as the summary of actions, whose main focus is Wenceslao. *Awakening* →	Complete summary of actions, mostly focalized on Wenceslao. ← *Awakening*.
	The text remains open
II (28 pages)	VII (4 pages)
Wenceslao goes to Rogelio's house	Wenceslao returns from Rogelio's house
III (57 pages)	VI (32 pages)
Mid-day meal (fish)	Supper (lamb)
IV (65 pages)	V (20 pages)
Nap, dream and Wenceslao's "delirious story" Passage to the text's "other scene"	Wenceslao's dive into the river

This dual organization of the story's larger units in terms of an opening/
closure schema of sequences (departure/return; mid-day meal/supper; day-
break/day-break) should not make us lose sight of the fact that we are dealing with an open text, which is virtually infinite and, for this reason, full of
lacunae. It is sequence IV, the sequence of Wenceslao's nap, that occupies
the central position; this is the longest and the one that plays a decisive role
in the story: it exposes its deepest matrix, stages the work of *condensation,
displacement, considerations of representability* or *figuration and secondary elaboration.* In this sequence the text produces such a tight recipro-
cal implication of materials and procedures that it becomes hard to tell
which of the two has priority. As the emblematic *limonero real* (royal/real
lemon tree) that yields flowers and fruits simultaneously, the discrete series
of materials and the limited series of narrative situations are also simultaneous in their re-elaboration, as if there were no "blank page" preexisting
them. The "first series" (in the order of a lineal reading) unfolds as a whole
in section VIII through a syntactical matrix (having a diagrammatic value)
of the type "*ha* + a, b, c . . . n;" that is, as a list, of which I quote a brief extract below:

> ha escuchado primero que nada la respiración de ella que ha parecido, du-
> rante treinta años, despertar cada mañana, una fracción de segundo antes
> que él, y después se ha levantado, se ha vestido, ha dejado . . . ha intentado
> convencerla de que debe dejar atrás el tiempo del luto . . . ha atravesado el
> río en la canoa amarilla, ha visto las postas del enorme surubí despedazado
> por Rogelio . . . , ha atravesado remando plácido, el río . . . , ha entrado en
> el dormitorio, . . . y ahora, en medio de un rumor de viento y de lluvia, sa-
> biendo que ella, como todas las mañanas, se ha despertado una fracción de
> segundos antes que él, *está sentado en la cama, el corazón latiéndole de un
> modo violento*, en el reciento incoloro, porque amanece con los ojos abier-
> tos. (LR 222–27, my emphasis)

> [Before all else he has heard her respiration, she, who for thirty years, has
> seemed to wake up a fraction of a second before him, and then he has gotten
> up, dressed and left . . . he has attempted to persuade her to leave her mourn-
> ing behind . . . he has crossed the river in the yellow canoe . . . he has rowed
> placidly, the river . . . he has entered the bedroom, and now amidst the
> rumor of rain and wind, knowing that she, like every morning, has awoken
> a fraction of a second before him, is sitting on the bed, his heart beating vi-
> olently, in the colorless room, because he wakes up with his eyes open.]

This sequence declines a list of actions in the past perfect; it unfolds a set
of already completed actions up to the point where it "returns" to the in-

2 / LITTORAL, LITERAL

dicative present, the verbal tense in which the story's enunciation is situated. *El limonero real* narrates a series of completed actions and events that took place on December 31, but it does so from a point difficult to localize and although called "the next morning," is part of the expansion of the present that the generative cell establishes as a temporal horizon.

In section IV the "story of narrating" (Jitrik) reaches a turning point. I claim that this section is the staging of the dream work and of its operations (not the narration of a dream or of its contents)[28]: the processes of condensation and transformation that desire (the "beehive," *colmena*) produces and of the marks it stamps on the text's surface. That the story modulates the effects of an affective magma and that it also touches the deepest "archeological" layers of storytelling is evident in the typographical figure (plastic figure), the black square that marks a passage to the *other scene*, or to the other of discourse. At the heart of the text, there is a figure that does not belong to the order of language.

THE LETTER'S JOY

The sequence in section IV presents a series of states linked to drowsiness and a parallel series of hypnagogic images, midway between wakefulness and sleep, which become the dream's content. The sequence ends in the dissolution of language, of its articulations, and the passage to *another scene* signaled by the insertion of the black square. This square, whose surface is reminiscent of abstract paintings (Malevitch's black squares), introduces a plastic space alien to reading: the square is something to be "seen," even if it indicates that there is "nothing" to be seen; the letters surrounding it do not make up any intelligible lexical units (there is no message there). The square that marks the passage to the other of discourse introduces a nonlinguistic figure within the space of language.

On the other side of this black square, a marvelous tale is awaiting the reader, which combines a cosmogony (LR 139); a theodicy, an eschatology, and a political economy (LR 141–45); the fluvial gaucho's tour told according to the *Odyssey*'s epic model, but also sprinkled with elements of *gauchesca* literature. This epic tour includes the return to the home (LR 150) and the blessings of a Golden Age (whose emblem is the lemon tree) that suddenly ends in tragedy with the son's death after being drafted.

The sequence focuses on Wenceslao and presents a series of "mental states" that result from a splitting of body and mind: "Ha de haber sido el sol cayendo a pique lo que me tumbó. Ha de haber sido el sol" (It must have been the sun that knocked me down. It must have been the sun [LR 132]). The scene is a soliloquy in which a subject tries to explain to himself his current state by means of causal explanations, just as the story is about to dismantle the classic narrative causality; it therefore evinces a subjective split. Given that its chronological and causal situation is highly problematic, we must treat the sequence as an oneiric story in which the subject presents himself as both spectator *and* actor.[29] It is possible to associate the states that the story refers with experiences of déjà vu (paramnesia, recoiling temporal structures, a-chronology) and *amnesia* (contradiction, erasure by repetition, "enjambement" of sequences). The repetition of diegetic situations, the frequency of prolepsis, and the mixing up of intertexts that are at first repeated only to be erased are the common denominator of these two experiences.

Freud has shown that a dream is the work (working) of desire and that it results from applying a *force* upon a text: desire does not speak but forces the order of language. This is a primordial rather than an accidental violence: desire's imaginary fulfillment consists in a transgression that repeats what has occurred and does not stop occurring in the original phantasm. The figure entertains a double relation with desire: on the margin of discourse, it is the density behind which the subject hides what he states, while at the very core of language the figure is its "form." *Phantasie* is the dream's "façade" for Freud, a form shaped in its background. It is possible to locate a "seeing" there that, although at the heart of speech, is irreducible to language. What I wish to retain from the dream work (*Traumarbeit*) is the fact that it "does not think, does not calculate and, generally, does not judge; it just transforms (*umformen*)."[30] The dream work is a set of operations that one applies on the text's signification (*Traumgedanke*); defiguration or displacement (*Enstellung*) plays a crucial role since a dream is "the (distorted) fulfillment of a (repressed) wish."[31]

Sequence IV plays out the four major operations of the dream work: *condensation, displacement, considerations of representability or figuration,* and *secondary elaboration.* A brief summary is in order here. According to Freud, condensation produces a collision or juxtaposition of signifiers, signifieds, or both; it is the result of an "energetics" that treats the units of an "original text" "with freedom" (regarding the constraints of any linguistic message). Condensation supposes a change in state; its end product is opaque, dense, and hides its dark side. In the case of Wenceslao's dream, we have a text that violently juxtaposes each of the story's themes (a desire to forget everything, an infanticidal desire, a feeling of guilt, a desire to bring the dead son back to life, and an incestuous desire). The story's matrix is compressed and condensed in the space of seven pages.

The dream's second operation, displacement, is the "dream-work's essential part,"[32] prior to condensation; it consists in the transmutation of all values and a disguise of meanings, which produces a "textual difference" between manifest and latent contents. It is precisely here that Freud situates the overdetermination that results from transposition or deformation (*Entstellung*). In Wenceslao's dream we find a transposition and deformation of actions, settings, temporalities, and desires. Inasmuch as the characters are *figurants* of unconscious processes and not representatives of a social class, their features can be combined and, in fact, the text allows us to do so. Rogelio is the "good father" and thus doubles Wenceslao's relationship with his dead son, but Rogelio also enacts the sacrifice of his son Rogelito, which also doubles Wenceslao's "crime." Agustín is the "bad father" who wishes he had thrown his handicapped son into the river the day he was born and thus expresses an infanticidal desire that finds resonance in Wenceslao's dream. In the dream, he sees himself coming across a body floating in the river (the fragment of skin he sees is similar to the image he remembers of his dead son) that he fights against and kills. Finally, Agustín, the drunkard, (after the death of his own son Wenceslao says he also used to go home drunk) is the incestuous father; incest finds its correlate in Wenceslao's joyful dance with his young niece Teresita, the only one of Augustin's daughters who did not become a prostitute. In a sense Wenceslao's dream condenses and displaces all the contents of the family romance.

Through considerations of representability (*Rücksicht auf Darstellbarkeit*) the dream expresses how it establishes relationships among thoughts (*Gedanken*): simultaneity, causal relations, disjunctive conjunction, opposition, and contradiction. The considerations of representability are nothing other than the organization of an "original" text with a double purpose: to illustrate the text or to substitute some of its segments with figures. In the first case, the figure is outside the text and text and image are, in principle, presented alongside one another. In the second case, as in the *rebus*, we have the substitution of fragments of a "primary text" by its corresponding figures. The text must be transformed into something "with images." A text "in images" is a discourse very close to a figure. The major linguistic figures are the expression of a general disposition of experience and the phantasm is the matrix of such a cut, of the *rhythmia* imposed on all that happens in the order of "reality" and expression. These figures "present" a "first" figure; it is thanks to them that discourse can establish communication with images that supposedly are "external," but that in fact depend upon the same signifying matrix as discourse for its organization. As an example of the work of figuration, Freud mentions poetry, understood as an immanent rhythmic force; a "distribution and selection" of signs takes place in the dream and in poetry.

Finally, secondary elaboration transforms the dream into a daydream; it provides the dream with an order that conforms to the laws of intelligibility. It is interesting to note that Freud does not deal with this fourth operation as if it were the final term of the process, but as something simultaneous to the other three operations. The façade this operation erects, the order it must impose upon the chaos left by the other three operations can already be found in this particular element of the dream-thoughts' materials (*Traumgedanken*) that Freud calls *Phantasie* and whose "analogue in the daytime is the *Tagtraum*, the romance (novel), stories or tales. It is out of what the phantasm erects from these memories, and not out of the memories in themselves that hysterical symptoms develop."[33]

What lies on the dream's surface is the same as what can be found in its deepest reaches: phantasms. The "romance" or "novel" is not an ulterior ordering, but an archaic one in which the recollections (of primary scenes) are articulated: the phantasm is both façade *and* ground. For Freud secondary elaboration entertains the same type of relation with the dream content that preconscious thinking entertains with the materials of perception: a drivelike ordering that erases the difference between what is given and what is expected and that prevents any true giving; it is in discourse that Freud situates the function of the *pseudein*.

Although the sequence in question focalizes on Wenceslao, it is important to recall that as a *figurant* of the story's own processes of production, it can refer only to the two key instances of the text: first to language or the a-temporal "I" which is the text itself and, second, to an instance that rejects infanticidal (and incestuous) phantasms that language has put into circulation. This second instance tries to repress these phantasms but, *at the same time and in the same gesture*, seeks to satisfy those drives that the work sets in motion.[34]

In *El limonero real,* this staging of the complex interplay between primary and secondary processes induces a differentiation in the "self" between a physical and mental instance. Perceptions are felt as sensations localized in a particular region of the body and as processes of the immediately adjacent outer world:

ella venía corriendo desde el paraíso . . . ;
Ahora hay una mancha tirando a blanco atrás de un vidrio empañado;
Ahora veo de golpe el farol y las dos mariposas blancas

[she came running from the tree; Now there is a whitish stain behind a
clouded glass; Now I suddenly see the lantern and the white butterflies.][35]

The corporal "I" thus re-experiences an archaic phase while the mental "I"
dominates the process, acting as if it were an observer and interfering in the
hallucinatory enjoyment that the first instance, immerse as it is in a primitive state of satisfaction, experiences. Censorship rejects this enjoyment
because it is a substitute for a genital incestuous enjoyment. This incestuous desire is substituted by another phantasm that refers to infantile stages,
as in the case of the return to the womb, which in the text appears clearly
marked by recurrent isotopies: the "larva en el interior de un capullo"; the
"cuña afilada que hubiese penetrado en la masa compacta de la tierra"; the
"caverna reducida" (larva inside a cocoon, LR 27 and 165; the sharp
wedge that would have penetrated the compact mass of earth, LR 42 and
107; the narrow cavern, LR 42) and the waters/fluid of the amniotic river.
The two tendencies are fulfilled: the desire to kill the son (and of killing
and burying the memory of the dead son) and the desire to bring him back
to life (literally and metaphorically, as in gestation):

De a ratos todo se me borra . . . de a ratos se me aparece todo otra vez . . .
matamos al animal hace catorce años y después fuimos caminando despacio zac y nos zambullimos. Empezamos a nadar . . . Ahí entonces
chocamos con algo duro que estaba parado en el fondo con las piernas
abiertas y que después se nos prendió de un tobillo y empezó a tirar hacia
abajo cosa de llevarnos también a nosotros zac zac zac y dejarnos ahí . . .
Pero nosotros zaaaaac zaac zac nos prendimos y nos afirmamos y empezamos a apretar hasta que el otro cedió y empezó a patalear cada vez
más débil hasta que al fin zac no se movió más del todo y aflojó del todo y
se fue boyando zac. Quedamos nosotros solos adentro de la espiral de
barro hecha polvo que subía zac desde el fondo. No había lugar para nadie
más. Salimos del agua y nos acostamos a dormir la siesta. Y después
veníamos en la canoa verde bajo la llovizna finita. Hará como unos veinte
años, o sea seis años después que matamos al cordero. O sea veinte años.
(LR135–36)

[Things get fuzzy from time to time . . . from time to time things re-appear
. . . we killed the animal fourteen years ago and later we walked slowly zac
and we dove. We began to swim . . . We came up against something hard
that was standing in the bottom with its legs wide open and later latched on

to our shins and started to pull us down zac zac zac and leave us there . . .
But we zaaaaac zaac zac grabbed on and stood firm and began to squeeze
until the other one began to give up and began to kick less and less until at
last zac it no longer moved and it let go and began to float zac. We were
left alone the two of us inside the spiral of mud that rose zac from the
bottom. There was no room for anyone else. We came out of the water and
lay down for a nap. Afterwards we were in the green canoe under the light
rain. It must have been some twenty years ago, or six years after we killed
the lamb. That is, twenty years.]

A los muertos hay que rechazarlos más que a la bosta. Para mí la ley es lo
que uno quiere. (LR 154)

[One must reject the dead more than shit. For me the law is what one wants
it to be.]

Ha de haber sido el sol cayendo a pique lo que me tumbó . . . ella venía corriendo desde el paraíso, vestida de negro . . . ahí debo de haber caído. Y después siento los brazos que me empiezan a palpar . . . Siento por encima de
los gritos el ruido de los pieces que siguen corriendo en dirección al río,
mientras unos brazos me palpan y tratan de soliviantarme . . . y después no
oigo más nada. Nada. Porque estoy esperando, porque estoy esperando que
venga la explosión de la zambullida, porque estoy esperando que venga la
explosión de la zambullida del cuerpo que salió de ella idéntico saltando al
agua para buscar lo que yo dejé que la corriente se llevara hace catorce
años. (LR 133–34)

[It must have been the sun that knocked me down . . . She came running
from the tree, dressed in black . . . I must have fallen there. And later I feel
the arms that begin to touch me . . . above the shouts, I hear the noise of feet
running toward the river, while arms grope me and try to help me up . . .
and later I hear nothing else. Nothing. Because I am waiting, because I am
waiting for the explosion of the dive, because I am waiting for the dive's
explosion, the body that came out from inside her the same plunging into
the water to look for what I let the current take some fourteen years ago.]

The story stages the operations of the dream-work; it condenses, displaces
and explicitly sets down the norms for the "considerations of its representability" (figuration).

El limonero real's sequence IV provokes a desire for a time "before"
language, what we could call regression.[36] The hallucinatory satisfaction is
regressive because it supposes a reverse path of the psychical apparatus,
the opposite of a specific action that begins with an excitation that then

passes through memories, verbal traces, motor activities, produces a trans-formation of reality, and finally fulfillment as an external discharge. In the hallucinatory satisfaction, instead, excitation crosses the layers of the psy-chical apparatus in the opposite sense, "charging" the recollection with very intense perceptions and thus causing a hallucination. The displace-ment of energy toward the perceptive pole instead of the verbal-motor pole is regressive then and results from the principle of immediate discharge. But there is regression in a historical sense too: a reactivation of the first satisfaction takes place and therefore a return to the infantile experience. This regression is characterized fundamentally by the use of "primitive modes of expression and figuration instead of the normal ways."[37]

The attraction that the visual recollection exerts upon a thought process separated from consciousness, as well as the censorship's supplementary intervention, cause the regression: the elaboration of dis-figured figures in-stead of recognizable figures and the *rebus* instead of a text. This regres-sion to more elementary or "primitive" forms of storytelling (marvelous, popular, and fairy tales) follows the dissolution of language and covers up the phantasm's appearance—the death of the infant son (always remem-bered as a young boy):

> Ahora se me borra otra vez todo. Ahora abro los ojos otra vez y veo el farol, pero no las mariposas blancas. Las mariposas negras grandísimas se mueven negadas al necho y a la nared. Zddzzzzzzzzzz. Ahora se me borra todo otra vez zdddzzzzzzz. Todo borrado. Nono nonado. Enanan nenadas nas nos nuna nene none nena nana na ona none nanina. Nanién nanuno nenado nenacón. Zac zac
> zaczac   zddzzzz   zddzzzzzzzz   zac   zac   zddzzzzzzzzzzzz
> zaczaczac   zddzzzzzzzzzzzzzzzzzzzzzzzzzz   zzzzzzzzzzzzzzaaac
> zzzzzzzzzaaaaaaaaaaaaac
> zddzzzzzzzzzzzzz

>   aaaaaaaa
> aaaa   aa   a   a   agtth   srkk   srkk   aaaa   aaa   aatth   srk . . .
> Era vea un solo ver agua. Agua y después más nada. (LR 138–39)

[Now everything becomes fuzzy again. Now I open my eyes again and I see the lantern but not the white butterflies. The huge black butterflies moved stuck to the ceiling and the wall. Zddzzzzzzzzzz. Now everything becomes fuzzy again. zdddzzzzzzz. Everything is gone . . . Zac zac zaczac zddzzzz zddzzzzzzz zac zac zddzzzzzzzzzzzz zaczaczaczddzzzzzzzzzzzzzzzzzzzzzzzzzzz zzzzzzzzzzzzzzaaac zzzzzzzzzaaaaaaaaaaaac zddzzzzzzzzzzz [black rectangle] aaaaaaaa aaaa aa a a agtth srkk srkk aaaa aaa aatth srk . . . It was, you see, water all around. Water and then nothing else.]

The dreamer (writer) is only an entity that writes (in the very moment of writing), that confuses itself with "lalangue," the maternal language (material and body) and with the text (its organization) he shapes while composing its unique textual *corpus*. By exhibiting the drives that underlie the story, the writer exposes the connivance between desire, its figure, and the phantasm; like Wenceslao, he can do no more than kill his son (*infans*) / the work. The text, a cycle of eight stories and *not* of nine (an interrupted gestation), is experienced as a process of separation and disintegration that the form called *El limonero real* can do no more than negate.

From then on, it is the text that dreams (about) itself, that hallucinates itself, that is written as a covering up: the marvelous tale in which Wenceslao goes to Paradise (*Paraíso*) and meets with his own father and his dead son is the simple transformation of the signifier /*paraíso*/ (a tree) that loses its leafy materiality to become a compensatory scene.[38]

The reader cannot retrieve an "origin" (neither of language, nor of the story itself) from a text that, unlike the mythic foundations of the precursors (Carpentier, García Márquez, Borges), repeats a deep matrix that is both surface and background. Desire does not work on a "clean slate" that is later distorted: what we have from "the start" is a text worked by desire, a mixture of what is legible and visible. The reader who believes, as Wenceslao first does, that at the center of the island or of the text lies a virginal and original page ("a portion of wet land that no one has seen," LR 81) will have to give up her desire of plenitude because "the three deep marks, regular, identical" (LR 99) that Wenceslao finds later in that very same spot, and which signal that no such origin is possible, will surely disappoint her. Saer's text does not exhibit its mechanisms of construction as a way of setting the stage for a hallucinatory coincidence between text and origin. This explains why he must return once and again to the same themes, scenarios, configurations, and even obsessions.

3

Saer's Fiction:
"A Speculative Anthropology?"
The Witness (El entenado)

En ese lugar sin nombre al que el nombre de pasado,
de tan fácil pronunciación, parece cuadrar tan bien,
sin que haya, sin embargo en el reverso de los sonidos
que se expelen al proferirlo o de los rastros de tinta
que se dejan al escribirlo, ninguna imagen precisa
para representárselo.

—Saer, Glosa

[In that nameless place which the name past—so easy
to pronounce—seems to suit so well, without there
being however, in the underside of the sounds emitted
when uttering it or in the traces of ink that are left
when writing it, a precise image to represent it.]

We are a sign, unreadable,
we are without pain, and we have
almost lost language in a foreign place.

—Hölderlin, "Mnemosyne"

Is there a place for the bastard in onto-theology or in
the Hegelian family?

—Derrida, Glas

In this house you will learn that it is hard to be a
foreigner. You will also learn that it is not easy to
stop being one. If you regret your country, each day
you will find here more reasons to regret it; but if
you manage to forget it and to love your new home,
you will be sent back to your country where, once
again displaced, you will start a new exile.

—Blanchot, "The Idyll"

THE TURN: FOUNDATIONS
AND LITERARY FOUNDERS

JUAN JOSÉ SAER'S REFLECTIONS ON LITERATURE ARE COLLECTED IN A
text with the suggestive title *Una literatura sin atributos* (*Literature Without Attributes*).[1] This collection of essays revolves around a number of key
issues that are crucial for understanding Saer's poetics: writing's autonomy;
a critique of magical realism and its most recent versions; a questioning of
the cultural presuppositions underlying the concept of "Latin American
Literature," especially those critical discourses that tend to substantivize
the adjective and subordinate the priority of the literary. To these essays we
must add "El concepto de ficción" (The Concept of Fiction) (1991) and
"*Zama*: Di Benedetto entre la incomprensión y el olvido" (*Zama*: Di Benedetto between Incomprehension and Forgetting) (1986) that, although not
included in *Una literatura sin atributos*, are especially revealing of Saer's
theory of fiction. In the first essay, written within the context of a polemic
against certain contemporary positions that subordinate writing to the demands of either a doctrinaire truth or of the publishing industry, Saer attempts to define fiction as follows:

> No podemos ignorar que en las grandes ficciones de nuestro tiempo, y
> quizás de todos los tiempos, está presente ese entrecruzamiento crítico
> entre la verdad y la falsedad, esa tensión íntima y decisiva . . . como el
> orden central de todas ellas, a veces en tanto que tema explícito y a veces
> como fundamento implícito de su estructura. El fin de la ficción no es ex-
> pedirse en ese conflicto sino hacer de él su material . . . A causa de su as-
> pecto principalísimo del relato ficticio, y a causa también de sus inten-
> ciones, de su resolución práctica, de la posición singular de su autor entre
> los imperativos de un saber objectivo y las turbulencias de la subjetividad,
> podemos definir de un modo global la ficción como una *antropología es-
> peculativa*. Quizás—no me atrevo a afirmarlo—esta manera de concebirla
> podría neutralizar tantos reduccionismos que, a partir del siglo pasado, se
> obstinan en asediarla. Entendida así, la ficción sería capaz no de ignorar-
> los, sino de asimilarlos, incorporándolos a su propia esencia y despoján-do-
> los de sus pretensiones de absoluto. Pero el tema es arduo, y conviene de-
> jarlo para otra vez.[2]

> [We cannot ignore that in the major fictions of our times and, perhaps, in
> those of any time, this critical crisscrossing between truth and falsehood,
> this intimate and decisive tension, not free of comicality or gravity, is pre-
> sent as the organizing center; sometimes, as an explicit theme, at others as
> the implicit ground of their structures. Fiction's purpose is not to solve this

conflict, but to treat that conflict as its material and to shape it "in its own way." Because of this central aspect of fictional narrative and because of its intentions and practical resolution, the singular position of its authors is caught between the imperative of an objective knowledge and the turbulence of subjectivity; because of all these factors, then, we may define fiction in general terms as a *speculative anthropology*. Perhaps—I do not dare to affirm it emphatically—this way of conceiving fiction neutralizes the multiple reductions that, since the last century, have been holding it under siege. Thus understood fiction would be able to assimilate these reductions by incorporating them to its own essence and consequently deprive them of their absolutist pretensions. However, the topic is difficult and it is best to leave it for another time.]

The complexity of the problem, Saer's caution, his abrupt way of stating a definition that, to my knowledge, he never returns to in his essays, and finally the overdetermined nature of the formula *speculative anthropology* forces us to pause and ask how one should read it, which of the two terms should be stressed, how should the concept, the figure of "man," be thought for an anthropology that duplicates itself in the fold of speculation and, finally, how one should deal with the speculative effects of "speculation"?

In what follows, I propose an elucidation of the term *speculative anthropology* through a reading of Saer's *The Witness* for which, or from which, this expression seems to have been coined. I propose a hypothetical equivalence: *"The Witness = speculative anthropology"* or *"The Witness* or the concept of fiction *as speculative anthropology."* Because I begin not knowing what to understand by "anthropology" and by "speculation," and even less by *speculative anthropology*, this formula will not constitute a frame of reference able to both contain and solve every paradox put into play by *The Witness*. The hypothetical equivalence between the text, the concept of fiction and the phrase that aims to be its definition, does not pretend to be absolute. Consequently, the whole weight of my reading cannot but fall upon the *as* that allows me to put the different terms into a series, as if they were an analogical relation.

Saer's critical essay, *"Zama*: Di Benedetto entre la incomprensión y el olvido," helps to clarify these preliminary considerations. This essay seems to present no more than a critical reading of Antonio Di Benedetto's homonymous *nouvelle* and takes a stand against a group of critics who reduced *Zama* to a historical novel. However, the movement of the essay goes beyond a simple revaluation of Di Benedetto. Written in 1986 and in an almost Borgean gesture, this critical piece on a totally extemporaneous text (*Zama* was published in 1956, although reedited in 1985) posits, on the one hand, a hyperbolic valorization of Di Benedetto, a "writer from the provinces" who kept himself, as did Saer, on the margins of the *Boom* and whose work marks an important turning point in fictional writing. According to Saer, *Zama* is a *nouveau roman avant la lettre* that signals a departure from the dominant sociological and existentialist orientation of realist fictional writing. This valorization transforms itself into the tracing or establishment of a lineage: Di Benedetto is part of a "family of writers" that includes Jorge Luis Borges, Felisberto Hernández, and Juan L. Ortíz. But more elliptically, on the other hand, through *Zama* Saer proposes an encoded reading of *The Witness*. *Zama* is a text that shares certain thematic and technical preoccupations with Saer's text and can be considered its textual precursor. One may also affirm that this self-reading anticipates a series of interpretations of *The Witness* that have crystallized in the last years and of which I will have more to say in a moment. Saer claims that:

> Toda narración transcurre en el presente, aunque habla, a su modo, del pasado. El pasado no es más que el rodeo lógico, e incluso ontológico, que la narración debe dar para asir, a través de lo que ya ha perimido, la incertidumbre frágil de la experienda narrativa que tiene lugar, del mismo modo que su lectura, en el presente. El esfuerzo de Di Benedetto tiende, por lo tanto, a exaltar la validez del presente y a hacerla más comprensible mediante un alejamiento metafórico hacia el pasado.[3]

> [All narration takes place in the present, although it speaks, in its own way, of the past. The past is simply a logical detour, a turn (*rodeo*), even an ontological one, that narration must make in order to grasp, through what has already vanished, the fragile uncertainty of the narrative experience which takes place in the present. Di Benedetto's effort tends, therefore, to exalt the validity of the present, to make of it something more comprehensible through a metaphorical distancing toward the past.]

The movement at issue here, designated by the expression "past *as* turn or detour," exposes narration to an interstitial space from which the past can be neither nostalgically recuperated nor overcome by the simple expression of a progressive optimism. Narration marks a retreat of the *present* as a condition *to present* what sustains and alters presence. Therefore, the "turn" does not produce a content that could become the product of a formal reconstruction or revision of the past but rather points to a modality of relating to the past that supposes a double narrative strategy. On the one hand, writing appropriates some of the loci of a literary tradition that is perceived as closed, but from which it is possible to separate (in the chemical sense of the expression) the essentialist presuppositions and mystifying elements underlying them. In what follows, special attention will be paid to the modalities of the "turn," of which we have an index *speculative anthropology* that displaces the category of "(new) historical novel" as a possible frame of reference.[4]

THE "PRIMAL SCENE OF THE RIVER PLATE"
(HETEROLOGIES AND THE *CHRONICLES*)

In *The Witness*, the "past *as* turn" involves an event of the colonization of the River Plate that is still highly disputed by historians: the attack of Juan Díaz de Solís' expedition by a presumably anthropophagous tribe.[5] In his *El río sin orillas* (1991) Saer refers to this event as the "primal scene (*escena primitiva*) of the River Plate" (RO 56). Although I plan to unfold the implications of this Freudian term (*Urszene*), for now it is important to point out that as both the limit and the condition of possibility of narration, and as the marker of a differential temporality redefining the notion of "present," the term *Urszene* indicates the problematic status of the (narrative) event in Saer. In addition, "primal scene" also indicates the peculiar position that *The Witness* occupies in Saer's corpus, since it is a text that produces its reorganization *aprés coup* and whose inter- and intratextual effects are still operative both in *La ocasión* and *Glosa*.[6]

The "turn" in question takes place under a double modality: cannibalism and the invention of the other.[7] By the former, *The Witness* parasitizes the classical heterological textual paradigm. I locate the "logical turn" at this level since what is at stake here is another way of writing the other beyond any logic. By the latter, *The Witness* exceeds the classical heterology, not without leaving the whole economy of invention untouched. At this level, I locate the ontological dimension of the "turn."

To parasitize the classical heterology means to situate *The Witness* in a peculiar relation to a long textual chain "on the other" inaugurated by Herodotus. This chain finds its most decisive re-articulation during European modernity with Jean de Léry's *Histoire d'un Voyage faict en la Terre du Bresil* (whose sources are *La Brevísima Relación de Indias* by Bartolomé de las Casas and the *Historia Natural de las Indias* by López de Gómara) and whose effects can be read in Montaigne, Rousseau, and Lévi-Strauss. Jean Lestrignant suggests that "The interest of Léry's work lies in the gaze and the conscience that emerge in the face of the other, in the course of an arduous ocean voyage that takes the narrator into the midst of a naked and cannibalistic peoples. We could say that Léry's *Histoire* combines the *Bildungsroman* with the adventure novel, provided we do not forget that *it is a testimony whose truth is affirmed at each point*."[8] Both de Léry's *Histoire* and Montaigne's essay "Du Cannibales" employ the same model of narrative authority: they claim to be the testimony of a trustworthy witness. Also, both texts share the structure of a travel narrative that, according to Michel de Certeau, is articulated in three stages: a trip toward the unknown, the description of a savage society such as it is seen by a true and reliable witness, and the return to the realm of the familiar, the home (the *oikos*).

The structuring moments of this threefold structure are as follows: the first produces a rhetoric of distancing, what the sixteenth century called the "insólito" (marvelous), endowing both the alterity of the savage with substantiality and the text with a force to speak from elsewhere, another place, and still be able to control the reader's belief. The third stage supplements this narrative authority by making the act of speaking in the name of the other legitimate. The second and central stage contains the "ethnological" description of savage society seen from the viewpoint of a "true witness." This description revolves around two issues: cannibalism and polygamy. The end product of this travel is the graphic configuration of the savage.[9]

Montaigne's essay "Du Cannibales" allows us to delineate a topology of the text on the other. If one assumes that the underlying question of "Du Cannibales" is the place the other occupies, one can conceive the essay's textual operations as spatializing ones. "Du Cannibales" produces two kinds of spatializing operations: first, a displacement of the borders delimiting different cultural fields (in this particular case the familiar versus the strange; proximity versus distance); and second, a re-articulation and revaluation of the internal divisions organizing a culture. These two spatializing operations are proper to the texts *"on* the other," to the classical heterology, whose archaeological history, according to de Certeau, should include Herodotus's *Histories* as their "fundamental textual precondition," since it "combines a representation of the other and the fabrication and accreditation of the text as witness of the other."[10]

We can now begin to assess the ways in which *The Witness* situates itself regarding the classical heterology. Two sets of preliminary considerations are necessary: first, the English translation of *El entenado* is *The Witness*.[11] This title privileges the juridical aspect of the narration and also draws on the archaeological form of legitimation that links Saer's story with the series of texts I have mentioned above. However, such a translation is asymmetrical with respect to the title in Spanish since it tends to legitimate one narrative form for which the question of origination or origins is vital: witnessing.

The title in Spanish is neutral regarding any of the multiple narrative modalities the text employs, while *The Witness* reduces the opacity at play in *El Entendo* (who, what?). In addition, *El Entendo* is a crucial lexical form, since it opens the problematic chain on origins that recurs throughout the text and for which Saer's French translator, proposes *L'ancêtre*,[12] thus preserving the semantic field of *entenado* (*ante natus*) and allowing the title to open up, by condensation, the long chain on origins and births that supplements the meanings of orphanhood, bastardy, and adoption implicit in the word "entenado." This word, at least in the River Plate area, has the value of a linguistic monument. One could force the entryway to this monument or crypt by fissuring its inscription: *entel nado*-a (being/ nothing), an operation that will allow us to read this text in a register that exceeds that of testimony. Consequently, it is both necessary to take into account the refusal to translate "entenado" by any of its equivalents (orphan, bastard, stepson), as well as to question the testimonial narrative regime that the English translation presents as the organizing motif: what is it that *gives itself* (here I emphasize the giving of) to be read as a testimony—if there is something like a testimony—and how? Second, the relation of *The Witness* with the classical heterology is not a simple one: the text occupies some of the loci of the classical text "*on* the other" while, at the same time, it displaces others. But, fundamentally, *The Witness* disarticulates the structure of the heterological text in order to inscribe within its blanks the possibility of another text that exceeds any hetero-*logics*.

The paradigm of the heterological text is inscribed in the very paratext of *The Witness* in the form of an epigraph taken, not by chance, from Herodotus's *Histories*: "más allá están los Andrófagos, un pueblo aparte, y después viene el desierto total." (further away are the Androphagi, a people apart, and then comes the desert [4:277]).[13] In other words, the archaeological precondition of the text "*on* the other," to recall de Certeau's words, appears as the textual ancestor of *The Witness*. The mention of the "desert" through Herodotus takes back the Argentine literary ideologeme "desierto" to an a-topical past, and it opens it to a broader series than the one chronologically circumscribed by del Puerto's *Memorias* and Schmidel's *Derrotero*.

This is the only direct and explicit citation, although throughout the text it is possible to recognize textual operators of the classical heterology. For example, the dialogue between the narrator-protagonist and Father Quesada parallels the narrative structure of the classical ethnographic interview, especially the chapters of de Léry's *Histoire*, "Sur le Cannibalisme" (chapter 15) and "Sur la Hospitalité" (chapter 18).[14] Nevertheless, there are two noteworthy strategies through which *The Witness* complicates the narrative structure of the classical heterology. The first affects the circularity of the travel narrative that entails the heterological reduction of the other to the same, of the other as the same (the bringing home of the other, strange, savage), while the second prevents the hypostasis of the narrative voice with that of the protagonist, the narrative overlapping that sustains the testimony's veracity, by targeting the traditional authorization of the classical text on the other.

My reading of *The Witness* forces me to question the critical interpretations that reduce Saer's text to a simple rewriting of the *Crónicas de Indias* to a new historical novel or to the commemoration of the first cultural encounter in the River Plate area.[15] Although there seems to be room for these interpretations, it seems to me that they lose sight of the operations that the text performs in order to open up the closure of the invention of the other outside or in the margins of what is calculable and to produce an encounter with the real (*lo refractario*).[16] In other words, I suggest here that what *The Witness* proposes is a different invention of the "invention of the other." Like Di Benedetto's *Zama*, *The Witness* functions as a "turn" whose implications cannot be fully accounted for by the strong referential orientation of the critical readings mentioned above. Only an examination of cannibalism and the invention of the other will allow us to delimit the implications of this "turn" in Saer's poetics.

EATING THE OTHER:
THE RHETORIC OF CANNIBALISM

> I practice a cannibal style.
> —Flaubert, *Correspondence*

> The cannibal is the other too similar to oneself, a
> mirror in which one refuses to stare at oneself. The
> savage's monstrosity consists in a desperate effort to
> establish a difference at any cost. It should be
> stressed that for the Indians themselves the cannibal
> is also the other: the most serious judgment that the
> Guayakis, who are themselves anthropophagous, can
> pass on others, is to say they are man-eaters.
> —Isabelle Combès, *La tragédie cannibale*
> *chez les anciens Tupi Guarani*, 46

Two sequences recur throughout *The Witness*: a cannibalistic feast (a scene filled with debauchery, blood, and gore) and its direct contrast, an apparently idyllic scene in which a group of children play at the banks of a river alongside the feast.[17] To be more precise, the feast is constructed as a recurrent scene in the form of "a recurrent memory." The horizon of both sequences is temporality. While the first sequence inscribes a circular recurrence, the second one undermines the illusory nature of a continuous temporality. In relation to the second sequence we read:

> Uno de esos recuerdos es, cosa curiosa, el de los niños que vi al día siguiente de mi llegada, jugando lejos del caserío, en la orilla del agua. En diez años, los niños cambiaban pero como los grupos se formaban con criaturas de todas las edades, los más chicos iban creando la continuidad, de modo tal que parecía siempre el mismo grupo que había visto el primer día . . . Debo haber visto jugar a esas criaturas cientos de veces pero, en mi memoria, es siempre el mismo recuerdo, el del primer día, el que vuelve cada vez más obstinado y más nítido.

> [Curiously enough, one of these memories is of the children I saw the day after my arrival far from the huts, on the river's bank. I often saw them happily playing the same game beneath the quiet sun. In my ten years there the group changed. But since the group was made up of children of all ages, the smaller ones created a kind of continuity, so that it always seemed to me to be the same group I had seen on that first day. And it is true that they did try to keep everything the same at all times and thus create an illusion of immobility.] (W 137)

A detailed description of the game follows, which is a description of the transformations of a circle into different figures:

> Tanta terquedad por perdurar en la luz adversa del mundo sugiere, tal vez, alguna complicidad con su esencia profunda. Ha de ser, sin duda, la cifra de cosas elementales, como la forma del tiempo o la razón del espacio, atravesadas por el ir y venir de la misma sangre humana entre sobresaltos, maravilla y titilaciones. Pero aun cuando ninguna cosa oculta se revele, una y otra vez, en la imagen de esos juegos, su reaparición constante en mi memoria, cada vez con mayor simplicidad, va gastando, poco a poco, la borra de los acontecimientos que contiene, para dejar la limpidez geométrica de esas figuras que las criaturas trazaban, con sus cuerpos. (E 137–39)

> [Such obstinacy to endure in the unfriendly light of the world suggests, perhaps, some complicity with its deepest essence. It must have been,

without question, the cipher of very elementary things, like the form of
time or the reason for the existence of space. But even if no hidden meaning were revealed, every time, in the image of those games, its constant
reappearance in my memory, each time in an ever simpler form, is wearing
out, little by little, the sediment of the events it contains so as to simply
leave the geometrical lines of the figures that the children formed with
their bodies on the sand.] (W 138–39)

Critics have pointed out the importance of the figure of play in Saer's fiction. The game is a ciphered figure of the narrative itself, of its economy
and tropological transformations. On the one hand, play points to the narrative's movement that folds and unfolds upon itself, transforming its own
materials.[18] On the other hand, the play of figures undermines the hierar-
chical relation between lived experience and its own remembrance that apparently articulates the narration. The narrator-protagonist talks about "the
sediment of events" (*la borra de los acontecimientos*) and of the "geometrical lines of the figures" (*limpidez geométrica de las figuras*) and thus signals that the recurrence of an event, the narrative recurrence of a recurring
event, is presented within an economy of decantation in which the event,
through repetition, is divested of its aleatory elements. What remains are
the traces of figures as well as the trace of the tracing of figures.

The text constructs itself not as the remembrance of a lived experience
but fundamentally as the "experience" of a construction that makes problematic the very possibility of recollecting an event without remainder.
Further, a consideration on the nature of memories frames the sequence
quoted above. These are presented either as "clear forms" or as "chaotic
series." In the sequence in question memory is a "clear form." However,
the clarity of this form is nothing more than the textualization of this form.
In other words, the becoming-clear of the memory is a textual effect. By
pointing to the ontologically irresolute nature of what is narrated, *The Witness* exposes the aporias proper to a classic form of memory (*anamnesis*):
"todo lo que creo saber de ellos [los indios] me viene de signos inciertos,
de recuerdos dudosos, de interpretaciones. Mi relato puede significar
muchas cosas a la vez, sin que ninguna de ellas sea necesariamente cierta"
(E 160). [All I believe I know about them (the cannibals) comes from uncertain signs, from doubtful memories, from interpretations. My account
may mean many things at once, without any of them being necessarily true
(W 160)]. The narration questions the very provenance of its own materials and thus exposes itself to uncertainty, while memory will be referred to
as atopic and autonomous.

The cannibalistic feast recurs with the temporality of the cycle ("I lived with them for ten years and ten times I saw them seized by the same madness" [W 82]). For the narrator-protagonist, cannibalism is an object of reflection, of *speculation*. He tries to understand its roots and, in so doing, constructs a narrative, an ontology of the cannibals based on an understanding of their language. To understand cannibalism is to understand the cannibal order and the narrator-protagonist's own place within that order. His place is also lexically marked by a sequence of sounds from the language of the Indians, "Defghi," which is how the cannibals refer to him and, more importantly, appeal to him. The interpretation of cannibalism, the deciphering of a name, and an understanding of the narrator-protagonist's position are all activities placed under the regime of writing, of a type of writing that questions representation.

Although *The Witness* presents sequences that seem to thematize the theme of the "noble savage," as for example when Father Quesada defines the Indians as being "la descendencia putativa de Adán" (the supposed offspring of Adam), the cannibal is treated neither under a moral register nor under an ethnological one. The narrator-protagonist refers to them as to "the only true (*verdaderos*) men" and as "the only real (*reales*) men." The cannibal is therefore framed within the problematic of the real. The status of the reality of this real is submitted to speculation's vertiginous play. The cannibals are the only real/true men and, yet the narrator indicates that they are at an ontological impasse:

> Que algo les faltaba era seguro, pero yo no alcanzaba, viéndolos desde afuera, a saber qué. Espiaban el día vacío, el cielo abierto, la costa luminosa, con la esperanza de recibir, del aire que cabrilleaba, un llamado o una visión. Como sin centro y sin fuerzas derivaban esperando. La substancia común que parecía aglutinar a la tribu, dándole la cohesión de un ser único, se debilitaba amenazándola de errabundeo y dispersión. (E 75)

> [It was obvious that they were lacking something, but I could not fathom what. They kept a watchful eye on the blank day, the clear sky, the luminous coast, in the hope of receiving some message or revelation from the dancing air. With nothing to cling to, they drifted in passive expectancy. The common substance that glued the tribe together, that gave them the cohesion of a single being, grew weaker, threatening them with errancy and dispersion.] (W 78)

An unnamable lack is the defining trait of cannibalism. The problem of naming, of the name of this lack, is not an aleatory one. For the Indians, the articulation of the name of what is lacking cannot take place, it can only be deferred by the cyclical return of (the act of) eating the other, whose most notorious effects are the absolute oblivion of its excess and transgression. For the narrator, the attempt to articulate it produces more storytelling or makes the storytelling to be subjected to a *mise en abîme*. This *mise en abîme* takes place within the context of the scene of an appeal that unfolds in two stages.

According to Jacques Lacan, the appeal always supposes a desire for recognition but "the demand in itself concerns something else than the satisfaction it calls forth. It is a demand for a presence or an absence."[19] The first part of the scene in question presents the demand as something incomprehensible, not without exposing the force of its unconditional and non-transitive character:

> Objeto de atenciones o de indiferencia, de obsequiosidad súbita y pasajera, de *demandas incomprensibles* o de desdén persistente, yo derivaba entre ellos, convencido de que lo que parecían esperar de mí, si es que esperaban algo, no lo obtendrían con mi muerte sino más bien con mi presencia constante y mi atención paciente a sus peroratas. (E 70)

> [Treated attentively and indifferently by turns, or with sudden, fleeting obsequiousness, the object of incomprehensible demands or persistent disdain, I drifted amongst (the Indians), convinced that what they seemed to expect of me if, that is, they expected anything at all, would not be achieved through my death but rather through my constant presence and my patient attention to their harangues.] (W 70)

The second part having to do with comprehension, is that of the *mise en abîme*; one year after his arrival in the New World, the cycle of human hunting and cannibalism repeats itself, and the narration turns upon itself as well:

> Pero yo no venía en esas embarcaciones—venía, eso sí, un hombre vivo, que tendría tal vez, mi edad, y se mantenía rígido e inmóvil entre los remeros. Def-ghi, Def-ghi, le decían algunos apenas pisó tierra, cuando el desórden y la multitud les impedían aproximarse a los cadáveres que los miembros de la expedición desembarcaban . . . El prisionero los ignoraba y si de vez en cuando se dignaba mirar a alguno, lo hacía con desdén calculado y menosprecio indiferente. Def-ghi, Def-ghi, insistían los otros, señalándose a sí mismos para atraer la atención del prisionero hacia sus personas. Las mismas sonrisas acarameladas que yo conocía tanto le eran dirigidas, las mismas bromas de mal gusto . . . la misma *ostentación teatral*

para configurarse un personaje fácilmente reconocible desde el exterior.
Adrede el prisionero ignoraba esos actos de seducción, lo cual contribuía a
estimularlos, incitándolos a tanta variedad que en un determinado momento no se sabía *si* el cambio de actitud era verdadero o fingido y si el
paso de la hilaridad a la rabia, del sentimentalismo a la violencia, de la al-
tanería a la obscenidad, *era causado por el deseo que tenían de componer
una actitud que podía ser aprehendida de immediato,* una modificación
deliberada *o si,* en realidad, movidos por la indiferencia del prisionero y
por la ansiedad que su presencia parecía infundirles, llenos de incertidumbre y de confusión, *eran como una substancia blanda e informe que el
vaivén del acontecer moldeaba en figuras arbitrarias y pasajeras.* (E 79)

[But I did not come in those ships . . .—a man would arrive that had my
age, perhaps, and would remain rigid and immobile . . . Def-ghi, Def-ghi
some would say to him as soon as he touched ground, pointing to themselves in order to attract the attention of the prisoner . . . I saw them use the
same theatrical display in order to configure an easily recognizable character from the outside, but it was hard to say if the change of attitude was
genuine, or if it was caused by the desire they had to construct a pose that
could be immediately grasped.] (W 79)

The narration folds and repeats the scene of the narrator-protagonist's
arrival. This specular fold points to what is at stake in cannibalism: the
very possibility of representation as the fiction of speculative reflection.
Cannibalism is a metonymy for a desire of presence understood as immediate representation: an (impossible) desire for a fiction of representation,
for fiction as representation. Within the frame of fiction desired as representation the thing lacking produces its effects, which are structured as the
narrator's explanations of cannibalism's roots.

These explanations take the form of a narrative that presents the history
of cannibalism as the passage from autophagy to alelophagy. This passage
came about, according to the narrator, by "some archaic disaster": "if they
acted this way, it was because they had experienced the weight of the void"
(*el peso de la nada*). The question underlying cannibalism is therefore an
ontological one:

*Lo exterior era su principal problema. No lograban como hubiesen
querido, verse desde afuera . . .* En los primeros tiempos me daban la impresión de ser la medida exacta que definían, entre la tierra y el cielo, el
lugar de cada cosa . . . Daban la impresión envidiable de estar en este
mundo más que toda otra cosa . . . Lentamente, sin embargo, fui compren-
diendo que se trataba más bien de lo contrario, que, para ellos, a ese mundo

que parecía tan sólido, había que actualizarlo a cada momento para que no
se desvaneciese como un hilo de humo en el atardecer. Esa comprobación
la fui haciendo a medida que penetraba, como en una ciénaga, en el idioma
que hablaban. Era una lengua imprevisible, contradictoria, sin forma
aparente . . . En ese idioma, no hay ninguna palabra que equivalga a *ser* o
estar. La más cercana significa *parecer* . . . Como tampoco tienen artículos,
si quieren decir hay un árbol, o que un árbol es un árbol dicen *parece*
árbol. Pero parece tiene menos el sentido de similitud que el de descon-
fianza. Es más un vocablo negativo que positivo. Implica más objeción que
comparación. No es que remita a una imagen ya conocida sino que tiende,
más bien, a desgastar la percepción y a restarle contundencia . . . Para los
indios todo parece y nada es. (E 121–22)

[The outside was their principal problem. They could not, as they would
have wished, see themselves from the outside . . . There is no equivalent in
their language for "to be." The closest equivalent they have means 'to
seem' (*parecer*). But 'seem' has more a sense of untrustworthiness than of
sameness. It is a negative word more than a positive one. It implies an objection more than a comparison. It does not refer to an already known
image but tends to erode perception and diminish its force. Also, the same
word with a change in pronunciation names presence and absence. For the
Indians everything seems /appears and nothing is.] (W 122)

Cannibalism is practiced in order to dissimulate the fragility of the real, to
defer the question on the "appearance of what appears." However, in the
narrative of cannibalism as a history having two moments, it is possible to
detect a paradox:

De esa carne que devoraban, de esos huesos que roían y que chupaban con
obstinación penosa iban sacando, por un tiempo, hasta que se les gastara
otra vez, su propio ser endeble y pasajero. *Si* actuaban de esa manera era
porque habían experimentado, en algún momento, antes de sentirse distin-
tos al mundo, el peso de la nada. Eso *debió ocurrir* antes de que empezaran
a comer a los hombres no verdaderos, a los que venían de lo exterior.
Antes, es decir en los años oscuros en que mezclados a la viscocidad general, se comían entre ellos. Eso es lo que recién ahora, tan cerca de mi
propia nada, comienzo a entender: que los indios empezaron a sentirse los
hombres verdaderos cuando dejaron de comerse entre ellos. (E 129)

[For a time, until again it lost its power, they drew from the flesh they devoured and the bones they chewed and sucked at with such terrible perse-
verance their own frail and transient sense of being. If they acted in this
way it was because at some time, before they felt themselves different

from the world, they had experienced the weight of the void. That must
have happened before they began eating the flesh of those who were not
true men, those from outside. Before, when in the dark years they floun-
dered with the others, they used to eat each other.] (W 129)

The narrator makes a distinction between "hombres verdaderos" (true, real
men), and "hombres no verdaderos" (untrue men). However, the narrator
writes about the subjects of his narrative, "the true, real men" under a conjectural modality.

What is "eating the other" for the Indians? "Eating the other" is an attempt to exteriorize oneself, to distinguish oneself from an outside where
they cannot see themselves. However, the vicious circle in which the Indians are trapped does not provide any guarantee that such a process of differentiation will take place. If the Indians are in an uncertain outside, they
partake of the uncertainty of both the outside as well as the process of exteriorization. In other words, the Indians are compelled to turn upon themselves in order to both demarcate and differentiate themselves from the
outside.

This turning upon themselves—this speculative turn and, at the same
time, this trope of speculation—does not offer any guarantee either. From
the other's flesh they attempt to extract the "certainty of being" (*certeza de
ser*), of being as immediate presence. However, the act of eating the other
implies a shift from the mouth to the eye, given that what is at issue here is
representation: a folding of the outside. Not eating oneself and exterioriz-
ing oneself are simultaneous acts but we know that, for the Indians, the
outside is improbable and that, consequently, they must succumb to an autophagic cannibalism—a displaced autophagic cannibalism, it is true, since
they do not eat each other literally, but the digestive effects of the cannibalistic meal are those of an orgy during which all taboos can be trans-
gressed. For this reason, the act of eating the other is considered to as a de-
ferral, detour or turn: "they took, in order to rediscover that archaic flavor,
an immense detour through the outside." Eating the other is eating (one)
self, because only the Indians are "true men." Eating the other's flesh,
eating an other whose reality is dubious, is to ruminate in the void; to experience or again taste the "archaic disaster." The cannibalistic ritual, the
act of eating the other, is therefore one of deferment:

Si, cuando empezaban a masticar, el malestar crecía en ellos, era porque
esa carne debía tener, aunque no pudieran precisarlo, un gusto a sombra
exhausta y a error repetido. Sabían, en el fondo, que como lo exterior era
aparente, no masticaban nada. (E 129)

[If, when they started to chew, uneasiness grew in them, it was because that flesh must have had, although they were not able to specify why, a flavor of exhausted shadow and repeated error. They knew, deep down, that since the outside was apparent, they were not chewing anything.] (W 129)

An empty gesture providing an illusory guarantee, the cannibalistic feast points to a limit: the representation of the other; the other is an impossibility. The other's impossibility is, at the same time, the impossibility of grounding oneself. The cannibal feast is the commemoration of an impossibility: no longer being able both to eat oneself and to eat the other.

For the cannibals, the process of exteriorization is not successful or complete. The cannibals cannot fix an image of themselves by themselves, they cannot give themselves an image of their selves, and they cannot be formed—informed—as idea or image by themselves. They are forced to recur "to a secret pact," to another gaze: that of a witness, narrator or Defghi, according to the series that the narration seems to establish. They must recur to someone or something that finds itself in a no less precarious situation than themselves. We must remember here that when the Indians massacre the expedition, the narrator-protagonist is the last survivor. Immediately after the massacre we read, "with the death of the men who participated in the expedition, the certainty of a *common experience* disappeared and I was alone in the world to settle all the difficult problems its existence implied" (W 27).[20] The rhetoric of cannibalism has allowed us to unfold the paradoxes underlying the representation of the other within the economy of the same or, in other words, within the frame of the classical heterology, whose economy is doubled in the cannibals' "experience."

WRITING AND THE LAW OF THE FATHER

> There is, perhaps, no humanity (and, perhaps, no
> animality) that does not include representation—
> although representation may not exhaust what, in
> man, passes infinitely beyond man.
> —Nancy, *The Birth to Presence* 15

Cannibalism is a failed introjection; it points to a complication in the incorporation/exteriorization opposition. The narrator states that after ingesting the other's flesh and after being part (although paradoxically without sharing each other) of an orgiastic rage, the Indians make no reference to these acts until the cycle of man-hunting returns to haunt them. The Indians remain in total oblivion about cannibalism and its effects. It would be easy to conclude that writing constitutes the memory of the Indians, as if writing were able to supplement and accomplish an incomplete process of incorporation. The fact that the narrator interprets the Indian's desire as that of being their witness or narrator may easily lead one to this conclusion. However, the status of memory and its relation to writing is more complex in this text.

How are writing and cannibalism articulated? In *The Witness* writing appears marked in three ways. First, the narrator writes while telling the story; writing and relating are simultaneous activities. Second, the text inscribes an economy of writing against which it works. Finally, the narrator's act of writing takes place after he sets up a printing house for his adoptive sons. For the moment we have to pay attention to the first two articulations, I will read the third one in conjunction with the sequence of the eclipse, which comes at the end of the story.

The narrator-protagonist learns to read and write under the direction of Father Quesada ("a fine and open philosopher, a patient and exact thinker" [W 100]). Both Father Quesada and the narrator-protagonist profit from this relationship, which is thematized as a father/son, master/disciple relation. Through dialogues with his disciple, the master, Father Quesada, composes a didactic and informative work titled "Relación de Abandonado." The disciple benefits by learning how to read and write: "the only act that could justify my life." In this pedagogical relationship, however, some things resist exchange by remaining on the margin or outside its economy:

El Padre Quesada me hacía, de tanto en tanto, durante las lecciones, preguntas que a veces me desconcertaban, pero cuyas respuestas él anotaba, haciéndomelas repetir para obtener detalles suplementarios. ¿Tenían gobierno? ¿Propiedades? ¿Cómo defecaban? ¿Trocaban objetos que fabricaban ellos con otros fabricados por tribus vecinas? ¿Eran músicos? ¿Tenían religión? ¿Llevaban adornos en los brazos, en la nariz, en el cuello, en las orejas o en cualquier otra parte del cuerpo? ¿Con qué mano comían? Con los datos que fue recogiendo, el padre escribió un tratado muy breve, al que llamó *Relación de abandonado* y en el que contaba nuestros diálogos. Pero debo decir que, en esa época, yo estaba todavía aturdido por los acontecimientos, y que mi respeto por el padre era tan grande que, intimidado, no me atrevía a hablarle de tantas *cosas esenciales que no evocaban sus preguntas.* (E 103)

[From time to time during my lessons Padre Quesada would ask me disconcerting questions and note down the answers, often making me repeat them to glean further details. With the information he gathered, Padre Quesada wrote a very brief treatise that he titled "An account of the adventures of a child lost in the world" in which he set down our dialogues. I should say, however, that at the time I was still stunned by what had happened to me, and my respect for Padre Quesada was so great that I felt too intimidated to speak to him of many essential things his questions failed to elicit.] (W 103)[21]

What remains untold is precisely what constitutes this other "experience" of writing or what resists confession: the "essential things" that exceed Father Quesada's economy of inquiry. In other words what cannot be placed under the Father's tutelage constitutes writing. Father Quesada composes the *Relación*[22] through the questions he asks and makes the acts referred to credible by the presence of a "legitimate survivor." In this way, Father Quesada authorizes the traditional paradigm of the text *on* the other. However, by displacing the "essential things" from the sphere of paternal writing, *The Witness* questions "ethno-graphy," the authority of the ethnological interview—the modern textual invention for writing *on* the other— as a form of bringing the other into representation.

The disciple learns to write, but cannot write under the Father's law since for Father Quesada "[writing] was like tongs destined to manipulate the incandescent world of the senses (*la incandescencia de lo sensible*). For me, fascinated as I was by the force of contingency, it was like going out to hunt a beast that had already devoured me" (W 99). Here we can read two ways to understand writing: one as a *tekhné* that shapes the real and second, as a fascination with what resists symbolization. In addition, this trope figures writing outside the realm of possibility. Nothing can be achieved with writing since its instrumental power is neutralized by the peculiar temporality of fascination; a type of interruption always already at the heart of writing's desire to apprehend the real that, in this case by metalepsis, decomposes the causality at play in instrumental reason. This trope enables us to delimit the inscription of writing as what exceeds the economy of possibility. Writing neither operates as a tool to produce a cognitive delimitation of the real nor depends on *adæquatio* as its standard of truth.

The sequence on comedy complements this undermining of representation and of writing's subordination to representation. After Father Quesada's death, the narrator-protagonist joins a theater company, and the troupe's director decides to represent the narrator's story, reserving for him "[his] own role, as if it were a natural attribute of a still empty entity" (W 110). The encounter with the theater company is narrated as follows:

Una paz imprevista, sin embargo, en un lugar cualquiera, me esperaba. Una noche, en un comedero, unas personas que se emborrachaban en la mesa de al lado, después de la cena, entraron, ya no me acuerdo cómo, en conversación conmigo. Eran dos hombres, uno viejo y uno joven, y cuatro mujeres. Al observar que yo había estudiado un poco pensaron que era un hombre de letras, y supe que ellos, en cambio eran actores. El vino nos acercó. Iban de pueblo en pueblo, de ciudad en ciudad, representando co-medias para ganarse *con ese juego infantil,* una vida miserable. Pero el viejo, que rengueaba un poco y que a pesar de su pobreza poseía cierta dig-nidad, era inteligente y no desdeñaba el placer de la conversación. Cuando se percató de que yo conocía, el latín, el griego, que no ignoraba ni a Teren-cio, ni a Plauto, me propuso que me uniese a ellos para compartir peligros y beneficios. El joven, que era su sobrino, llamaba primas a todas las mu-jeres. Sin dejar translucir que para mí se trataba de elegir entre el teatro y los basurales, y con el coraje que infunde el vino nocturno, acepté la pro-puesta. Salimos de ese modo a los caminos. (E 106-7)

[An unexpected peace awaited me. One night at an inn, a group of people eating and getting drunk at the table next to mine got to talking once their meal was over—I no longer remember how. There were two men—one old and one young—and four women. Realizing that I was a person of some learning they took me for a man of letters and I, in turn, learned that they were actors. The wine drew us closer. They traveled from village to village and town to town putting on plays and scraped a living for that childish employment. The old man limped slightly but had, despite his poverty, a certain dignity. He was intelligent and not immune to the pleasures of con-versation. When he realized that I knew Greek and Latin and had some knowledge of Terence and Plautus, he proposed that I join them to share what dangers and profits came their way. The young man, his nephew, ad-dressed all the women as "cousin." Without revealing that for me it was a choice between a life in the theater and one spent scavenging rubbish dumps, and encouraged by the night's wine, I accepted his proposal. And so it was that we set off along the highways.] (W 106–7)

This sequence is the symmetrical double of the scene of the children play-ing by the river and, at the same time, adds a new twist to the series of family and origins. As a scene of adoption, this is the symmetrical opposite of Padre Quesada's adoption of the narrator-protagonist. (However, if in the convent it was the narrator-protagonist who kept secret "essential things" [self-censorship], here it is the company's director who imposes a form of censorship.) Nevertheless, in both cases censorship operates under the law of the same: as a response to the ethnocentric structure of the ethnographic inquiry about the other, on the one hand, and as a response to the audience's phantasmatic expectations on the other:

Empezamos a representar. Después de las primeras funciones, dondequiera que íbamos nuestra fama nos precedía . . . Yo me maravillaba. Viendo el entusiasmo de nuestro público, me preguntaba sin descanso si mi comedia transmitía, sin que yo me diese cuenta, algún mensaje secreto del que los hombres dependían como del aire que respiraban, o si, durante las representaciones, los actores representábamos nuestro papel sin darnos cuenta de que el público representaba también el suyo, y que todos éramos los personajes de una comedia en la que la mía no era más que un detalle oscuro y cuya trama se nos escapaba, una trama lo bastante misteriosa como para que en ella nuestras falsedades vulgares y nuestros actos sin contenido fuesen en realidad verdades esenciales. El verdadero sentido de nuestra simulación chabacana debía estar previsto, desde siempre, en algún argumento que nos abarcara . . . (E 108–9)

[We began to represent. After the first few shows, fame preceded us wherever we went . . . I was astonished. When I saw the audiences' enthusiasm for the play, I kept wondering if, without my knowing it, it was not transmitting some secret message that proved as vital to men as the air they breathed. Or perhaps during the performances, we actors played our parts unaware that the audience were also playing theirs; perhaps we were all characters in a play of which my play was nothing but an obscure detail and whose plot escaped us, a plot mysterious enough for our commonplace baseness and empty actions to pass for essential truths. Long, long ago the true meaning of our cheap parody must already have been written into a more encompassing plot that also encompassed us.] (W 108–9)

The testimony of the "direct witness," as well as the comedy of the "authentic survivor," obliterate differences, since they are articulated from the point of view of the same. Both of them speculate and calculate their results and profits. For them the other operates within the field of what can be calculable. The "scene of representation" (of the comedy, of the representation of representation, of its specular sending off) signals the passage to another scene in which writing exceeds the economy of representation as *adæquatio*. The double fold of speculation begins to present an uncanny edge.

TESTIMONY: THE SCENES OF WRITING AND THE INVENTION OF THE OTHER

> . . . lo desconocido—lo que más allá del don fugaz de lo empírico, es transfondo y persistencia.
> —Saer, *Glosa*
>
> [. . . the unknown—that which beyond the gift of the empirical is inconspicuous and persistent.]

Having discussed the modalities by which the text complicates representation, we can now elucidate the narrator-protagonist's place within the cannibal order, as well as the question of the invention of the other. The lexical marker "Defghi," which the Indians use to refer to and designate the narrator-protagonist, is open to the play of the signifier. The narrator states that it means several things at the same time and these are even contradictory. It is thus circumscribed to the *sema* of duplication; a kind of doubling in which the terms *narrator-witness-survivor* converge in order to form a chain:

> Después de largas reflexiones, deduje que si me habían dado ese nombre, era porque me hacían compartir, con todo lo otro que llamaban de la misma manera, alguna esencia solidaria . . . Amenazados por todo eso que nos rige desde lo oscuro, . . . querían que de su pasaje por ese espejismo material quedase un *testigo* y un *sobreviviente* que fuese, ante el mundo, su *narrador.* (E 133–34)

> [After long reflection I decided that the reason they had given me that name was because they wanted me to share some common essence with everything else that was *def-ghi* . . . Threatened by everything that controls us from the dark, the Indians wanted there to be a witness to and a survivor of their passage through this material mirage, their own narrator.] (W 143–44)

It is important to remember that the text we read is presented as the written memoirs of the narrator-protagonist and that this reminiscence is written after the conquistadors massacred the cannibals (an event in which the narrator-protagonist is implicated by accident). Therefore, the testimony of this witness is the testimony of an absence. Is it possible to be the witness of an absence? Is it possible to bear witness fifty years after the fact, after the events in question took place?

If we return to de Certeau's observations and accept that a classical heterological account is a way of constructing a discourse *on* the other authorized by that very other, it is also legitimate to ask about the authority of the supposed testimony of the narrator-protagonist. *The Witness* is not the product of a circularity in which the production of the other and that of the text *on* the other are homologous. When the narrator-protagonist decides to abandon the troupe he makes a deal with the director: "his nephew could interpret my own role [that of the "authentic survivor"] even assuming my identity and I agreed to change my name" (W 140). This pact affects the narrative status of the testimony in two ways. First, every testimony presupposes a subject determined by certain figures of subjectivity: someone or something that, when saying "I testify that . . ." breaches the gap separating the utterance from its proffering. In other words, the testimony supposes a myth of interiority. Moreover, the Judeo-Christian testimony, which supposes a vivification of the name and a regeneration of presence, possesses a paradoxical narrative structure. It is an immediate form of memory whose immediacy is absolute, irrecoverable, and ungraspable. The testimony's paradoxical narrative structure impugns what has been testified to in the very act of bearing witness.[23]

What form of memory is told in *The Witness*? A detour through one of Borges's short stories may help to shed some light on this problem. Borges's "La noche de los dones" (The Night of Gifts) makes the possible convergence of the event and its verbal recollection problematic. This convergence is dissolved in the fundamental uncertainty of a memory unable to distinguish between the event and its narrative. In Borges's story this takes place within the context of a discussion on the nature of knowledge (Plato and Bacon are invoked at the beginning of the story) and in regard to particular types of objects: "dones" (gifts). At stake here is the possibility of knowing something about love and death that, in the words of one of the narratees, are unique and unrepeatable experiences. However, after retelling the story of this night of gifts, the narratee states that, "The years pass and I have told the story so many times that I no longer know if I truly remember it or if I only recall the words with which I told it."[24] The story's repetition, whose subject is the "dones" (gifts)—what by definition cannot be repeated and is unique—opens a gap between events and words. To remember the words one uses to tell a story entails a face value declaration of what this act amounts to: the telling of a story of words; words telling words, as well as what this telling produces: the disappearance of the narrative witness as the ground of the story.[25] As in Borges's story, in Saer's *The Witness* the testimony is grounded on "atopic memory": a memory of words that "manda imágenes no se sabe cómo, ni de dónde, ni por qué" (E 58) [sends images one knows not how nor from where, (W 127)]. The narrative voice is neuter[26] and exceeds the telling of the narrator-protagonist:

> De esa manera, sueño, recuerdo, y experiencia rugosa se deslindan y se entrelazan para formar, como un *tejido impreciso,* lo que llamo sin mucha euforia mi vida. Pero a veces, en la noche silenciosa, la mano que escribe se detiene, y en el presente nítido y casi increíble, me resulta difícil saber si esa vida ha tenido realmente lugar, llena de continentes, de mares, de planetas y de hordas humanas o si ha sido, en el instante que acaba de transcurrir, una visión causada menos por la exaltación que por la somnolencia.

Que para los indios *ser* se dijese *parecer* no era, después de todo, una distorsión descabellada. Y, no pocas veces, algo en mí se plegaba, dócil y bien hondo, a sus certidumbres. (E 148)

[In that way, dream, memory, and harsh experience become unloosened and intertwined to form the piece of loosely woven web I unenthusiastically call my life. But sometimes in the silence of the night, my hand stops its writing and in the clear, almost ungraspable present, I find it hard to know if that life full of different continents, seas, planets and human hordes really did take place or if it was just the vision of a moment provoked more by my drowsiness than by any exalted frame of mind. *The Indian's use of "seem" for "to be"* was not after all such a wild distortion. Quite often something in me gave way to what they believed to be true.] (W 159)

I have shown that *The Witness* displaces and disrupts the narrative economy of the classical heterologic account, but the question concerning the re-invention of the invention of the other still remains. In Saer's text a more "original" (but not in the sense of a ground or foundation) approach of the other is inscribed. This approach is signaled as "unnarratable" and here we are no longer dealing with a personified other, with the other as prosopopoeia.

The undecidable nature of this unnarratable event appears as the "memory" of something impossible, as an impossible memory or as the impossible event *of* memory: "the Indians' eyes betrayed that unnarratable memory." What this memory betrays unfolds within the context of a scene of forgetting. The coming together of forgetting, the unnarratable nature of memory and the unique nature of this event are all features that exceed but, at the same time, sustain testimony. They are more original, since they are the nonsignifying signs of the "archaic disaster." This scene unfolds the eminently poetic nature of any testimony and, at the same time, points to the derivative nature of its constative dimension.[27]

Further, the unnarratable nature of this memory marks a cæsura, an interruption of narration and a displacement of speculation's economy outside the play of the model and the copy. This interruption takes place in/as the sequence of the eclipse, a closing sequence that opens narration to a dimension of language that I call the *poem*, if by such a term we understand, following Alain Badiou, language's ability to present the pure notion of "there is."[28] One must remember that, in the language of the Indians "eclipse" and "to resemble, to appear" are expressed with the same words:

En ese idioma [el de los indios], no hay ninguna palabra que equivalga a *ser* o *estar.* Las más cercana significa *parecer.* La misma palabra que designa la apariencia designa lo exterior, la mentira, los eclipses, el enemigo. También *una misma palabra con variante de pronunciación, nombra lo presente y lo ausente.* Para los indios *todo parece y nada es.* (E 122)

[There is no equivalent in their language for *to be.* The closest equivalent they have is *to seem (parecer).* The word used to designate appearance also means exteriority, a lie, an eclipse, an enemy. They share the same word for what is present and what is absent, which can be distinguished by a slight difference in their pronunciation. For the Indians everything seems and nothing is.] (W 130–31)

In his *Diccionario Crítico Etimológico de la Lengua Castellana,* L. Covarrubias gives "derivado incoativo de *parere"* (to see, to appear) as the etymology of *parescere. Parere* is also the infinitive form of *pario*: to bring forth, produce, give birth. Covarrubias states that *apparescere* is a derivative form of *parescere.* In Spanish *parecer* can be used as a masculine noun or as a verb. As a noun, its semantic field not only covers "apariencia" (outward appearance, usually of a physiognomic type), but also opinion, judgment, and sentence on a given matter. In addition to judging *parecer* as a verb means "to appear or let something be seen," "to give signs of what something is or includes," and "to be found somewhere, to let oneself be seen there." In *parecer* appearing or coming to light, the semblance, and the saying on/of the appearing-appearance converge.

"THE TRUE MEASURE OF OUR HOMELAND": ABANDONMENT, PROCLAMATION, AND BIRTH TO PRESENCE

The sequence of *The Witness* mentioned above tells the event of a lunar eclipse, emphasizing its point of maximum intensity and the (un)veiling of light: "la claridad que [la luna] difundía, ni nocturna, ni diurna, parecía tener un tinte de inminencia" (E 197) [the clarity that the moon distilled, neither nocturnal nor diurnal, seemed to have the color of imminence, W 197]. This neutral light transforms narration into the space of a "waiting" followed by an "epiphany." Interrupted and intensified by the poetic saying, narration lets itself be read as a mode of access to the phenomenon of the world and to the appearance of things; as an "it appears/seems *(parece)"* that is not the expression of a subjectivity deprived of certainty, but uncertainty as the constitutive horizon of appearing:

Parece tiene menos el sentido de similitud que el de desconfianza. Es más un vocablo negativo que positivo. Implica más objeción que comparación. No es que remita a una imagen ya conocida sino que tiende más bien a desgastar la percepción y a restarle contundencia. (E 122)

["seems" has more a feeling of untrustworthiness than sameness. It is more a negative than a positive word. It implies an objection more than a comparison. It does not refer to a known image but rather tends to erode perception and diminish its force.] (W 130)

Here there is a theory of analogy that does not allow for comparison but constitutes a *comparecencia*—the "how" of presentation. This "how" can only be indicated in the saying of the poem, since it is a summons to be the place of the appearing/appearance:

Al fin podíamos percibir el color justo de nuestra patria, desembarazado de la variedad engañosa y sin espesor conferida a las cosas por esa fiebre que nos consume desde que comienza a clarear . . . *Al fin* palpábamos en lo exterior la pulpa brumosa de lo indistinto . . . *Al fin* llegábamos, después de tantos presentimientos, a nuestra cama anónima. Por venir de los puertos, en los que hay tantos hombres que dependen del cielo, yo sabía lo que era un eclipse. Pero saber no basta. El único justo, es el saber que reconoce que sabemos únicamente *lo que condesciende a mostrarse.* (E 155)

[*At last* we could perceive the colors of our native land, *at last* we could faintly touch, in the outside, the foggy mass of the undifferentiated, *at last*, after so many presentiments, we reached our anonymous resting place . . . I knew what an eclipse was, but knowing is not enough, the only real knowledge is the knowledge that recognizes that we only know what condescends to be shown.] (W 200)

The poem as language of the event ("At last . . . At last . . . At last . . .") is the letting appear of what seems/appears; it says by indicating (by pointing) but without representing. It is a pure saying; an uttering that exceeds its utterance, and an exclamation that leaves things in their openness without rendering them into a theme.

The language of fiction understood as *speculative anthropology* does not assign any substantial determination but instead opens up a space that disarticulates any pre-established knowledge about the human: the space of "what condescends to be shown." This unfolds in a sequence endowed with a particular linguistic "relief," as if it were floating or suspended in a space adjacent to the story; a scene of forgetfulness (the eclipse) in which "being-born-as-already-abandoned" (*entenado*) and the birth to presence are intertwined. For this reason, the formula *speculative anthropology* can be re-read in the following way: *The Witness* and Saer's fiction can be conceived as an allegory of the birth to presence, if by presence we understand an interruption of representation (presence being the "primal scene" of representation). The "object" of this fiction, as a form of *anthropology*, would be the figures of what exceeds representation: "what condescends to be shown": an inerasable exteriority (*imborrable, refractaria*) which is not the prerogative of anybody's memory, recollection, or incorporation. What is told/written "takes place" between the letter (the print)[29] and the stars (the space of dissemination): an irreducible outside, that of the text as an a-topic memory and as a place of errancy:

> A lo que vino después, lo llamo años o mi vida—rumor de mares, de ciudades, de latidos humanos, cuya corriente, como un río arcaico que arrastrara los trastos de lo visible, me dejó en una pieza blanca, a la luz de las velas ya casi consumidas, balbuceando sobre un encuentro casual entre, y con, también, a ciencia cierta, las estrellas. (E 201)

> [What came later I call years or my life—the rumor of seas, of cities, of human heartbeats, whose current, like an archaic river which would seem to drag the remainders of the visible, left me in a white room, by the light of candles that were almost spent, babbling about a casual meeting among and with . . . the stars.] (W 201)

4

Voices and Tones
History, Memory and
Trauma in *Glosa*

—Socrates: Why do you think that I mentioned the
mix of pain and pleasure proper to comedy?
—Plato, *Philebus*

Why is man better able to utter many voices, while
other animals of one and the same species utter only
one voice? Does man really have only one voice,
but many forms of speech?
—Aristotle, *Problems*, X, 38

Ungrateful earth . . . although not quite.
—S. Beckett, *Endgame*

WRITING THE EVENT:
AN ETHICS OF WRITING

IN THIS CHAPTER, I WILL DISCUSS THE ETHICS OF WRITING IN SAER'S *Glosa*
(1986), a novel that explores the relation between the event and narration.
The event is what Saer's fiction seeks to name and although it is precisely
what subtracts itself from narration, it nevertheless leaves its trace. In Saer,
there is an ethics of writing because his texts configure encounters with the
real. In this fidelity to the event's indiscernible character lies Saer's ethics
of writing: "estamos de acuerdo en que todo esto pertenece al orden de la
conjetura. La evidencia se enciende y apaga más allá o más acá de las palabras" (we agree that all this is conjecture. The evidence goes on and off
nearer and farther from words [G 238]). To say that the event is indiscernible means that it subtracts itself from any type of marking and cannot

be treated like an object. The event's indiscernible character demands the production of a poetic image or name; in this production the very possibility of encountering the real occurs as an ethical instance.

The novel's point of departure is the second-hand retelling of an apparently trivial episode: a birthday celebration for Washington Noriega that neither of the two protagonists (the Mathematician and Leto) has attended. An untrustworthy witness, Botón, tells the "story" of what happened that night to the Mathematician, and is later corrected by Tomatis, who delegitimizes himself because of the tendentious manner in which he communicates the facts. The question that organizes the knot of the story is: what really happened the night of Washington's birthday? And the emphasis here is on the adverb "really."

The reader finds himself with a familiar pragmatic situation: a version of the get-together of friends that is an oft-repeated scene in Saer's texts. This time, however, they find each other by chance and the pretense is to talk precisely about a get-together. The reader also finds here another twist on that pragmatic situation: the dispersion of friends due to the experience of exile.[1] What is unexpected about this narration is that it highlights the problematic status of the intrigue, an element often ignored by Saer. This emphasis on the intrigue itself becomes part of the narration's constructive procedures: the focus on the intrigue and its motives will remain open, allowing for reflection on language and narrative devices.

This episode, which opens up a series of questions on experience, memory, and the narrative account of fragments of memory and experience, is linked to events in recent Argentine history (the historical materials treated in the narrative are the "dirty war" of the 1970s and 1980s). The apparent banality of the episode of the birthday celebration contrasts markedly with the seriousness of the historical events: the defeat of the militant Left at the hands of the dictatorship, torture, death, and exile; what could be called "the end of the novelistic history of history."

Where one would have expected a "re-writing of history" that denounced the "official story" in a semi-epic or semi-tragic tone, or even a moral judgment that reorganized the representation of the past, we find a story that puts into question the notion of representation and therefore the very possibility of an epistemologically justified reorganization of the representation of reality. Nevertheless, in *Glosa* there is a dimension that allows us to see another way of writing "history." That is why when César Aira says that in *Glosa* the recent Argentine past has the aspect of "a hackneyed political detail, of bad taste, almost in the style of a Galeano,"[2] this judgment can be taken at face value: the topical character of political facts indicates that the event exceeds novelistic representation. In Saer it is not a matter of "how to know the real," as most critics maintain, emphasizing the "how" over above the status of the real. Although Saer's fiction puts into play an epistemological frame, the two dimensions in which it operates are the real and truth, which are always in excess with respect to the order of knowledge.

Glosa is self-figured in terms of an aesthetic that is not that of representation, but rather the pictorical aesthetic of dripping (the abstract art of Jackson Pollock or Juan Pablo Renzi). When Leto contemplates an abstract painting, the narrator declares:

> no son formas, sino formaciones—rastros temporariamente fijos de un fluir incesante, aglomeración sensible, podría decirse, en un punto preciso de la sucesión, que relacionando tensa y frájil, sin anularlos, azar y deliberación, le añade liberadora, a lo existente, delicia y radiaciones. (G 217)

> [These are not shapes, but formations—temporarily fixed traces of a never-ending flux, a sensible agglutination, one could say, at a precise point of a tense and fragile succession that, relating chance and purpose without canceling them out, liberally adds, to what exists, delight and energy.]

The narrative voice glosses the space of the abstract painting and translates its intensities into a narrative space that will do justice to the double demand of "chance and necessity."

Glosa: The Knot
of Voices

These two poles allow the story to relate the series of shared daily life (a daily life which is shared only through word and story) and those of historical events. This is done under the modality of comedy, according to the terms which Saer's dedication sets forth:

> A Michel, Patrick, Pierre Gilles que practican tres ciencias verdaderas, la gramática, la homeopatía, la administración, el autor les dedica, por la sobremesa de los domingos, esta comedia: *but then time is your misfortune father said.*

> [To Michel, Patrick, Pierre Gilles who practice three true sciences, grammar, homeopathy, administration, the author dedicates this comedy to them: *but then time is your misfortune father said.*]

In this comedy there is a reflection on the status of instinct, whose coordinates are autonomy and servitude, as if the central question in *Glosa* were, how can one be free by/with/in language instead of what really happened the night of Washington's birthday? Finally, the dedication links the signifier "comedy" to a quote in English that introduces what seems to be a dimension proper to tragedy or tragic philosophy: that of finitude and death, phrased in terms of fall or "loss of grace." This is the dimension of "better not to have been born" ($\mu\eta \ \phi\iota\nu\alpha\iota$) that, from Sophocles to Nietzsche, characterizes the tragic condition of human beings.[3] The question therefore becomes, how can comedy take responsibility for what should properly be called "tragic"? What does comedy as a form or tone offer this problem that at first appears to be tragic?

The organization of the story along the axis of chance and necessity also points to, on the one hand, the compulsion of the characters, all marked by trauma, and on the other, the contingent ("tense and fragile") status of memory. This is a comedy that must be read as a gloss or a *Glosa* that must be read as a comedy.

Glosa, the word, the concept, and the thing, orients the reading in the direction of the question of language: a gloss (*glosa, γλωσσα*) is language. *Glosa* also signifies "strange word with abstract or obscure meaning," an ancient word that has fallen in disuse, is difficult to comprehend, and therefore requires an explanation. These difficult words included some that belonged to provincial or literary dialects. In *Glosa* the series of Washington's birthday celebration produces an idiomatic residue: the expression "like Washington's mosquitoes" that will be used years later by Pichón Garay and by the Mathematician. The meaning of this expression is not explained since the story of Washington's birthday celebration does not disclose the "secret" of Washington's dialectical argument. *Glosa* produces an idiomatic residue that speaks in, with, and of the language spoken the night of Washington's birthday. Years later, when the Mathematician and Pichón are in Paris as part of a group of Argentines protesting state repression, they walk together and

> Sin saber cómo, habían empezado a hablar del cumpleaños de Washington, tal vez porque de esa noche, había quedado una expresión, *es como los mosquitos de Washington* . . . y que Pichón había empleado unos momentos antes aplicándola a las promesas de una posible ayuda a los refugiados por parte del gobierno francés . . . No se sabía quién había utilizado por primera vez la expresión, ni cúando, pero, en aquellos años, después de la famosa noche, aparecía seguido en las conversaciones, y una vez, incluso maravillado, el Matemático se la había oído emplear a alguien que no únicamente no conocía a Washington ni a ninguno de sus allegados, sino que tampoco podía estar al tanto de la historia. (G 160–61)

[Not knowing how, they had started talking about Washington's birthday, maybe because of the expression that remained from that night, *it's like Washington's mosquitoes* . . . and that Pichón had used some moments ago when referring to the possible promise of aid to the refugees by the French government . . . No one knew who had used that expression first, nor when, but during that time, after that famous night, it frequently appeared in conversations and one time he was astonished when the Mathematician had heard it used by someone who not only did not know Washington or any of his friends, but also could not have known the story.]

Additionally, "gloss" condenses all the senses of commentary, explication, rectification, and note added to a text. In this sense a gloss can be common; that is to say, it can occupy a marginal position in relation to the text commented, or be interlineal, between the lines of the text. In any case, the function of the gloss is to clarify or illuminate the text and therefore to offer an interpretation. Although the gloss is a type of commentary, it maintains a relation of proximity with the original since it treats it literally.

The Mathematician's narrative activity and Leto's interpretative one, as well as Tomatis's malicious and pejorative comments (all the corrective measures utilized in order to present "what really happened the night of Washington's birthday") can be included in the meaning of the word "gloss." This word also has a poetic meaning since it refers to a rhymed parody of a poem that repeats the last verse of every stanza. Finally, by extension, gloss means story. An exercise on language, writing on writing, interpretation, parody and story, all come together in the word "gloss;" a word that means language, word and story; a word that self-signifies itself and is part and whole, the retelling of the part in the whole and of the whole in part.

Where does *Glosa* begin and where does the gloss that provides the title for the story begin? In the first place, the story presents the gloss that the Mathematician makes of Botón's story (there is a referred and interfered voice, which is the voice of the other: a voice of the desire of the other which will be linked to that of the same). The Mathematician tells Leto what Botón told him about what happened at Washington Noriega's birthday party, while he also passes review of the narrative and reorganizes its elements. Botón attended the party while the Mathematician was traveling through Europe; Leto did not attend because he thought he had not been invited. A second witness who did attend the party will question Botón's version of the event, but this new version will also be glossed and reviewed by the Mathematician and Leto. The Mathematician sees Leto on the street and calls to him. Leto will accompany him for fifteen of the twenty-one blocks of his walk (the story is divided into three sections whose length is measured in a series of seven blocks). During the walk, the Mathematician tells Leto what Botón told him the Saturday before about Washington's birthday party.[4]

The narrative frame of the story is the following: a heterodiegetic narrator ("the undersigned," "yours truly" [*el que suscribe, un servidor*]) narrates the encounter between the Mathematician and Leto, which takes place one October morning in the city of Rosario. That morning Leto had decided to step off the bus and to walk in the direction of the city center instead of going to work. That same morning the Mathematician is on his way to the offices of the local paper in order to publish a press release on the trip that the students from chemical engineering had made to Europe. Although the narrator shares certain characteristics with the traditional omniscient narrator, toward the end there are important differences since the story, especially what concerns Washington's birthday party, is inconclusive and the narrator cannot affirm any type of knowledge over "what happened"; on the contrary, he exhibits a nonknowledge. This can be called the negative dimension of *Glosa*.

The narrator does not mediate between the different versions that claim to account for what happened at Washington's birthday party, since there is no discursive synthesis. But this negative dimension is only apparent, because the irresolution displaces and reinscribes the enigma not in terms of decipherment or reconstruction (of filling in the clues) but rather in that of an event: the interruption of the conversation and of the conversation about the conversation (the Mathematician's and Botón's on the one hand and the Mathematician's, Leto's, and Tomatis's on the other) makes evident that the things talked about were heard, but not in the presence of the "thing itself." *Glosa* unfolds in absentia.

The detailed reconstruction of what happened—how Washington finally refutes the thesis on the "necessity of the instincts" (that Basso bases on the supposed "tripping of Noca's horses," the fisherman's story) with the story of the three mosquitoes—does not reveal its "secret." This reconstruction constitutes the narrative plot sustained by the following question: is the conversation moved by a secret that is subtracted from language and can be represented by facts? Or is the conversation what produces the secret and therefore the event is no more than one of the expressions or versions that circulate in language, as if they were language itself; that is, the propagation of an absence, of a lack of origin and end? The alternatives arising from this type of question, rigorously speaking cannot be resolved. The detailed reconstruction of the facts does not shed light on what happened during Washington's birthday party. It is not a matter of reconstructing but of subtracting: language differs from conversation and from itself and therefore it is impossible to assign the "secret" a fixed place.[5]

The production of an image or the naming of an event displaces the localization of what cannot be localized toward the question of contingency, the opposite pole to the "necessity of the instincts"; in *Glosa* this is called by the name *devenir* (becoming) or *acontecer* (event):

El Matemático despliega frente a sí el brazo, aferrando en la mano el hornillo de la pipa . . . y trazando en el aire un movimiento semicircular, designa lo presente, es decir, las veredas, la calle, las hileras de negocios, los letreros luminosos . . . la multiplicidad incesante y clara que podría ser también, y por qué no, una expresión nueva para eso.
—El acontecer—dice.
Visitado por una locuacidad repentina, Leto responde:
—La niña bonita de los filósofos. Era esta calle. Este momento. (G 185–86)

[The Mathematician unfolds his arm before him, holding the pipe in his hand, and tracing a semicircular movement in the air, designates what is present, that is, the sidewalks, the street, the row of stores, the marquees . . . the incessant and clear multiplicity that could be, and why not, a new expression for that.
The event he says.
Overcome by a sudden loquacity, Leto responds:
The philosophers' pretty girl was this street, this moment.]

Becoming or the event is named in common, everyday language (the expression "la niña bonita" [the pretty girl] is used to symbolize numbers in games of chance) and as the effect of a sudden urge to talk. This name is accompanied by the production of an image: the two characters turn themselves around and walk in an unnatural manner—backwards or with their backs to the sidewalk (G 187–88).

Glosa's narrative frame echoes Plato's famous banquet, at the beginning of which Glaucon intercepts his friend Apolodorous on an Athens street and asks him to tell him what happened at the feast in Agathon's house, a feast which Glaucon did not attend and only knows about through the stories told by Aristodemous and Socrates. But unlike *The Symposium* in *Glosa* no one requests a story to be told. Although it does not achieve narrative resolution, the question of instinct is the central episode in Washington's party that points to a decisive dimension of Saer's writing: the real, the drive, and trauma as the coordinates of the event.

Glosa glosses itself. The constructive principle of this text is the commentary and expansion of a few verses that, placed as epigraphs of the story, will be recited by Tomatis to the Mathematician and Leto: "En uno que se moría/ mi propia muerte no ví, / pero en fiebre y geometría / se me fue pasando el día/y ahora me velan a mí" (In one who was dying / my own death I did not see / but in fever and geometry / the day went by / and now a wake is being held for me).[6] Although referring to a serious topic (the themes of finitude and death traditionally found in the tragic genre and in tragic philosophy), these verses do so in a light and jovial tone.

The verses mark three moments and speak of the noncontemporaneity of one's "own" death, but do so from the perspective of the beyond. The poetic voice speaks as though it were already dead, as if it could see itself in wake and were in the process of mourning.[7] The poetic voice signals the delay of death and, in a certain way, anticipates its own process of mourning. It is important to add that Tomatis gives the Mathematician a copy of the verses as a gift and the latter will keep it as though it were a relic only to read it, years later, during his trip into exile. The poem is a link that binds two series: the meeting of friends and that of history (the moment of dispersion, exile) and it does so in terms of the death drive and of trauma, the modalities in which history is ciphered. Finally, the story *Glosa* glosses Saer's text: it comments, expands, and rewrites spatio-temporal nuclei of the zone that are rearticulated in terms of Place (*Lugar*). The constitutive narrative scene in Saer's narrative—the meeting of friends—is rewritten from the perspective of the dispersion occasioned by exiled.

Glosa is a strange text since it glosses the epigraph, a part of the text that is written twice: first as an epigraph, a separate part, almost a textual relic— the compulsion to repeat is a generative element of the text—and, second as a turning point in the plot. The part of the text that cites and recites itself at the same time is the gloss of a part of the text as well as the gloss of the text as a whole. *Glosa* self-signifies itself, it is part and whole, the retelling of the part in the whole and the whole in part. The title *Glosa* is as much outside as inside the text, thus producing a principle of instability that is parallel to the uncertainty of the referent: what happened the night of Washington Noriega's birthday party, what is the status of the event?

TRAUMA

Two people meet and one tells the other the story of Washington's birthday party not firsthand, but by way of Botón's story, who was present at the party. The Mathematician tells the story and Leto listens, but the story and its reception are marked by "asides" in which the narrator focuses on the

thoughts of both protagonists. The referred or interfered voice ties itself to
the inferred voice that supposes the enigma of the one and the knowledge
of the other; a reticent voice that is at times didactic. But these two voices
are also tied to the deferred voice: the voice of difference (the rumor of language that the heterodiegetic narration spreads throughout the story) that
makes it impossible to decide with certainty on the status of the event.
These two adolescents of different social backgrounds are both affected by
such an intense trauma that one could say that the text exhibits a *Trauma-
arbeit*.

It is important to note that for Freud the concept of trauma has a physi-
ological and psychical value that denotes a violence perpetuated by an external entity. At the same time, it is an economic concept that refers to a
massive cathexis of an external stimulus that fissures the protective shield
of the perception-consciousness system and therefore, supposes shock and
surprise. Lacan reformulates the concept of trauma in terms of a subjective
contact with the real that shatters the economic unity of the ego and sus-
pends the pleasure principle temporarily. In what psychoanalysis calls traumatic neuroses, the original scene of trauma is compulsively and unconsciously repeated in nightmares, insomnia, and obsessive thoughts.

We should remember that when much younger the Mathematician suffers a narcissistic blow at the hands of a well-known poet from the city
who was supposed to meet with him to discuss his views on poetry and
poetic meter, but the Mathematician is "stood up" (the narrator refers to
this as "the episode"). The Mathematician returns to this episode obsessively when he interrupts the narration and later recounts a nightmare that
concerns the identity of that well-known poet. It is also important to recall
that Tomatis is going through a depressive crisis and he suffers from insomnia, which in the daytime manifests itself in his unkept appearance and
bad mood. Years later when Tomatis visits Leto underground he will also
find the latter in a state of depression. Finally, Leto, who is in the process
of mourning because of his father's death, returns constantly to those
episodes that have to do with the father's suicide. The story that circulates
between the three characters—Washington's birthday party—is not
common to all or founded on common experiences, but the *trauma-arbeit*
is a common element that both separates and unites them. At the beginning
of the story we read, "el hombre que se levanta a la mañana, que se da una
ducha, que desayuna y sale, después, al sol del centro, viene, sin duda, de
más lejos que su cama, y de una oscuridad más grande que la de su dormi-
torio (G 16) [the man who gets up in the morning, showers, eats breakfast
and goes out,later, under the city sun, no doubt comes from much farther

than his bed, and from a darkness much greater than that of his bedroom]. The work of trauma is a sign of this anteriority, which traverses the subjective position of Saer's characters.

In *Glosa* a character is the intersection of a trajectory, a personal history that belongs to the dimension of the *Trauma-arbeit* (and for which there are linguistic signs) and of an "object-narration" (the characters review and weigh the benefits of the narrative modalities used in order to tell a story). The trajectory lasts twenty-one blocks (fifteen of which will be shared) from the south toward the center of Rosario; the personal histories form a framework with three points whose signs are as follows:

1. "El que ha sufrido tanto" [He, who has suffered so much (G 19–26)], a phrase pronounced by Isabel in reference to Leto's deceased father and which reverberates in his head;
2. The Mathematician's "episode," "esa quemadura que había transformado su interior en una llaga viva" [that burn that had transformed his insides into an open wound (G 46)];
3. Tomatis's "si de todos modos voy a . . . y el universo entero tarde o temprano va también a . . ." [if in any case I'm going to . . . and the entire universe sooner or later will also . . . (G 126)].

The three characters obsessively return to these indexes, so much so that one could affirm that in *Glosa* not only is the story of Washington's birthday party glossed, but every character glosses the effects of the Thing (*das Ding*). There is a weaving together of the fragments of the personal histories with the fragments of the story of Washington's birthday, as well as of recent Argentine history. The three threads are interwoven on the same plane: the story/history (*la historia*) does not have an *a priori* objective value in Saer's fiction.

The importance of this subjective level, the dimension of trauma, should not be underestimated. It is not by chance that in less than two pages there are two mentions of the uncanny (*unheimlich*), given that trauma inscribes the encounter with the real in terms of the Thing. It is also not by chance that the threat that Tomatis feels is referred to as "el naufragio de las cosas—o la Cosa" (the shipwreck of things—or the Thing (G 124)]. According to Lacan, "*das Ding* is at the center . . . [but] it is central only in the sense that it is excluded. One must posit *Das Ding* as something external, as the pre-historic Other which is impossible to forget—the Other that, although at the heart of the I, is Other than the self."[8] The unconscious traumatic effect of the relation with *das Ding* is the residue that escapes the cognitive power of the subject[9] and, at the same time, modulates the imbrications of two series: the story of Washington's birthday and the story of contemporary Argentine society.

TRAGEDY AND COMEDY

These imbrications appear to be unjustified: the pretension to treat painful facts in comedic form. Here it would be necessary to do an analysis of the place of tragedy in modern thought (from Schelling to Benjamin passing, on the one hand, through Hegel, Nietzsche, and Kierkegaard and through Freud, Heidegger, and Lacan, on the other) and of what Peter Szondi has called "tragic philosophy" or what Jacques Taminiaux calls "the theater of the philosophers." However, I will limit myself only to pointing out that as a result of the Kantian critique, the aesthetic begins to have the function of a bridge between practical or moral reason (the domain of liberty) and pure reason (the domain of nature or of knowledge). In this context, tragedy is conceived as the apex of aesthetics. For Schelling "tragedy's essence is an actual and objective conflict between freedom and necessity [in which] they both manifest in a perfect as simultaneously victorious and defeated."[10] Although beyond the limits of this chapter, it is important to remember what allows tragedy to be promoted to the rank of mediator of critical faculties: the question of finitude and the meaning of life. Tragedy is conceived as an aesthetic form capable of filling the void produced by the "death of God." It is through tragedy and the paradigm of tragic philosophy that a certain history of finitude is written and whose most important trait is heroism. Heidegger and the revolutionaries on the Left are allied in this version of finitude since for both death is understood as a possibility. In Heidegger *Dasein* is linked to death thanks to the resolute anticipation through which destiny and historicity can be assumed and the union between necessity and freedom achieved.[11]

If in *Glosa* there is an "announced and anticipated death," it does not belong to the register of tragic philosophy, but to that of comedy. Additionally, there are two deaths that are narrated under the paradigm of tragic philosophy: the suicide of Leto's father, which supposes a transgression ($\alpha\tau\eta$), and that of Leto himself, which is a mockery of heroism. Both deaths share a common trait: they result from the wish to make desire and action coincide.

In comedy, on the other hand, finitude appears in a different light: death is no longer a possibility (of impossibility), but an impossibility (of the possible).¹² To conceive death as impossibility means that "resolute antici-pation" is no longer operative, that possibility ceases to be contemporane-ous to the subject's power and that, consequently, finitude escapes the grasp of the concept. By inscribing life between two deaths, *Glosa* shows that the tragic-heroic transgression fails to affirm finitude and that the life of comedy can only be recognized in its bitter humor. Comedy is not the triumph of life, but life escaping us; a putting into scene of the failure of the will to make desire and action coincide. Comedy is then the suspension or parody of all catharsis or tragic heroism. Solitary heroism collapses in the shared joy of comedy:

> —la comedia, ¿no?, que es, si se piensa bien, tardanza de lo irremediable, silencio bondadoso sobre la progresión brutal de lo neutro, ilusión pasajera y gentil que celebra el horror en lugar de maldecir, hasta gastar la furia inútil y la voz, su confusión nauseabunda. (G 235)

> [Comedy, which is, if you think about it, the delay of what is irremediable, a kind silence on the brutal progression of the neuter, a fleeting and gentle illusion that instead of cursing to the point of exhausting a useless fury and the voice, celebrates horror, its nauseating confusion.]

If *Glosa* employs the tone of a comedy it is because one can read an in-scription of the end: "Leto is history." In other words, in *Glosa* there is a certain inflection of the "end of history," not in the sense that Francis Fukuyama understands this notion, but rather in that of a certain suspen-sion of history understood as sense, direction, and finality. History can no longer be thought as the narrative of the collective destiny of humanity since "our time" is that of the suspension of history: permanent wars, gen-eralized genocide, the production and administration of poverty on a plan-etary scale by the financial institutions of "advanced" nations—all signs of the destruction without possibility of a dialectical sublation of negativity. "Our time" cannot be considered the time that will "make history" or "will produce the greatness of history."¹³

We could say that in *Glosa* the series of Argentine history (which Saer first develops in *Responso* and later in *Cicatrices*, *El limonero real,* and *Nobody Nothing Never*) closes with Leto's suicide (due to state terrorism) and with the dispersion of the group of friends in exile.¹⁴ This closure marks the suspension of a history that is a reduplication at the level of the story: the story of what happened the night of Washington's birthday is in-terrupted. The history and the novelistic representation of history share the "same history"—the history *of* the (hi)story. But there is something that one can read on this or that side of the history of the end of history and the end of its novelistic representation.

Glosa's temporality wrests the narration from the temporality of novelistic history, which has been the main suture of Argentine literature; in this way it allows the narration to encounter the event ("lo imborrable," or inerasable). In other words, *Glosa* allows us to see what the material status of the event may be—what we must still call "history"—once this mode of understanding history is interrupted by the indiscernible dimension of the event that leaves its traces in the empty peripetiae of the story. *Glosa* spatializes time, it makes time a spacing (a Place) in which one can read the "language of the absent" as the event of a dispersed community.[15]

5
"Regia victoria":
Affects and Percepts

. . . las *victorias regias* que flotaban cerca de las orillas . . . evocaban un cordón umbilical . . . Les hicieron pensar a Pichón a causa de esa flor un poco separada del círculo verde pero un poco dependiente de él, igual que un planeta y su satélite en esas *diosas arcaicas y solitarias* que, *fecundándose a sí mismas parían*, por entre sus miembros vigorosos, *un dios menor*, blanco, espigado y frágil, *con el que se elevaba en vuelo nupcial antes de abandonarlo a la mesa del sacrificio para hacerlo despedazar y perpetuar de ese modo su propio culto.*
—Saer, P 69, emphasis mine.

[. . . the water lilies (*victorias regias*) floating near the river banks . . . brought an umbilical cord to mind . . . [they] reminded Pichón, because of that flower slightly separated from the green circle yet dependent upon it, like a planet and its satellite, of those *archaic, solitary goddesses* who, fecundating themselves, gave birth between their vigorous limbs to a *minor god*, white, frail, slender and graceful, *with whom they rose in nuptial flight before abandoning him on the sacrificial altar to be hacked to pieces and thus perpetuate their own cult.*] (I 66–67)

. . . el sol y la muerte, dicen, nadie puede mirarlos de frente, pero a la *distorsión sin nombre* que pulula en el reverso mismo de lo claro . . . todo el mundo prefiere ignorarla.
—Saer, P 28, my emphasis

[. . . the sun and death: no one, they say, can look
them in the face, but as for the *nameless distortion*
that teems on the other side of what is clear . . .
everyone prefers to ignore it.] (I 31)

The real? It is what resists, insists, exists irreducibly
and gives in subtracting itself as enjoyment, anxiety,
death or castration.
                                 —Leclaire, *Démasquer le réel* 11

"POR LA VUELTA":
FOR A CRITIQUE OF CULTURE

IN *THE INVESTIGATION* (*LA PESQUISA*, 1994) THE READER ONCE AGAIN FINDS
familiar signs of Saer's fictional universe: the story unfolds in the "zone"
and focuses on Pichón Garay, who after a twenty-year absence returns to
his birthplace and recounts the crimes that occurred at the Leon Blum
Square in Paris, as well as the investigation that Inspector Morvan con-
ducted to solve them. It is telling that in what appears to be a detective
story (the crimes, according to Pichón, "occurred in my neighborhood"
and "appeared in all the papers") there is an abundance of commentary regarding Parisian society:

> Bien al abrigo en los anocheres de invierno . . . los que en otras épocas
> habían nacido para ser personas y ahora se habían transformado en meros
> compradores, en unidad de medida de los sistemas trasnacionales de
> crédito, en fracciones de los puntos de audiencia de la televisión y en
> blanco sociológica y numéricamente caracterizados de las tandas publici-
> tarias . . . confundían el mundo con un archipiélago de representaciones
> electrónicas y verbales. (P 32)

> [Snug and cozy on winter nights . . . those who in other eras had been born
> to be persons and had now been transformed into mere consumers, into
> units of measurement of transnational credit systems, into fractions of
> points of television audiences and a numerically defined social target of
> advertising campaigns . . . confuse the world with an archipelago of elec-
> tronic and verbal representations.] (I 32)

Morvan's investigation takes place on Christmas Eve, a date which fore-
grounds the question and search for meaning (the incarnation of the Word
in man), so even if that date motivates Pichón's criticism of consumer society and the society of the spectacle, the tenor of his statements have little
to do with the conventions of the "classic" detective story.[1] Pichón, the nar-

rator, sets the coordinates with which the story seeks to give an account of the *"impenetrable depths (fondo impenetrable)* in which the ephemeral days that civilizations endure are rooted" (I 80/ P 81, my emphasis) and to which one remains "deaf and blind" (I 80/ P 81). The text establishes an oppositional relation between the social situation (that Pichón signals intradiegetically) and the situation of three characters of *The Investigation* (Pichón, Tomatis, and Soldi), for whom, according to the external or extradiegetic narrator,[2]

> únicamente *la conversación los ha hecho olvidarse* un par de horas del calor enbrutecedor, *del tiempo inquietante y oscuro* que los atraviesa, continuo y sin cesuras, *como un fondo constante y monocorde* . . . durante un par de horas han obligado a *las fuerzas que tiran hacia lo oscuro* a quedar fuera de sus vidas, sin dejar de saber ni un solo instante que, en las inmediaciones, dispuestas como siempre a arrebatarlos, esas fuerzas *palpitan todavía.* (P 171–72, my emphasis)

> [Conversation alone has made them forget for a few hours the mind-numbing heat, the disquieting, dark time that traverses them continuous and unbroken, *like a constant, monotonous background accompaniment* . . . for a couple of hours they have obliged *the forces pulling down toward darkness* to remain outside their lives, while at the same time never ceasing for a moment to know that, all around, close at hand, ready as always to carry them off, those *forces still throb*.] (I 179)

There is an opposition here between a refusal of the *real*, characterized by a saturation of images and representations, and that of an opening, whose privileged, although precarious vector, is language (the conversation and the story that begins to be told). The text establishes its cultural coordinates: it speaks in the present, in the context of a disillusioned contemporary world that is caught between the inexpressive *ennui* of media illusions and the desire for a fragile word that could offer some protection from the outside and is willing to run the risk of encountering the real (even in its less attractive manifestations). Against the pale brightness of stereotypical and pacifying images that fail to shield us from the violence that inhabits them, *The Investigation* posits the "dim splendor" (*resplandor apagado*) of a vision (I 66/ P 69). This vision detaches itself from the "society of the spectacle's" sado-masochistic roots and functions as a barrier against its violence, while at the same time allowing us to see the "distorsión sin nombre que pulula en el reverso mismo de lo claro" [the *nameless distortion* that teems on the other side of what is clear, [I 131]).

How can writing today encounter the *real*? This is the question that underlies all the evaluative utterances of the internal or intradiegetic narrator (Pichón). Let me state from the outset that the prospects seem to be disheartening: the novel genre (the most regressive forms of detective fiction, the historical novel, the family romance, and autobiographical texts), as well as the movies of the big studios and TV (the products of the "culture industry"), provide the schemas that shape our thoughts and emotions. These schemas respond to two criteria only: gratification and rentability; thus their need for happy endings, since they tend to affirm a general feeling of nothing really happens here. In the era of televised simulacra (embedded journalism and its symmetrical twin, reality TV), "reality" is a byproduct whose *veracity* is simply affirmed by marketing techniques and by the debris of novelistic discourses still shaped by nineteenth-century conventions, as if the achievements of the avant-gardes and neoavant-gardes had no currency whatsoever. "Reality" is the novels and discourses modeled on nineteenth-century novelistic "realist" codes; they not only condition the stereotypical roles we play in our lives, but also their low affective level of investment. If we adapt one of Lacan's formulations, it is possible to claim that "reality" is structured like a fiction.

This fiction is marked by the use of prose as an "instrument of the State" (NO 54). Saer conceives his narrative prose against the state and its "reign of communicability," as well as against the reductive assimilation of the theory of prose and the theory of the novel, confusion with which

> se busca siempre . . . la coincidencia de texto y referente. En música, en artes plásticas, en poesía, la ausencia de referente es, por distintas, razones toleradas. La novela no goza de ese beneplácito: *está condenada a arrastrar la cruz del realismo*. A decir verdad, nadie de un modo claro sabe qué es el realismo, pero se exige de la novela que sea realista por la simple razón de que está escrita en prosa. Casi que me atrevería a definir el realismo como el procedimiento que encarna las funciones pragmáticas generalmente atribuidas a la prosa. (NO 58, my emphasis)

> [a coincidence between text and referent is sought. In music, in the plastic arts, in poetry, the absence of a referent is, for different reasons, tolerated. The novel does not enjoy this blessing: *it is condemned to carry the cross of realism*. To tell the truth, nobody really knows what realism is, but it is demanded that the novel be realist for the simple reason that it is written in prose. I would almost dare to define realism as the procedure that incarnates the pragmatic functions generally attributed to prose.]

If the double colonization by the state and market threatens to transform realism into a dead weight, neutralizing its critical dimension in favor of a pragmatic economy, how can the conditions for encountering the real be created? This is the recurring question in Saer's texts. My hypothesis is that Saer's texts create the fiction *of* this fiction (of "reality") and that in that split, they cancel it out. This operation allows it to touch a point in the real where the sense of experience (death, desire, finitude) can still speak at a time when it seems to have lost its valence. The *impossible* and *unsayable real* is what keeps Saer's writing in permanent tension.

Always inhabited by the latent *poem*, in Saer narrative prose passes through the sieve of poetic procedures (rectification or isolation of certain words, intensive expansion of a memory, phrasing of variables) in order to extract from it what the state represses: the unsayable. His writing gives consistency to the unsayable and does so in the realm of the modern poem. To speak of the unsayable does not suppose making Saer a mystic or a romantic, but stresses his kinship with a modernity for which the revelatory power of literary language is structured like an enigma whose "mystery is precisely that all poetics have at their center what cannot be represented."[3]

The Investigation provides valuable clues as to how Saer's writing encounters the real. First, because it utilizes literary forms that do not seem to fit well within its project, such as the detective story in its classic and closed form: the filling in of an initial void produced by the supposed narrative ordering of partial information, the reduction of an enigma to an explanation that supposes a transparent and intelligible universe and the elimination of all ambiguity or opacity through the intervention of the Great Detective who imposes his absolute, final and true word.[4] Although detective fiction presents a series of formal problems, *The Investigation* allows us to see the sadomasochistic side of the "happiness" that the "society of the spectacle" promises. The historical novel is another form included in *The Investigation*. Titled *In the Greek Tents* (*En las tiendas griegas*), its plot is recounted by another character to Pichón, who does not make it part of his own narrative at first, but later introduces it in the context of a debate over the "truth of fiction" and the "truth of experience." One should not overlook that *In the Greek Tents* refers to the homonymous poem by César Vallejo and therefore inscribes the interplay between the poem and prose. It also ciphers the singular affective dimension that I call "the writing of the affects."

In *El río sin orillas*, an autofictional text written in the same period as *The Investigation*, there is an explicit reference to Vallejo's poem that occurs in a significant context: when Saer reflects on the effects that names have on reality and the "realist reduction" that is at the heart of official state rhetoric. In this context the quotation from the poem has a double function: it breaks the link between prose, realism, and the state and gives testimony to the remainder that resists assimilation. Saer calls this remainder "la más oscura terminación nerviosa" (the darkest nerve end), which he elaborates on with the following quote: "*Allí en el desfiladero de mis nervios!*" como se queja dulcemente César Vallejo comparando sus estados de ánimo con un campamento griego antes de la batalla. (RO 112–13) ["There in the cliff of my nerves!" as César Vallejo gently complains comparing his mood with a Greek camp before the battle.]."[5] We will see that these "estados de ánimo," which I refer to as the "writing of the affects," are a central concern in *The Investigation* and frame Pichón's story.

In its desire to explore the "*impenetrable depths* (fondo impenetrable) in which the ephemeral days that civilizations endure are rooted" (P 81), I will also show that *The Investigation* exhibits the place of the subject ("Place") and its concomitant pain and horror; the site through which and in which it seeks to differentiate itself from the chaos ("the forces exerting their pull toward darkness," P 179). Here it is a question of an incandescent, unbearable limit, between inside and outside; the I and the other on this side of the phantasm (the reality and violent drives that subtend it) that only "art" (or what is left of it) can find and preserve in a fragile *vision*.

The Investigation is a highly structured story whose narrative plot is constantly threatened with dissolution by "the forces pulling down toward darkness." Within a narrative representation, the themes of pain and sorrow are a testament to the affects that come from layers deeper than symbolization or narrative representation itself. The latter stages a perverse theater, plotted as an Oedipal story with interpretative clues included (although outwardly frustrated). Saer's story is a machine that puts the reader's desire to work; what must be determined then is the scope of this work of desire, what its law is and what limits it transgresses.

Saer's writing belongs to the tradition of modern literature since it performs a descent into the foundations of the symbolic universe in a world devoid of the promise of the Other. *The Witness* is a good example of how the writing of fiction (understood as a speculative anthropology) retraces the fragile frontiers of the speaking subject and touches that bottomless point of the real that is primary repression. In this experience, "subject" and "object" reject and confront each other in order to relaunch themselves, inseparable and contaminated, toward the very limit of what is sayable or thinkable. *The Investigation* unfolds at the limit where writing seeks to encounter the real. In what follows, I will make the articulation of desire that this machine puts into effect explicit. First, through an analysis of the story's construction in order to then show that, if a detective/ Oedipal story (Oedipus could be read as the first detective) exhibits the roots of the phantasm proper to our contemporary "reality," the text inscribes an inassimilable margin which I call the writing of the affects, a "*regia* (albeit fragile) *victoria*," on this side of the phantasm.

By phantasm I understand an imaginary scene in which the subject takes himself as object in order to exhibit his unconscious desire and, by so doing, to block the anguish that *jouissance* causes him. By writing of the affects, I understand the remainders of formations that are older than the symbolic order, that survive it and which the Oedipal story cannot totally assimilate. While the phantasm is trans-subjective because it is structured by the order of language as well as by the Oedipal metanarrative, the affects and its figure (the vision) exceed the Oedipal metanarrative and are singular.

CONSTRUCTION
(ON THE OBJECT-NARRATION)

> Unicamente una imagen lo obsedía: un recién nacido rojizo, ciego y ensangrentado, saliendo de entre las piernas abiertas de la mujer que durante nueve meses lo fabricó . . . que aterriza en este mundo para manchar de sangre la sábana blanca de la maternidad.
>
> —Saer, P 21.

> [Only one image obsessed him . . . a beet-red newborn babe, blind and bloody, emerging from between the parted legs of the woman who for nine months had made it . . . that lands in this world to stain with blood the white sheet of the maternity hospital.] (I 15)

Incipit(s): Frames and Stories

There is no anguish over the blank page in *The Investigation*. A voice assumes the function of narrator and we are introduced to his story *in media res*: "Allá, en cambio, en diciembre, la noche llega rápido. Morvan lo sabía" There, however, in December, night comes on swiftly [I 2/ P 9]). This sentence elliptically condenses the beginning of the traditional realist story: where, who, and when. Even though it is not until twenty pages later that certain details about that narrative voice appear, for the moment it is possible to establish some parameters in relation to the pragmatic context: a voice establishes a gap between the here of the enunciation and the there of the utterance, between the now of the enunciation and the night in December of the story; between the night of the act of telling and that of the intrigue told. It is not until after the three nuclei of the incipit are expanded and filled in that Morvan the detective and his "family romance" are clearly framed and localized and the narrative voice makes its appearance: "ustedes se estarán preguntando qué posición ocupo *yo* en este relato" (you must be wondering what place I occupy in this story [I 15/ P 22]).

Although without identity and still lacking the traits of a character, this "I" is simply a position and, above all, a taking of position. The story that passes for an "oral tale" treats the voice as its object, it folds on itself and in a metanarrative turn institutes its autonomy. The voice that narrates marks the conventional character of an omniscient heterodiegetic narration which still preserves what makes it homologous to the organization of any utterance: the presence of a "movil, ubicua, múltiple y omnipresente" [mobile, ubiquitous, multiple and omnipresent [I 21/ P 20]) consciousness that serves as organizing principle. The voice is object *and* subject, product and production, absence and presence. The constructed character of the story, of the first story in the order of reading, becomes patent; it is a construction that plays with the gap between word and inscription. We should add here that this "oral tale" or this story that presents itself as the effect of the voice is balanced out by a metanarrative frame and is therefore a narration to the second degree, self-aware of the conventions and the rules of detective fiction it will use. The articulation of this metanarrative dimension does not hinder the story's telling. On the contrary, it gives the impression of the histories' clear progression, erasing the complex system of modalization that structures them.

The incipit which functions both as the beginning of the story, but also as a story of beginnings, consists of only one sequence in Morvan's history (which comprises around thirty-two pages) and expands only one narrative nucleus: the scene in which Morvan returns to his office after lunch, looks out the window, observes the coming snowstorm, and sees the bare sycamore trees. This scene introduces the mythological reference to Zeus's rape of Europa through the mediation of an illustrated mythology book. The reference to the mythological story ("porque fue bajo un plátano que en Creta el toro intolerablemente blanco, con las astas en forma de medialuna, después de haberla raptado en una playa de Tiro o Sidón . . . violó, como es sabido, a la ninfa aterrada" (because it was beneath a sycamore tree in Crete that the unbearably white bull, with half-moon shaped horns, after having abducted her on a beach in Tyre or Sidon . . . raped, as is common knowledge, the terrified nymph [I 2/ P 9]) becomes the generative cell of the detective story and the axiom of Morvan's fantasm.[6] The story is centered on Morvan and the search for a serial killer who is characterized by his horrific treatment (rape, murder, and mutilation) of twenty-eight elderly Parisian women (*viejas*).[7]

The first part of *The Investigation*, which consists of three parts, closes without the reader knowing the identity of the speaking voice, where it is uttered, and for whom. And it will not be until well into the second part that the principal narrator, who encompasses the narrator of Morvan's story, introduces the second investigation (concerning the identity of the author of *In the Greek Tents*). Focusing on Pichón, this principal narrator establishes the basic pragmatic situation on which Morvan's story depends: "quienquiera haya sido el autor—hasta ese mismo momento en que están sentados a la mesa tomando la primera cerveza de la noche con Soldi y Tomatis . . . no se le ha ocurrido [*a Pichón*] ningún nombre" (whoever the author may have been—until this very moment when he [Pichón] is sitting at the table drinking the first beer of the night with Soldi and Tomatis, no name has come to mind [I 60/ P 63]). This second part is the responsibility of an omniscient heterodiegetic narrator with multiple focalizations (although the focalization on Pichón's affective state is the central one) and in contrast to the first part there is an abundance of direct transcriptions of dialogues. This narrator establishes the basic pragmatic situation: those present at a beer garden in the city of Santa Fé—Pichón, the narrator of Morvan's story; Tomatis, his old friend; and Soldi, a new character who belongs to a different generation than the others and who will link the plots of the two investigations.

The sequence is a long analepsis: after a morning boat trip to Washington's house (in order to investigate the identity of the author of *In the Greek Tents'*) and the return trip from Rincón Norte at sunset

> cuando han bajado de la lancha en el Yacht Club . . . han decidido venir a comer al patio en el que están ahora . . . después de las nueve . . . se encontraron en el patio [cervecero]" (P 170–71)

> [once they got out of the boat at the Yacht Club they decided to go to dinner at the beer house where they now are . . . it was past nine when they met again in the beer house,] (I 176)

they pass by the house (and by the location of Saer's other text *Nobody Nothing Never*), which years before belonged to Gato, Pichón's twin, who has since disappeared along with Elisa. One could argue that *The Investigation* is a long semi-diegetic analepsis constructed out of Pichón memories and appropriated by the heterodiegetic narrator.

The first narrative sequence of this second part corresponds to the "moment" immediately following the return from Rincón Norte, when the three characters briefly separate and then meet again for dinner. This means that the story told by Pichón, Morvan's investigation of the serial killer's identity, should actually be framed by the investigation of the historical novel's author. But in fact it is "un-framed" and enjoys certain autonomy, since it is not until the third and final section that Morvan's story appears explicitly included in the basic narrative (hypodiegetic narration): "Pichón *sacude de un modo enigmático la mano* por encima de su vaso de cerveza y continúa. *Sin hacer ningún gesto Morvan esperó que Lautret se decidiera a hablar*" (P 86, my emphasis) [Pichón shakes his hand enigmatically above his half-empty glass of beer and goes on: *Not making a single gesture, Morvan waited for Lautret to make up his mind to speak* (I 85/ P 86)]. In the absence of quotation marks, this transition is marked by the chiasmus gesture/voice.

Kidnappings and separations

The Investigation, in the singular, unfolds into two investigations whose common characteristic is "who?"—a question of authorship and of identity.[8] On the one hand, there is a detective story (a whodunit) which seeks to find the identity of a serial killer; on the other, there is a text that narrates Pichón's return to Santa Fé after a twenty-year absence (his return is due to the sale of family property which is his last and only link to his place of birth) and deals with the authorship of *In the Greek Tents*. In the singular *The Investigation* is a double-edged, unframed story, given that if Pichón's return contains Morvan's story, as told by Pichón, the reader will not know this until he has read half the book.

This peculiar structure or variation on the traditional framed story (metadiegetic narration) forces the reader to focus on another investigation which now concerns the identity of the narrative "source." The narration itself becomes the object of the investigation ("object-narration") and questions the function of Pichón's story (what it evades or includes). Given that the detective story is first in the order of reading, the "investigation" names one of the components that structures the traditional detective story, which includes the story of a crime and the story of its in-

vestigation.[9] The title, in singular form, names a part of the whole but
according to the peculiar temporality of the detective story, comes after
the (always vacant) story of the crime.[10] The "investigation" encompasses the two stories of what *The Investigation* in turn, encompasses,
links, and juxtaposes, not without eroding the logic of the frame and what
is framed.[11]

It is highly significant that the boat trip to Rincón Norte and the visit to
Washington's library frames the knot of the intrigue of Morvan's story and
that it comes first in the order of reading. This sequence is centered on the
"zone-place": the text re-writes *Nobody Nothing Never,* as Saer himself
says in *La narración-objeto,* and produces a transformation of the "zone-
birth place" into "Place."[12] Taking the presuppositions of hyperrealism and
the nouveau roman as its point of departure, *Nobody Nothing Never* had already made use of the detective story plot by inserting it in a text that rejected intrigue, psychological and revealing dialogue, and the significant
anecdote. If the differences between *Nobody Nothing Never* and *The Investigation* are obvious, they nevertheless share a common characteristic:
the interplay between writing and discourse in which form plays a critical
function. The form becomes the "criticism" of discourse because it is a
philosophy of narration and not because it proposes a philosophy in the
story. The "object-narration" contains (or is) the intra-philosophical max-
ims that it exhibits as its own proper object, instead of proposing a series of
extrinsic and pre-existent discursive utterances with which to coincide.
Nobody Nothing Never postpones the outcome of the detective story and
unfolds only after a multiplicity of repetitions and multiple conflictive versions of what happened; this dilutes its cognitive power and dissolves the
closed form that subtends it. In *The Investigation,* on the other hand, the
detective story props up a writing of the affects that is not totally absorbed
by it.

The Investigation's temporal unity comprises twelve hours and the spatial frame includes the city of Santa Fé, the Paraná River, and Rincón Norte
(the "zone"). These unities of place and time are integrated into a peculiar
structure: an "un-framed" story imbued with a series of figures that hold
together its formal coherence. Two paternal deaths organize two "family
romances," Morvan and Julia's, Washington's daughter. These in turn
serve as the front for an undisclosed death, the cause of Pichón's trip and
the two authorial investigations, which are themselves also investigations
about origins. Two kidnappings (Europa's by Zeus and Helen's by Paris,
which according to tradition is a restitutiton of the first),[13] link the story

told by Pichón and the summary of the plot of *In the Greek Tents,* as told by Soldi, but also serves as a front for the "kidnapping" (disappearance) of Gato and Elisa (a couple that is ghostly doubled in the sporadic disappearances of Francesito, Pichón's son, and Alicia, Tomatis's daughter), and the failed investigation of their whereabouts which has left "scars" in Pichón and Tomatis's friendship.[14] Finally, the snow and the rain of white papers (the letter shredded by Lautret) in Pichón's story and the white butterflies that close the basic story function as metonymic or diegetic metaphors that take their vehicle from the narration itself (or from the text) and not from a preexisting referent.

A story told by Pichón and the summary of an unpublished text related to him by Soldi make up the narrative structure of *The Investigation.* Pichón brings the story from Paris and, thanks to the correspondence he maintains with Tomatis, he also knows of the existence of an unpublished novel in Washington's archives. Pichón has access to the manuscript and from its perusal the heterodiegetic narrator states that

> lo que le ha llamado antes que nada la atención [a Pichón] es que la novela empieza con puntos suspensivos, y que en realidad la primera no es una frase sino el miembro conclusivo de una frase de la que falta toda la parte argumentativa: "*. . . prueba de que sólo es el fantasma lo que engendra la violencia . . .*" (P 62, my emphasis)

> [what has, above all else, attracted (Pichón's) attention is the fact that the novel begins with ellipsis dots, and that the first sentence is not really a complete phrase but, rather, the concluding clause of a sentence, all of whose supporting arguments are missing: "*. . . proof that it is only the phantasm that engenders violence.*"] (I 58–59, translation modified)

If the beginning of *In the Greek Tents* can be read as a *mise en abîme* of Pichón's story and of *The Investigation,*[15] it is significant that in the order of reading the epigraph comes before the oral summary of the plot related by Soldi. The epigraph is a floating supplement of meaning that by an *après coup* effect resemantizes the detective story told by Pichón (which according to the order of reading Pichón *has been telling* even before his visit to Rincón Norte). If the phantasm is what engenders violence, what is Pichón doing when he formulates a phantasm that does *precisely* what it says (engenders violence)? What happens between the acts of *engendering through narration* and formulating a phantasm that *engenders narration*?

"IN THE CLIFFS OF MY NERVES":
THE *WRITING OF THE AFFECTS*
OR *ON THIS SIDE* OF THE
"ORIGINARY PHANTASM"

Y el General escruta volar
 siniestras penas
allá . . . .
en el desfiladero de mis nervios!
     —César Vallejo, "En las tiendas griegas."

[And the general scrutinizes flying
sinister sorrows
there . . . .
in the cliffs of my nerves!
     —César Vallejo, "In the Greek Tents"]

Identifying a literary phantasm in a literary text and
designating it by its name has no value as
recognition . . . The analysis of unconscious
phenomema in literature never touches the drive's
raw reality but constructs or models a representation
which the reader imagines from the viewpoint of his
unconscious.
     —Pierre Glaudes, "Après coup" 240

When dealing with the phantasm it is above all a
question of trying to see what is behind it. This is not
an easy task since behind it there is *nothing*.
However this is a nothing that can assume a variety
of aspects.
     —Jacques-Alain Miller, "Dos dimension
     es clínicas: síntoma y fantasma" 13

No hay, al principio, nada. Nada.
[There is, in the beginning, nothing. Nothing.]
     —Saer, NNN 1

The Oedipus complex founds the Law and Desire in which the father figures as support of the former and the mother is the prototype of the object (first object of desire and of the signifier).[16] In Morvan's story the Oedipus complex is overcodified and a sadistic scene is played out. The sadism that Saer's texts often display can be read as a defense from the maternal—those elements predating the process of symbolization and which survive it: affects or energies—and is linked to a desire for self-generation.

There is an unresolved Oedipus complex in Saer's works: a fusion of the writer with the work, of which he would be the creator and the work his offspring. A sort of perfect incest, the work being, in turn, the mother, the offspring, and its own entrails, born of itself. It is not convincing to treat the Oedipus complex, the modern myth par excellence, as a hermeneutic key that allows one to identify and name Saer's phantasm, as recent critics would suggest.[17] And this for two reasons: first, because his writing can be read as "consciously" illustrated with symbols and psychoanalytic structures (as if it were Morvan's illustrated mythology book) and with an anecdote that has a psychoanalytic-mythical base. Second, because the work guarantees its own (partial) decoding by making use of the discursive intertext provided by Freud: the mystery and the clues are given to us "almost" simultaneously.[18]

Psychoanalysis teaches us that the Oedipus complex is the first narrative that tentatively provides the frame for processing and reconstructing an individual's past experience. The materials of this narrative are elements predating symbolization that, although sifted through the order of language, are ruled by desire. The narrative is a signifying structure that corresponds to the unification of the subject with respect to an actantial pole of the Oedipal triangle; this in turn results from the desire and castration articulated within that structure. This structure, overdetermined by the family triangle, filters and translates the unconscious energy flux or rests (affects) that remain outside of the Oedipus narrative. A fictive story repeats the constitution of the subject in the Oedipus complex inasmuch as it is a subject *of* desire and subject *to* castration, but the fact that it introduces what the Oedipal subject has repressed, what we call affects, is a clear indication that the repetition of the Oedipus story that Saer's fictions display occur in plain consciousness of its cause—cause of the Oedipus complex and the Oedipal cause of the fiction and, therefore, of the desiring and narrating subject. By representing and by putting into play what exceeds it, the "object-narration" traverses the Oedipal complex or, in what amounts to the same movement, the "object-narration" exhibits the limit of the Oedipal complex and for that reason transgresses it. And this is so only because it posits it *as* a limit and *not* as an end in itself.

Saer's themes are linked to a perverse sexual phantasm. The display of the maternal body and its possession exist in a latent and obsessive form and are frequent in his writing. However, it is important to clarify what we understand by phantasm, how his fictions treat that structure and if it has the last word in those desiring machines that are his stories.

Phantasm is a clinical term that points to an imaginary scene in which the subject figures, in a more or less deformed manner, the satisfaction of a desire that is ultimately sexual. Additionally, phantasm covers the field of particular imaginary formations whose comforting role was noted by Freud. The phantasm is at the same time the effect of an unconscious archaic desire and the matrix of actual desires, conscious and unconscious.[19] Following Freud, Lacan posits that the phantasm functions like a machine to turn *jousissance* into pleasure, because if left to itself the former would result in unpleasure. Lacan distinguishes three dimensions of the phantasm: its imaginary aspect, which corresponds to what a subject can produce as images and its symbolic aspect, since it consits of a short story that responds to certain linguistic rules of construction. Only when its profusion, the "dense forest of the phantasm,"[20] decants itself completely do we obtain its axiom (a phrase with grammatical variations). Finally, Lacan distinguishes the fundamental dimension of the phantasm: the real. To say that the phantasm is a real in the analytic experience is equivalent to saying that it is a remainder that cannot be modified.

The life of a subject is shaped by a "phantasmatics" and literature and art are the priviledged sites of its formulation, but *not* of its realization. The principal five phantasmatic scenes (*phantemes*)[21] at work in literary texts are seduction, castration, the family novel, the return to the womb, and the primal scene (*Urszene*); these scenarios express trans-subjective structures that the subject adopts in order to tell his story.[22]

What is the function of the phantasm in Saer? For Saer presenting an Oedipal phantasm is a way of reducing it to the rank of spectacle, given that it is a well established fact in literary culture that any determination of the Oedipus complex is already a construction.[23] Saer's writing constantly frustrates the mythical interpretation of psychoanalysis precisely because it is the writer who transforms himself into a mythical figure:

> . . . las *victorias regias* que flotaban cerca de las orillas . . . evocaban un cordón umbilical . . . les hicieron pensar a Pichón a causa de esa flor un poco separada del círculo verde pero un poco dependiente de él, igual que un planeta y su satélite en esas *diosas arcaicas y solitarias* que, fecundándose a sí mismas parían, por entre sus miembros vigorosos *un dios menor*, blanco, espigado y frágil, *con el que se elevaba en vuelo nupcial antes de abandonarlo a la mesa del sacrificio para hacerlo despedazar y perpetuar de ese modo su propio culto.* (P 69, my emphasis)

> [. . . the water lilies (*victorias regias*) floating near the river banks . . . brought an umbilical cord to mind . . . (they) reminded Pichón, because of

that flower slightly separated from the green circle yet dependent upon it, like a planet and its satellite, of those *archaic, solitary goddesses* who, fecundating themselves, gave birth between their vigorous limbs to a *minor god*, white, frail, slender and graceful, *with whom they rose in nuptial flight before abandoning him on the sacrificial altar to be hacked to pieces and thus perpetuate their own cult*.] (I 66–67, my emphasis, translation modified)

This sequence appears to invert the values of the mythical account of Europa's rape by Zeus and introduces an element which belongs not only to the space of the "zone" but also to its mythical universe (*irupé* or *victoria regia*), although without its legendary correlates.[24] This means that one must treat Pichón's idiosyncratic construction as a *vision*. One can read not only a nucleus which resists the narrative assimilation of the Oedipus complex there, but also the cipher of something located *on this side* of the phantasm: it is a question of self-engendering, birth and sacrifice; producers of a remainder that perpetuates an autonomous and sovereign cult.

Saer's writing incites a conflict that is not won on the side of the Oedipal identifications that the narration produces. As in *Oedipus King*, Morvan is the victim of narrative causality[25] or, if we agree with Tomatis's hypothesis, Morvan's phantasm functions because of the subjective intervention of the reader-writer Lautret ("his best friend").[26] By *formulating* this phantasm and the mechanism of its construction, Pichón's story exposes the sado-masochistic roots of the "society of the spectacle" (the cultural coordinates in which Pichón locates his story) and thus protects itself from the violence that it begets. But he does *not* achieve victory by exhibiting or formulating the phantasm.

If there is a victory in Saer's text, it is achieved by a series of profound and risky descents into the realm of the affects. These are legible at the level of the *dispositio* and *lexis*, in the marks they leave in narrative prose. In "La cuestión de la prosa" (The Question of Prose) Saer speaks about changing the function of the language of narration in order to break with the pragmatic colonization of the state and market. Saer's art of narration remits to the very limits of realist prose that the poets of the "alchemie du verbe" (Rimbaud, Mallarmé, Lautréamont, but also Vallejo) also had to confront: *"lo indecible* es aquello que no ha sido ni pensado ni dicho antes del advenimiento del poema y que no es producto tampoco de un descubrimiento intelectual suscitado logicamente" (*the unsayable* is what has neither been thought nor said before the advent of the poem; it is not the product of a logically provoked intellectual discovery [NO 59]). The poem's unsayable is the point of resistance of a prose that seeks to subtract itself from the prosaism of the state and market. If the destiny of the modern poem is played out in its becoming prose, for Saer the destiny of prose is played out in the realm of the prose poem, or the becoming poem of prose.[27] This is the reason his writing (its rhythm, syntax, concatenations) is closer to the inhumanity of the modern poet than to the verisimilitude of the writer of realist novels. A strange poet, it is true, since his themes are not derived from the great lyric tradition. In Saer horror, death, terror, madness, orgies, the repugnance and threat of the feminine are central. But he is a modern poet, above all, because of his way of implementing a set of neutral directives ("neither melancholic nor nostalgic") that concern the present condition of a writing that has left behind the "time of the promise" and knows that "nothing is promised to us but the power to remain true to what comes to us."[28]

Pichón's story exhibits a two-faced maternal figure: a giver of life *and* death. The old ("closed") feminine sex is contaminated by the cadaver and by a series of impure substances (excrement, blood, urine, and semen), but it is the closed sex that the madness of the criminal wants to reopen. Pichón's narration certainly exhibits a phantasm. The methodical pulcritude of the supposed killer, Morvan, contrasts with the chaos of the scene of the crime. Here *scene* should be read in the sense of a significant construction; the criminal stages a scene of intercourse, birth, abortion, and sacrifice in order to violently displace sexual difference and replace it with the violence of sacrifice and the ritual of purification. It also exhibits in an intransitive sense since the reader does not know if in fact it is Morvan's staging: Pichón's narration is inconclusive regarding the authorship of the crimes, not only because his gloss of the psychiatric report of "Morvan's case" decomposes its true value, but also because Tomatis proposes another interpretation (the murderer was not Morvan but his best friend Lautret who killed for pleasure and set a trap for the detective).

We must therefore show what function the detective story plays in *The Investigation*. The real or imaginary itinerary that Morvan traces and whose motivations he does not know, according to the narrator, are marked by indications and objects: a recurring dream, a phantasm structured in mythological form, a family romance marked by an Oedipal story, a small white piece of paper that points to him as the criminal. From the beginning Morvan's investigation folds over itself and becomes an investigation *of* Morvan, or a counter-investigation that does not seek to find the identity of the criminal but to frustrate the search. That is why Tomatis's comments interrupt the detective story's tedious convention according to which the detective takes control and summarizes the fundamental points of the investigation. In Saer the investigation substitutes the story of the crime and that of the investigation for that of the story *of* the story. *The Investigation* is the search for the story ("object-narration"): the true story consists in the display of the story, of the mechanisms that produce it—the formulation of a phantasm *and* the inscription of its unsayable, impossible *hither side.*

The story of Pichón, who is back after a long *separation* and who has returned in order to enact it by definitely doing away with what little remains of the family estate, assumes the separation proper to the symbolic function (which operates under the law of the father, the Oedipal form. It is not by chance that Pichón returns to his place of birth with his own son):

> En un fulgor instantáneo [Pichón] ha entendido por qué, a pesar de su buena voluntad, de sus esfuerzos incluso, desde que llegó de París después de tantos años de ausencia, *su lugar natal* no le ha producido ninguna emoción: porque ahora es al fin un adulto, y ser adulto significa justamente haber llegado a entender que *no es en la tierra natal donde se ha nacido*, sino en un lugar más grande, más neutro, ni amigo ni enemigo, desconocido, al que nadie podrá llamar suyo y que no estimula el afecto sino la extrañeza, un hogar que no es ni espacial ni geográfico, ni siquiera verbal, sino más bien, y hasta donde estas palabras puedan seguir significando algo, físico, químico, biológico y cósmico, y del que lo invisible y lo visible . . . no es en realidad su patria sino su prisión, abandonada y cerrada ella misma desde el exterior—la oscuridad desmesurada que errabundea, ígnea y gélida a la vez, al abrigo no únicamente de los sentidos, sino también *de la emoción, de la nostalgia y del pensamiento.* (P 78–79, my emphasis)

> [In a sudden flash . . . he has understood why, despite his good will, his efforts even since his arrival from Paris after so many years of absence, his birthplace has produced no emotion in him: because he is at last an adult and to be an adult means, precisely, having reached the point of understanding that *it is not in one's native land that one is born*, but in a larger, more neutral place, neither friend nor enemy, unknown, which no one could call his own and which does not stir emotions but strangeness; a home that is neither spatial nor geographical, nor even verbal, but rather, and insofar as those words can continue to mean something, physical, chemical, biological, cosmic, and of which the invisible and the visible . . . is not in reality his homeland but his prison, itself abandoned and locked from the outside—the boundless darkness that wanders, at once glacial and igneous, beyond the reach not only of the senses, *but also of emotion, of nostalgia and of thought.*] (I 76–77)

What better narrative "mode" than the detective story (which is highly formalized, with easily recognized conventions) and structured in psychoanalytic key (Oedipus, the first detective) in order to *formulate* it?[29] Even if from the reader's unconscious perspective one could see in the detective story the wish to present a less painful and more pleasing rendition of the primal scene (*Urszene*),[30] the type of crime that Pichón's story narrates seems to frustrate or perturb that very possibility.

He who separates himself (is separated)[31]—Morvan/Pichón—the son, "touches" the mother, but *The Investigation* is not ruled by the Oedipal triangle given that the subject of the phantasm, the writer (who is also the object), transgresses the three positions of the triangle and in this way inscribes a writing of the affects.[32] Intermittently, this lasts approximately as long as the story (twelve hours), like the *victoria regia*, "flor de un blanco rojizo que se había abierto en el atardecer, para *relumbrar con un resplandor apagado* durante la noche y volver a cerrarse al alba" (P 69, my emphasis) [the white flower with a pink tinge that had opened in the late afternoon, *to gleam with a dim splendor* during the night and close again at dawn (I 66)]: a crepuscular flower that condenses Pichón's vision, a sign of an impossible object, a threshold and a limit. This vision introduces a supplemental drive (*trieb*) of horror and death into the original phantasm (*Urfantasien*) that impedes the images from crystalizing as images of desire or of nightmares, dissipating them in sensation (pain) and rejection (horror) —the *affects*. The scene of scenes is the image of birth, a reverse incest, a shattered identity, horror and beauty, sexuality and the brutal negation of sexuality.

This vision and its writing of the affects is ambiguous: if it can be said to have a demarcating function, it is not able to totally separate the subject from what threatens it. The writing of the affects reveals it to be in permanent danger. From the archaic pre-objectal relation, from the immemorial violence with and by which a body separates itself from another in order to be, language conserves the signs of an "archaic disaster": the night in which the contours of the signified thing is lost and in which the affects are at work; what in *The Investigation* is called "*the forces pulling down toward darkness.*" Writing fails to transform this combat with darkness into a phantasm, and so the writer can do no more than constantly return to the same mechanism of symbolization. He does this not in order to find in the object he names the nothingness of the void, but rather in the operation itself: the "object-narration" that like the modern poem is without object.

Pichón's story formulates the *impossible* dimension of the phantasm (Oedipal incest as transgression of the limits of the proper), but the basic story (hypodiegetic) goes further and by displaying the attempt to symbolize the "origins" inscribes the other side of the paternal prohibition: pleasure and pain. *The Investigation* tells another version of the "Account of the adventures of a child lost in the world" (*Relación de abandonado*) that like *The Witness* exhibits the frame of the paternal law in order to inscribe its inassimilable remainder. *The Witness* erases the narrator-protagonist's gender and inscribes the "scene of writing" transforming the story into an "auto-fiction" that is played out in the rejection of the symbolic law represented by Father Quesada. The memories of the narrator-protagonist become an abject theater that, playing on the three poles of the Oedipal metanarrative in order to transgress it, touches the roots of the symbolic order and shows this side of the phantasm, the nothing which is "el color justo de nuestra patria" (E 155) [the true measure of our homeland].

As in *The Witness*, the *fascinum* of *The Investigation* is not the phantasm. Saer's text allows us to "see what is behind the phantasm": "the *nameless distortion* that teems on the reverse side of what is clear" (I 131, my emphasis) and which is one of the faces the nothing assumes in his narrative universe. That is why the vision (the affects) allows for a crucial operation that concerns the place of the writer—the Place: the subtraction of "birth place" from its representation ("the zone"). *The Investigation*, an "object-narration" *without* object, transforms the subject of writing into an object of its phantasm but by sacrificing it in order to pass to the other side and "*perpetuate its own cult*" (I 67/P 69, my emphasis) it finds (itself) *on this side* of the phantasm, with the unsayable-impossible *real* to which it gives its own body.

Notes

INTRODUCTION: A LITERATURE
WITHOUT ATTRIBUTES OR
FOR AN ETHICS OF WRITING

All translations are the author's except for extracts from *The Witness* and *The Investigation*.

1. Guy Scarpetta, *L'âge d'or du roman* (Paris: Grasset, 1996).

2. Juan José Saer, *El concepto de ficción* (Buenos Aires: Ariel, 1997), 9–17.

3. Severo Sarduy, *Barroco*, in *Obra Completa, II* (Buenos Aires: ALLCA XX/Editorial Sudamericana, 1999), 1195–1262.

4. Saer, *El concepto de ficción,* 198.

5. By the term *anomaly* I aim to condense developments by Theodor W. Adorno, in particular from *Notes to Literature*, (New York: Columbia University Press, 1992) and *Aesthetic Theory* (Minneapolis: University of Minnesota Press, 1997) as well as from Lyotard, who, corrects Adorno's *pathos*. See Jean-François Lyotard, *Driftworks* (New York: Semiotext(e), 1984); *The Postmodern Condition* (Minneapolis: University of Minnesota Press, 1984); *The Inhuman (Reflections on Time)* (Stanford: Stanford University Press, 1991) and Maurice Blanchot, "La littérature et le droit à la mort" in *La part du feu* (Paris: Gallimard, 1949) and *The Infinite Conversation* (Minneapolis: University of Minnesota Press, 1993). For a systematic reflection on the status of contemporary literature, Jean Bessiére, *Enigmaticité de la literature* (Paris: PUF, 1993) and *Quel statut pour la littérature?* (Paris: PUF, 2001).

6. "Lo central, en literatura, es la praxis incierta del escritor que no se concede nada ni concede nada tampoco a sus lectores . . . La verdadera reflexión sociológica sobre el arte moderno es la siguiente: ya no hay, justamente, centro, en la medida en que no existe un modelo único como en el arte clásico, sino una multitud de tradiciones y de búsquedas que coexisten en un espacio de libertad" (What is decisive in literature is the writer's uncertain practice that concedes nothing to himself or to his readers . . . The true sociological reflection in modern art is as follows: there is no longer any center insofar as there is no single model, as in classical art, but rather a multiplicity of traditions and experiments that coexist in a space of freedom), Juan José Saer, *Juan José Saer por Juan José Saer* (Buenos Aires: Celtia, 1986), 13.

7. Juan José Saer, "La literatura y los nuevos lenguajes" and " La cultura europea" in *El concepto de ficción*, 90–93.

8. Saer, *El concepto de ficción*, 276.

9. Saer's name has been frequently linked with "regional literature."

10. "Saer's literary choices appear to be marked by their unpredictability and by the possibility of establishing new configurations and relations between the literatures that his texts put into play. This can be seen in his work on the American detective novel in *Cicatrices* (a link that Piglia also establishes); the perspective of 'regionalism' in "Palo y Hueso" and *El limonero real* (a possible link with H. Tizón's texts and also M. Briante's); the inclusion of film techniques in *El limonero real* and *Nadie nada nunca* (a project that M. Puig also develops in another direction); the discursive, at times experimental, search in *La Mayor* (also proposed by L. Gusmán and N. Ulla) and the introduction of objectivism in Argentina, with *El limonero real*. From these brief observations, one can deduce that *Saer's production is integrated within the Argentine literary system in its most important characteristics*" Graciela Montaldo, *Juan José Saer. El limonero real* (Buenos Aires: Hachette, 1986).

11. It is important to remember that Centro Editor de America Latina, the publishing house in charge of *Historia de la Literatura Argentina* (1982), included a section on Saer in a chapter dedicated to the new generation of writers (see Mirta Stern, "Juan José Saer y la construcción de una teoría del relato." *Historia de la Literatura Argentina*, vol. 6 [Buenos Aires: CEAL, 1982], 656–60). It also published three volumes by Saer in its "Biblioteca Básica" series: *El limonero real* and *Narraciones* (2 volumes). This occured during the military dictatorship. The first reviews of Saer's work (by the critics Beatriz Sarlo and María Teresa Gramuglio) appeared in Argentina at that time in *Punto de vista*. With the return to democracy, Saer became a permanent part of the reading lists of the Argentine Literature courses at the University of Buenos Aires.

12. Juan José Saer, *La narración-objeto* (Buenos Aires: Seix Barral, 1999), 56.

13. Ibid., 58.

14. We will follow the avatars of these two sites of fiction as they are transformed from "zone" to "place" and finally to "Place." The transformation of these enclaves is linked to the experience of exile and its "existential" coordinates, but the progressive transformation is indicative of fundamental redefinitions in the scope of Saer's "literary space."

15. See Alain Badiou, *Conditions* (Paris: Éditions du Seuil, 1992), 41. I will return to this point below.

16. "*Lo indecible* es aquello que no ha sido ni pensado ni dicho antes del advenimiento del poema y que no es producto tampoco de un descubrimiento intelectual suscitado logicamente," Saer, *La narración-objeto*, 59.

17. Gabriel Riera, ed., "For an 'Ethics of Mystery': Philosophy and the Poem." In *Alain Badiou: Philosophy and Its Conditions* (Albany, SUNY Press, 2005), 61–85.

18. ". . . ser adulto significa justamente haber llegado a entender que *no es en la tierra natal donde se ha nacido*, sino en un lugar más grande, más neutro, ni amigo ni enemigo, desconocido, al que nadie podrá llamar suyo y que no estimula el afecto sino la extrañeza (. . . being an adult means to finally understand that one is not born in a birth place, but in a much bigger place, more neutral, neither friend nor enemy, unknown, which no one can call theirs and which does not elicit affects but rather estrangement), Juan José Saer, *La pesquisa* (Buenos Aires: Seix Barral, 1994), 78–79.

19. Alain Badiou, *Petit traité d'inesthétique* (Paris: Éditions du Minuit, 1999), 23.

20. According to the epigraph of *Las nubes*.

21. César Aira, "Zona Peligrosa," *El Porteño*, Buenos Aires: (1986): 185–87.

22. I take the pioneering essay by Beatriz Sarlo, "Narrar la percepción," *Punto de vista* 10 (1980): 34–37 as the point of departure for these reflections.

23. *Extimité* ("external intimacy") is a term that Lacan introduced to point to an irreducible kernel of the real at the very heart of the symbolic order. It was Jacques-Alain Miller who gave currency to this term in his unpublished *Semimar 1, 2, 3*.

24. "Percepts are no longer perceptions; they are independent of a state of those who experience them . . . The novel has often risen to the percept—not perception of the moor in Hardy but the moor as percept; oceanic percepts in Melville . . . " Gilles Deleuze and Felix Guattari, *What is Philosophy?* (New York: Columbia University Press, 1994), 172–74.

25. "la Realidad Previa al Texto da la impresión de ser de esencia semejante a la de la Causa Primera respecto de la aparición del mundo," Saer, *La narracion-objeto*, 23.

26. See Noé Jitrik, "Entre el corte y la continuidad. Juan José Saer: una escritura crítica," *Revista Iberoamericana* 102–3 (1978): 99–109. For a comprehensive study of hyperrealist aesthetics in the River Plate area see, Hebert Benitez Pezzolano, "Encrucijadas de la objetividad," in *Historia Crítica de la Literatura Argentina, 11. La Narración gana la partida*, ed. Noé Jitrik (Buenos Aires: Emece, 2000), 143–59.

27. See Enrique Foffani and Adriana Mancini, "Más allá del regionalismo," *Historia Crítica de la Literatura Argentina, 11*, 261–80.

28. See Saer, "El concepto de ficción," in *El concepto de ficción*, 9–17.

29. I borrow the idea of the two "slopes" (*versants*) of language from Maurice Blanchot's "La littérature et le droit è la mort," in *La Part du feu* (Paris: Gallimard, 1949), 291–331.

30. "era como una tenaza destinada a manipular la incandescencia de lo sensible," Juan José Saer, *El entenado* (Barcelona: Destino, 1988).

31. "era como salir a cazar una fiera que ya me había devorado," ibid., 68.

32. For example, in the case of the cannibals contemplating human flesh in *The Witness*; the case of Gina, who observes horses mating; the incestuous gaucho in *The Event;* or the Inspector Morvan's wanderings in *The Investigation*. I borrow the concept of *forcing* from Alain Badiou, who in turns borrows it from the mathematician Cohen. See Alain Badiou. *Conditions* (Paris: Éditions du Seuil, 1993). Lacan employs this same concept in his *Ethics of Psychoanalysis* in order to formalize a nonsymbolizable kernel of the real that becomes the inner limit of the symbolic order.

33. "lo que más allá del don fugaz de lo empírico es transfondo y persistencia," Juan José Saer, *Glosa* (Buenos Aires-Madrid: Alianza, 1986), 101.

34. "el modo en que una verdad se manifiesta es secundario. Lo importante es que la verdad se deje vislumbrar," ibid., 84.

35. Badiou develops the difference between knowledge and truth that he takes from Lacan in *L'Être et l'événement* (Paris: Éditions du Seuil, 1976) and also in *L'Éthique. Essai sur la conscience du mal* (Paris: Hatier, 1993).

36. Emmanuel Lévinas develops the difference between phenomenon and enigma. See his *En Decouvrant l'existence avec Husserl et Heidegger* (Paris: Vrin, 1970).

37. "estamos de acuerdo en que todo esto pertenece al orden de la conjetura. La evidencia se enciende y apaga más allá o más acá de las palabras," Saer, *Glosa*, 184.

38. Maurice Blanchot, *L'Entretien infini* (Paris: Gallimard, 1969), 1–113.

39. Jacques Lacan, "Lituraterre," in *Autres écrits* (Paris: Éditions du Seuil, 2001), 11–22.

40. Juan José Saer, "La perspectiva exterior: Gombrowicz en la Argentina," in *El concepto de ficción*, 18–31.

41. Saer, *El concepto de ficción*, 9–17.

CHAPTER 1. SAER BEFORE SAER: FROM ZONE TO PLACE

1. See Nicolás Rosa, "Julio Cortázar," in *Historia de la literatura argentina, Tomo 5* (Buenos Aires: CEAL, 1982), 97–120; Beatriz Sarlo and Carlos Altamirano, *Ensayos Argentinos. De Sarmiento a la Vanguardia* (Buenos Aires: CEAL, 1983); and Beatriz Sarlo, *Una modernidad periférica. Buenos Aires, 1920 y 1930* (Buenos Aires: Nueva Visión, 1988).

2. The "Argumentos" condense an important biographeme: Saer's departure to France, an event that leaves important marks on how he redefines and transforms his literary project. See in particular, "Me llamo Pichón Garay," "En el extranjero," and "La dispersión."

3. Juan José Saer, "La selva espesa de lo real," *El concepto de ficción* (Buenos Aires: Ariel, 1997, 267–71).

4. "In a sudden flash . . . he has understood why, despite his good will, his efforts ever since his arrival from Paris after so many years of absence, his birthplace has produced no emotion in him: because he is at last an adult and to be an adult means, precisely, having reached the point of understanding that *it is not in one's native land that one is born*, but in a larger, more neutral place, neither friend nor enemy, unknown, which no one could call his own and which does not stir emotions but strangeness; a home that is neither spatial nor geographical, nor even verbal, but rather, and insofar as those words can continue to mean something, physical, chemical, biological, cosmic, and of which the invisible and the visible . . . is not in reality his homeland but his prison, itself abandoned and locked from the outside—the boundless darkness that wanders, at once glacial and igneous, beyond the reach not only of the senses, *but also of emotion, of nostalgia and of thought* (I 76–77/ P 78–79, my emphasis). I will follow these shifts in more detail in the next chapters.

5. On this particular device, see María Teresa Gramuglio, "El lugar de Saer," in *Juan José Saer por Juan José Saer* (Buenos Aires: Editorial Celtia, 1986), 261–307; Beatríz Sarlo, "Narrar la percepción," *Punto de vista*, 10, (1980): 34–37, and Jorgelina Corbatta, "*En la zona*: germen de la praxis poética de Juan José Saer," *Revista Iberoamericana* 155–56 (1991): 557–68.

6. This periodization seeks to make dominant lines of reading valid. However, the temporality of writing is more complex since experiments of a diverse nature coexist there. In the "Entrevista de Princeton," Saer states: "I wrote two books at a rather fast pace, *Cicatrices* and more or less at the same time *The Event*—as Ricardo Piglia advised me—. Since I had lost the habit of writing things too quickly, Ricardo told me 'I think you have to test your reflexes.' It sounded like he was talking about a boxer, which totally

convinced me . . . besides there was some money at stake. I devoted the same time to the two books: twenty days for one; twenty nights for the other. I used to live in a house in Colastiné where we had many fruit-trees, mandarines, lemons, and a lot of oranges. I prepared a jar of orange juice and poured a bottle of vodka with lots of ice on it and I drank slowly from it . . . until I realized I was dizzy and then went to bed. The other books took me much longer, I wrote them at a slower pace: *Glosa* and *Nobody Nothing Never* took me four years each; *El Limonero real* nine years, although in the meantime I was writing other things (*Cicatrices, Unidad de Lugar*, a part of *La mayor*). The challenge thus consisted in keeping a formal and stilistic unity, which entailed a constant work of readjustement from one book to the other. But in the end, in 1972, I was almost done –I already had the end—and it took me a month to finish it. That was, with *Glosa*, the book that gave me the most trouble. *The Witness*, which is a short book, took me three years . . . from this we can conclude that my writing was slow. In the last years, my last three books—*Lugar, The Investigation* and *Las nubes*—which are shorter texts, took me between two and three years. Currently, I am writing a long novel which I think will take me a long time." Juan José Saer, "La entrevista de Princeton," *Juan José Saer: Conversación en Princeton, PLAS Cuadernos*, no. 6, Program in Latin American Studies (Princeton, NJ: Princeton University, 2003). Saer's last novel (*La Grande*) was interrupted by his untimely death in the summer of 2005.

7. "Antes, ellos, podían. Mojaban, despacio, en la cocina, en el atardecer, en invierno, la galletita, sopando, y subían . . .'"

8. "Una columna oblícua de luz que entra, férrea, por la ventana, y que deposita, sobre el piso de madera, un círculo amarillo, y en su interior un millón de partículas que rotan, blancas, mientras el humo de mi cigarillo, subiendo desde la cama, entra en ella y se disgrega despacio, en esta mañana de mayo, de la que puedo ver por los vidrios, el cielo azul: la vigilia."

9. On *Sur*, see John King, *Sur: A Study of the Argentinean Literary Journal and the Development of a Culture* (Cambridge: Cambridge University Press, 1986).

10. On *Contorno*, see Carlos Mangone and Jorge A. Warley, "La modernización de la crítica. La revista *Contorno*," in *Historia de la literatura argentina, Tomo 5* (Buenos Aires: CEAL, 1982). On the *Boom* see Angel Rama, "El *boom* en perspectiva," *Literatura y mercado: más allá del boom* (Buenos Aires: Folio, 1984); Horacio González, "El boom: rastros de un palabra en la narrativa y crítica argentina," in Noé Jitrik, ed. *Historia crítica de la literatura argentina, Tomo 11*, 405–30 (Buenos Aires: Emecé, 2000); and Hector Libertella, *Las sagradas escrituras* (Buenos Aires: Sudamericana, 1993).

11. "I became aware of Adorno's books in the 1960s, in Paraná City; one afternoon I was at a bookstore and found a book called *Notes On Literature* in which there were a series of essays that left an indelible mark on us. One of those essays was "On Lyric Poetry and Society," the other "Punctuation Marks," in which one can read a whole new conception of literature articulated in Marxist terms—we were all Marxists at that time—. During those years we were in search of a more complex conception of art than the one developed by Marxist theoreticians. Adorno's essays were innovative, irreverent and at the same time, they followed a path that did not totally sever art from society. We found new names that did not appear in the classical Marxist repertoire: Beckett, Kafka. It was the time of Lukács' polemic on "Kafka or Thoman Mann"; the time when some Marxist critics tried to broaden the terms of the discussion, as in 'Toward a Realism

Without Frontiers' by Roger Garaudy (who has now taken on a mystical position). For us (the 1960s generation) Adorno meant a way to think the complex interplay between art and society without falling prey to the habitual simplifications and without sacrificing the social problems we were facing. It is posible to say that this way of understanding literature produced a synthesis in Argentine culture since for the first time for the young writers on the Left Borges became part of the canon. Up to that moment there was a split: while the leftist theoreticians of the *Contorno* group rejected Borges's work, we instead accepted it (along with Arlt's) as the richest one, as the first milestone in our literary tradition." Saer, "La entrevista de Princeton."

12. On the 1960s, see Oscar Terán, *Nuestros años sesenta. La formación de la nueva izquierda intelectual argentina.1956–1966* (Buenos Aires: El Cielo por Asalto, 1993).

13. I am thinking of *Cuaderno San Martín*, *Fervor de Buenos Aires*, *Luna de enfrente*, *El tamaño de mi esperanza,* and even his *Evaristo Carriego*, especially the poem "Fundación mítica de Buenos Aires," to which Saer will ironically allude later on in *El río sin orillas* (1991).

14. Jorge Luis Borges, "El cuento policial," *Obras Completas, IV* (Buenos Aires: Emecé, 1996), 189–97.

15. This group of intellectuals gathers around *El Litoral* newspaper and the Instituto de Cine in Santa Fé. They take a strong position against the market and cultural institutions; they read Borges, Di Benedetto and Juan L. Ortíz and are well read in foreign literatures: Pavesse, Montale, Pound, Joyce, Kafka, Proust, Sarraute, Robbe-Grillet, Faulkner, and the hard-boiled novel. They reject traditional realism and naturalism and all forms of aesthetic populism.

16. The question of a literary language that must opt between the Spanish of the Iberian peninsula and the Spanish of the River Plate has one important antecedent: Borges's "El idioma de los argentinos," which is part of a long debate on "criollismo." This question was still part of an important discussion in *Contorno*, motivated in part by Cortázar's decision to model his literary writing on the colloquial Spanish of the River Plate. See Alfredo E. Rubione, ed., *En torno al criollismo. Textos y polémicas* (Buenos Aires: CEAL, 1983), and Oscar Massota, "Vocos, la lupa y el viejo mundo," *Contorno*, 3, Buenos Aires, September 1954.

17. These signs are syntactical breaks, moments when the self who is composing the poem focalizes herself as imagining facts or events, which suggests a problematic simultaneity.

18. Adeline "does not see" Leopold's face as is; she projects his genitals onto his face. It is when Adeline fails to see Leopold's shadow that she composes the poem's first verse.

19. It is true that these operations are still subordinated to a main focus and that they are not as visible as in *El limonero real*. However, the interplay between the poem and the narrative plot is not as smooth as one would expect and their juxtaposition creates some difficulties for a strict linear reading. We will see in the next chapter how these processes are the main focus of the story and how they refer to the "other scene."

20. Although it is true that poems already appear in previous stories, such as "Alguien se aproxima" and "Fresco de mano," this is the only time that we are present at "the birth of a poem" in Saer's stories; we will see later how the stories themselves become "latent poems."

21. See Jacques Lacan, *Seminar Book XI, The Four Fundamental Concepts of Psychoanalysis* (New York: Norton, 1981) and *Le Séminaire Livre 4, La relation d' objet* (Paris: Éditions du Seuil, 1990).

22. Saer's readers will know from reading "Amigos" that this voice is Tomatis's.

23. Marcel Proust, *A la recherche du temps perdu*, I, 42.

24. Ibid., I, 53.

25. I am thinking of stories like "The Other Sky" and "La noche boca arriba" by Julio Cortázar, as well as Borges' "The Garden of Forking Paths."

26. Stéphane Mallarmé, "Un Coup de dés," in *Collected Poems*, trans. Henry Weinfield, 142–43 (Berkeley and Los Angeles: University of California Press, 1994).

27. "Nuestros recuerdos no son, como lo pretenden los empiristas, pura ilusión: pero un *escándolo ontológico* nos separa de ellos, constante y continuo pero más poderoso que nuestro esfuerzo por construir nuestra vida como narración. Es por eso que, desde otro punto de vista, podemos considerar nuestros recuerdos como una de las regiones más remota de lo que nos es exterior" (Juan José Saer, "Recuerdos" [M 191–92, enphasis mine]). [Our memories are not, as the empiricists claim, pure illusion: however *an ontological scandal*, constant and continuous, separate us from them. This is a much more powerful scandal than our efforts to shape our life as a narration. For this reason, and from a different point of view, it is possible to consider our memories as one of the more distant regions of what is exterior to us.]

CHAPTER 2. LITTORAL, LITERAL:
THE JOYS OF THE LETTER

1. Mirta Stern, "Prólogo," in *El limonero real* (Buenos Aires: CEAL, 1981), I–XI and "El espacio intertextual en la narrativa de Juan José Saer: instancia productiva, referente y campo de teorización de la escritura," *Revista Iberoamericana* 125, 10–11 (1983): 965–81. A neo-formalist paradigm for which "the novel is an adventure of writing" (Jean Ricardou) inspires Stern's reading. In *Juan José Saer: El limonero real* (Buenos Aires: Hachette, 1986), Graciela Montaldo develops her argument along similar lines. The first critic to point to the risks at stake in this approach was Alberto Giordano in *La experiencia narrativa. Juan José Saer, Felisberto Hernández, Manuel Puig* (Rosario, Arg.: Beatriz Viterbo Editora, 1992).

2. See Maurice Blanchot, "Les deux versiones de l'imaginaire," in *L' espace littéraire* (Paris: Gallimard, 1955).

3. See Blanchot, "Le chant des Sirènes," in *Le livre à venir* (Paris: Minuit, 1963).

4. Noé Jitrik, "Entre el corte y la continuidad. Hacia una escritura crítica (sobre *El limonero real*)," *Revista Iberoamericana*, 102–3 (1978): 99–109.

5. Lacan coins the expression "lalangue" to distinguish the object of psychoanalysis from Saussure's "la langue" or the object of linguistics. "Lalangue" is the dimension of language where the subject of the unconscious tries to hear himself and write his symptom.

6. The functional unit in the organization of the unconscious is the letter, instead of the phoneme (the unconscious is "a-phonos"). Because it is localizable and differential, the letter offers itself as a pure symbol. The letter's materiality, which commemorates the

murder of the thing by the symbol, incites the subject to take it as the sign of the lost object and even as the object itself. Consequently, words can be treated as things and one can cut and paste them according to the play of "lalangue." See Philippe Lacoue-Labarthe and Jean-Luc Nancy, *Le titre de la lettre* (Paris: Galilée, 1983).

7. There are several signs of this simultaneous persistence of the "son in the father": a childhood memory of horror that returns every morning (the scene of a foggy morning that at first lacks clear focalization) and which is later focalized as follows: "ha recordado, mientras orinaba en el excusado, como si el acto de orinar tuviese una correlación refleja con ese recuerdo, la mañana de niebla en que puso por primera vez los pies en la isla, en compañía de su padre" (he has remembered, while he pees, as if the act of urinating had a reflex correlation with that memory, the foggy morning when he first set his foot on the island, with his father [LR186]); the fact that the family elders call him "Layo," a name with which his father uses in the scene above; his nephew momentarily assumes the role of son.

8. Wenceslao's wife is constantly fixing these black bands that symbolize a process of mourning that for Wenceslao is already completed; as a consequence, he does not want to wear the shirts.

9. Beatriz Sarlo, "Saer, Tizón, Conti: Tres novelas argentinas," *Los libros* 44 (January-February, 1976): 3–6.

10. In spite of Borges' sharp criticism in "El escritor argentino y la tradición," this type of literature was still popular in the 1970s, as *Santa Fé, mi país* by Mateo Booz clearly shows.

11. See Ernesto Sábato, *Tres aproximaciones a la literatura de nuestro tiempo: Robbe-Grillet, Borges, Sartre* (Santiago, Chile: Editorial Universitaria, 1968), and Juan Carlos Portantiero, *Realismo y realidad en la narrativa Argentina* (Buenos Aires: Procyón, 1961).

12. Jitrik claims that the novel "is a real summary of what was later artificially developed by Butor, Robbe-Grillet, Claude Simon, and all those who have of course received the acclaim that Vanasco, reduced to the nostalgic category of an unknown precursor, has yet to achieve." Noé Jitrik, "Prólogo" to Alberto Vanasco, *Sin embargo Juan vivía* (Buenos Aires: Sudamericana, 1967), 2nd ed., 14.

13. "Let's not forget that Antonio Di Benedetto had already written objectivist texts toward the 1950s without the faintest idea of something called *nouveau roman*." See G. Saavedra, "Juan José Saer. El arte de narrar la incertidumbre," in *La curiosidad impertinente. Entrevista con narradores argentinos* (Rosario, Arg.: Beatriz Bitervo, 1993), 177.

14. See Hebert Benítez Pezzolano, "Encrucijadas de la objetividad," en Noé Jitrik, *Historia crítica de la literatura Argentina, vol. XI. La narración gana la partida* (Buenos Aires: Emecé, 2000), 143–60.

15. At that time Saer was living in France.

16. See A. Perrone, "Borrar fronteras. Entrevista a J. J. Saer," *La Opinion cultural*, Buenos Aires, May 23, 1976. This conviction has to do with the constructive procedures proposed by the new novelists and their critique of the traditional novel's conventions. The essays in *El concepto de ficción* ("Notas sobre el *Nouveau Roman*" [1972], "Zama," [1973], "La novela" [1981] and "Antonio Di Benedetto" [1992]) confirm the importance of the *nouveau roman*, but also denounce their "dogmatism and theoretical contradic-

tions" (185). Two decades later, this conviction is less resolute: "I've used elements related to the aesthetics of the *nouveau roman* tangentially, like one more procedure. It is not a central procedure in my work. In any case, there are objectivist writers that I admire a great deal, but who I consider to be very different from each other. We realize that the name *nouveau roman* is above all a label given to certain writers for marketing purposes." G. Saavedra, 1993, 176.

17. Saer has not renounced this "conviction" to date. See his *La narración-objeto*.

18. For a systematic study of these devices, see Lucien Dällembach, *Le récit speculaire* (Paris: Éditions du Seuil, 1978).

19. According to the expression Barthes popularized to refer to what later became the *mouvance* of the *nouveau roman*. See Nelly Wolf, *Une littérature sans histoire. Essaie sur le nouveau roman* (Paris: Droz, 1995); Francine Dugastes-Portes, *Le nouveau roman. Une césure dans l'histoire du récit* (Paris: Nathan, 2001); Roger Allemand, et al. *Le nouveau roman en question* (1–4) (Paris: Lettres Modernes, Minard, 1992–1999) and *Le nouveau roman* (Paris: Ellipses, 1996). These books revise the doctrinaire phase of the *mouvance* that includes Alain Robbe-Grillet, *Pour un nouveau roman* (Paris: Éditions de Minuit, 1967) and Jean Ricardou, *Problèmes du nouveau roman* (Paris: Éditions du Seuil, 1967); *Pour une théorie du nouveau roman* (Paris: Éditions du Seuil: 1971); *Nouveau roman, hier, ajourd'hui* (Paris: 10/18,1972); *Le nouveau roman* (Paris: Éditions du Seuil, 1973) and *Nouveaux problèmes du roman* (Paris: Seuil, 1978).

20. See Beatriz Sarlo, "Narrar la percepción," *Punto de vista* 10 (1980): 34–37.

21. Juan José Saer, "Razones,"17, in *Juan José Saer por Juan José Saer* (Buenos Aires: Editorial Celtia, 1986).

22. "Pero lo que está ocurriendo en el tiempo, lo que está ocurriendo ahora, el tiempo de las historias en el interior del cual estamos, es inenarrable" (But what is happening in time, what is happening now, the time of the stories in which we are, is unnarratable). Hector's painting also functions as a concretization of objective *durée*. See Juan José Saer, "A medio borrar" in *La mayor*, 81–82.

23. Philippe Hamon, *Introducción al análisis de lo descriptivo* (Buenos Aires: Hachette, 1988).

24. Roman Jakobson, *Essais de linguistique générale* (Paris: Éditions de Minuit, 1969), Samuel Levin, *Linguistic Structures in Poetry* (The Hague: Mouton, 1972), and Nicolas Ruwet, *Langage, musique, poésie* (Paris: Éditions du Seuil, 1972).

25. See Juan José Saer, "La selva espesa de lo real," in *Una literatura sin atributos*, 267–68.

26. I borrow the term from Hamon (1988), who uses it to define a linguistic competence similar to narration.

27. The only segments that perform this type of transformation occur in the marvelous and fairy tales, whose position in the overall structure of the text is highly ironic and therefore becomes the target of parody.

28. Dreams are not uncommon in Saer's texts; in fact they play a structuring function in *Cicatrices*, *Nobody Nothing Never*, *The Event*, *Glosa,* and *The Investigation*, but they never highlight the dream-work as in *El limonero real*.

29. It can either be a floating narrative segment detached from its sequential context, Wenceslao's nap or, more likely, the dream that awakens Wenceslao the morning after he returns home: "ha dormido, respirando y roncando . . . *algunas horas*, y ahora, en medio

de un rumor de viento y de lluvia . . . está sentado en la cama, *el corazón latiéndole de un modo violento*, en el recinto incoloro, porque amanece, con los ojos abiertos" (LR 227, my emphasis) [he has slept, breathing and snoring . . . *a few hours*, and now in midst of a rumor of wind and rain . . . is sitting on the bed, his heart beating violently, in the colorless room, because he wakes, with his eyes open].

30. Sigmund Freud, The *Interpretation of Dreams* (New York: Norton, 1965), 241.

31. Ibid., 506.

32. Ibid., 342.

33. Ibid., 414.

34. Infanticide is overdetermined in the text: Wenceslao-Layo, who has the same name as Oedipus' father, kills a lamb; Rogelio plays at cutting his son Rogelito's throat; Agustín wanted to throw his son Agustín (the Ladeado) into the river. The doubling of the names in the last two cases signals contiguity between paternal and filial roles: the fathers are at the same time their own sons. Also note that there is a doubling of names in all the father-son, mother-daughter relations, except in the case of Wenceslao-Layo, whose double name condenses the father-son figure and fills the void of the name of the son (which is anonymous).

35. See LR 133, 135, and 137, respectively.

36. Freud, The *Interpretation of Dreams*, 2.

37. Ibid., 554.

38. The story also takes a stand against magical realism as a form promoted by the *Boom*.

Chapter 3. Saer's Fiction:
"A Speculative Anthropology?"
The Witness (El entenado)

1. Juan José Saer, *Una literatura sin atributos*, (Santa Fé, Arg.: Universidad Nacional del Litoral, Cuadernos de Extension Universitaria, 7, Serie Ensayo, 1986), later included in *El concepto de ficción*.

2. Juan José Saer, "El concepto de ficción," originally published in *Punto de vista*, 40 (1991): 3, later included in *El concepto de ficción*.

3. Juan José Saer, *"Zama*: entre la incomprensión y el olvido," originally published in *Clarín*, "Cultura y nación" (Suplemento Dominical) (Buenos Aires, 1986), later included in *El concepto de ficción*.

4. Although Saer has written a considerable number of books (short stories, novels, poetry, and essays), a cursory look at the critical bibliography shows that *The Witness* has received particular attention. Many critical interpretations of *The Witness* tend to be historicist: a rewriting of the chronicles of Indies, a commemoration of the Amerindians, or a new historical novel. Another set of critical readings follows S. Menton's ideas in his *Latin American New Historical Novel*. However, Menton's paradigm is problematic due to its empiricism: "The following list of 367 new and not-so-new Latin American historical novels published between 1949 and 1992 normally would appear in an appendix. However, by locating them in the prependix, I am foregrounding my preference for empirically rather that theoretically based scholarship" (1). And: "the empirical evidence

suggests that since 1979 the dominant trend in Latin American fiction has been the proliferation of New historical Novels" (14). Evidently this view does not elicit decisive questions about language and history. Finally, the distinctive traits Menton uses to characterize this new narrative mode, genre, or subgenre are so broad that one can include any type of novel under the category of "new historical novel."

5. In other words, we are dealing here with an event without archive (or at least with a very thin one). In a sense, there is an isomorphic desire that links *The Witness* to its supposed "referent" and the narrator-protagonist to his peripeteia: "The unknown is an abstraction; the familiar, a desert; but what is glimpsed (*lo vislumbrado*), the perfect site for desire and hallucination to unfold" (*es el lugar perfecto para hacer ondular deseo y alucinación*) (W 1/E 2).

6. Saer employs the expression "primal scene" to refer to Solís' fate in *El río sin orillas* and quotes Borges's verse: "Donde ayunó Juan Díaz y los indios comieron" (Where Juan Díaz fasted and the Indians ate) from "Fundación Mítica de Buenos Aires." This verse is followed by a commentary that parodies the criteria Borges uses: proximity to the foundational space and the writer's appropriation of this space. This parodical gesture transforms the logic of foundation since by opening it to the differential temporality of the *Urszene*; it becomes an interminable and abyssal process of supplementation of fictions of origins.

7. "Invention" in the sense of *invenire*: "The fortuitous advent of the wholly other beyond the incalculable as a still possible calculation, beyond the very order of calculation; this is the 'true' invention, which is no longer an invention of the truth and which only comes as finitude's chance. It invents and appears only from what fails in this way." *Invention* must be read in a strong sense and beyond the inventory of the archive. See Jacques Derrida, *Psyché. Les inventions de l'autre* (Paris: Galilée, 1986), 59.

8. Frank Lestringant, "The Philosopher's Breviary: Jean de Léry in the Enlightenment," *Representations* 35 (1991): 142–67. For a more detailed discussion of de Léry, see Frank Lestringant, *Le Hugenot et le sauvage*.

9. Michel De Certeau, "L'ethnographie, l'oralité, ou l'espace de l'autre: Léry," *L' écriture de l'histoire* (París: Gallimard, 1975), 218–20.

10. Michel De Certeau, "Montaigne's 'Of Cannibals': The Savage 'I,'" *Heterologies. Discourse on the Other.* (Minneapolis: University of Minnesota Press, 1986).

11. Juan José Saer, *The Witness*, trans. M. Jull Costa (London: Serpent's Tail, 1990).

12. Juan José Saer, *L'ancêtre*, trans. Laure Bataillon (Paris: Flammarion, 1983).

13. On Herodotus see François Hartog, *Le Miroir d' Herodote*, especially the chapter "Une rhétorique de l'alterité," 224–52.

14. In this series of texts we should include Hans Staden's chronicle of captivity among the Tupinambas of Brasil. Staden's book was written after de Léry's *Histoire*; historians point to the fact that Staden compared notes with Léry before publishing his book.

15. See Arcadio Díaz-Quiñonez, "*The Witness:* las palabras de la tribu," *Hispamérica* 23 (1992): 3–8; Rita de Grandis, "The First Colonial Encounter in *The Witness* by J. J. Saer: Paratextuality and History in Postmodern Fiction," *Latin American Literary Review* 41 (1992): 31–38; and "*The Witness* de J. J. Saer y la idea de la historia," *Revista Canadiense de Estudios Hispánicos* 18, no. 3 (1994): 417–25; Rita Gnutzmann, "*The Witness* o la respuesta de Saer a las Crónicas," *Iris* (1992): 23–36; and Florencia Garra-

muño, *Genealogías culturales. Argentina, Brasil y Uruguay en la novela contemporánea* (Rosario, Arg.: Beatriz Viterbo Editora, 1997).

16. "Sociological criticism tends to exaggerate the features of unreality it finds in literature. The data it extracts from literature is reduced and assimilated to the sociological domain while the fragments that resist (*los fragmentos que permanecen refractarios*) the reduction are often invalidated. In this sense the sociologist behaves as a common reader, a mere consumer: although he does not "skip steps," he interprets what he reads this way and constructs a work's arbitrary context, a context endowed with a fundamental unreality with respect to the work." Juan José Saer, "El largo adiós," *El concepto de ficción*, 254, my emphasis. If we replace "sociological criticism" for "cultural criticism," we recontextualize a reflection that is still pertinent today.

17. The bibliography on cannibalism is extensive and consequently I quote only some key critical studies: Bernardette Boucher, *La Sauvage aux seins pendants* (Paris: Hermann, 1977); Frank Lestringant, *Le Cannibale. Grandeur et decadence* (Paris: Perrin, 1994); Peter Hulmes, *Colonial Encounters. Europe and the Native Caribbean. 1492–1787* (London: Routledge, 1986); Roger Célestin, *From Radical to Cannibals* (Minneapolis: University of Minnesota Press, 1996); Claude Rawson, "Narrative and the Proscribed Act: Homer, Euripides and the Literature of Cannibalism," in J. Strelka ed., *Literary Theory and Criticism. Festschrift in Honor of René Wellek, Part II* (Bern, Switz.: Peter Lang, 1985). See also Rawson, "Indians and Irish: Montaigne, Swift and the Cannibal Question," *Modern Language Quarterly* 3 (1992): 43–76; and "Cannibalism and Fiction," *Genre* 10–11 (1977): 132–45. For an ethnological perspective, see Claude Lévi-Strauss, *Tristes tropiques* (Paris: Plon, 1955); Isabelle Combès, *La tragédie cannibale chez les anciens Tupi-Guarani* (Paris: PUF, 1992), 46; Pierre Clastres, *Chroniques des Indiens Guayakis* (Paris: Éditions du Seuil, 1984); Eduardo Viveiros de Castro, *Arawaté: os Deuses Canibais* (Río de Janeiro: Zahar, 1986); and Emmanuel Désveaux, "Eschatologie cannibale et anthropophagie saisonnière," *Critique*, 1990. The unclassifiable *Totem and Taboo* by Sigmund Freud should be included in this list, as well as the special issue of the *Nouvelle Revue de Psychanalyse*, *Destin du cannibalisme* (Paris: Gallimard, 1972). From this immense "cannibal text" written by captives, chroniclers, travelers, ethnologists, historians, social scientists, philosophers, psychiatrists, psychoanalysts, and poets, Saer selects and transforms some *topoi*, omitting some crucial ones: the motif of revenge that, according to de Castro, organizes the ritual cannibalistic meal and that is also the pillar of their temporal conception, disappears from Saer's text, which may explain the tragic dimension of his cannibals.

18. See Maria T. Gramuglio, "La filosofía en el relato," in *Punto de vista* 6 (1979): 3–8; Mirta Stern, "Saer: construcción y teoría de la ficción narrativa," *Hispamérica* 37 (1984): 15–30; and Jorgelina Corbatta, *"En la zona*: germen de la praxis poética," *Revista Iberoamericana* 155–56 (1991): 557–68.

19. Jacques Lacan, *Le Seminaire Livre IV: La relation d'objet* (Paris: Éditions du Seuil, 1994).

20. In the short story "Paramnesia" (1966), Saer explores the question of reality's "permanence" and memory's ability to validate it once the "normal" parameters of apprehension have been severed. "Paramnesia" already inscribes the topography of *The Witness*. It narrates the experiences of a Spanish expedition to the New World, whose fortress (*el Real*) has been destroyed and its men decimated by the Indians. In the context of such chaos, the friar's survival is subjected to a soldier's retelling of a story about

Madrid. But the story does not validate the "reality of its referent": "A ver , cuéntame, ya que dices ser de Madrid, cuéntame, suelta la taravilla . . . Hazme el cuento de que hay un océano y que nosotros lo cruzamos con el adelantado y el nos mandó en expedición hasta aquí . . . Cuéntame de los indios y de las picas envenenadas. Hazme creer que todo eso es real . . . Hazme creer que no hemos estado siempre tú y yo y Judas en este lugar, rodeados de carroña y que hay algún otro lugar que no sea éste." (CC 237) [Let's see, tell me, since you say to be from Madrid; tell me, loosen your tongue . . . Tell me the tale: that there is an ocean and that we crossed it with the captain and that he sent us on an expedition to this place . . . Tell me about the Indians and their poisonous lances. Make me believe that all of that is real. Make me believe that we haven't been, you, myself and Judas, in this place surrounded by rotting flesh and there is no other place than this one]. "Paramnesia: a disorder of memory: as a) a condition in which the proper meaning of words cannot be remembered; b) the illusion of remembering scenes and events when experienced for the first time"(*OED*).

21. The expression "child lost in the world," chosen by M. Jull Costa, does not seem to render all the resonances of "abandonado." Both the *Diccionario Crítico Etimológico de la Lengua Castellana* by J. Corominas and the *Diccionario de la Real Academia Española* give the French "abandonner" as the etymology of "abandonar" and add that the French "abandonner" (laisser à bandon) comes from the German "bann," which is related to the French "ban" (proclamation). We can say that the text unfolds between the narration (*relación*) and the proclamation of a more encompassing abandon.

22. "Relación" (from Latin *relatio*) refers to a sixteenth-century discursive modality in which the writer aims to give a personal testimony of the events he/she presenced and about which he/she writes.

23. Alexander García Düttman, *La parole donnée. Mémoire et promesse* (Paris: Galilée, 1989).

24. Jorge Luis Borges, "La noche de los dones," in *Obras Completas* (Buenos Aires: Emecé, 1986), 41–44.

25. There is an additional complication: love and death (the gifts) revolve around two characters: the Cautiva (a young prostitute) and Juan Moreira (an outlaw), but both characters are literary characters from key nineteenth-century Argentinean texts (E. Echeverría's poem *La Cautiva* and E. Gutierrez's *Juan Moreira*). The memories of the gifts are also intertwined with literature, as if the gift of memory were a gift of literature.

26. Maurice Blanchot, "La voix narrative (le "il," le neutre)," in *L'entretien infini* (Paris: Gallimard, 1959).

27. I disagree with Shoshana Felman's interpretation of witnessing in *Testimony. Crises in Literature, Psychoanalysis and History* (London: Routledge, 1992).

28. In the sense that Alain Badiou gives to the nonconceptual "notion" of *poetry*: "Poetry produces a truth out of the multiple and as a presence that comes to the limits of language. Poetry is language's singing as the ability to presenting the pure notion of "there is" (*il y a*) in the very effacement of its empirical objectivity," "Philosophie et poésie: au point de l'innomable," *Poe&sie* 64 (1994): 18–27.

29. The printing shop the old narrator-protagonist opens in his house after adopting the orphans of a murdered actress. The narrator protagonist writes his memoirs during the night, which indicates that Saer's story is, as Blanchot would put it, a quest for the experience of narration. See Maurice Blanchot, *L'espace littéraire* and *Le livre à venir*.

Chapter 4. Voices and Tones:
History, Memory, and Trauma in *Glosa*

1. On literature and exile, see Daniel Balderston and others, *Ficción y política. La narrativa argentina durante el Proceso military* (Buenos Aires: Alianza, 1987); Jorgelina Corbatta, *Narrativas de le Guerra Sucia en la Argentina* (Buenos Aires: Corregidor, 1999); Karl Kohut and Andrea Pagni, eds., *Literatura argentina hoy: de la dictadura a la democracia* (Frankfurt am Main: Verlag, 1989); Fernando Reati, *Nombrar lo innombrable. Violencia política y novela argentina: 1975–1985* (Buenos Aires: Legasa, 1992); Saúl Sosnowski, ed., *Represión y reconstrucción de una cultura: el caso argentino* (Buenos Aires: Eudeba, 1988), and Roland Spiller, ed., *La novela argentina de los años 80* (Frankfurt am Main: Verlag, 1991).

2. César Aira, "Zona peligrosa," *El porteño*, Buenos Aires (1986): 185–87.

3. For a discussion of "tragic philosophy," see Peter Szondi, *Versuch über das Tragische, Schriften I* (Frankfurt am Main: Suhrkamp, 1978) and Jacques Taminiaux, *Le théâtre des philosophes* (Grénoble, France: Millon, 1995).

4. *Glosa* can be defined as a peripatetic novel, among whose antecedents are *Adam Buenosayres* by Leopoldo Marechal and *El examen* by Julio Cortázar.

5. On the distinction between language and chatter, see Martin Heidegger, *Being and Time*, trans. John Macquarrie and Edward Robinson (New York: Harper & Row, 1962). On the impossibility of clearly distinguishing between them and their mutual contamination in literary language, see Maurice Blanchot, "La parole vaine" in *L'amitié* (Paris: Gallimard, 1971).

6. On the antinomy "fever/geometry" as a structural pattern of the story, see Raquél Linenberg-Fressard, "Fiebre y geometría en *Glosa* de Juan Jose Saer," in Claude Cymerman, ed., *Le roman hispano-americain des années 80. Les cahiers du CRIAR* 11 (1991): 103–8.

7. On the three times of the poem, see Sandra Contreras, "*Glosa*, un atisbo de fiesta," *Paradoxa* 6, no. 6 (1991): 43–52.

8. Jacques Lacan, *The Seminar Book VII. The Ethics of Psychoanalysis*, trans. Dennis Porter (New York: Norton, 1982), 96.

9. "Muchos años más tarde sabrá, gracias a evidencias sucesivas, que los que los otros llaman el alma humana nunca tuvo ni tendrá lo que otros llaman esencia o fondo; que lo que los otros llaman carácter, estilo, personalidad, no son otra cosa que repeticiones irracionales acerca de cuya naturaleza el propio sujeto que es el terreno en que se manifiestan es quien está más en ayunas, y que lo que los otros llaman vida es una serie de reconocimientos *a posteriori* de los lugares en los que una deriva ciega, incomprensible y sin fin va depositando, a pesar de sí mismos, a los individuos eminentes que después de haber sido arrastrados por ella se ponen a elaborar sistemas que pretenden explicarla . . . (Many years later he will know, thanks to the evidence, that what others call the human soul never had or will have an essence or ground; that what others call character, style, personality, are nothing more than irrational repetitions whose nature the subject, as the place in which they manifest themselves, ignores more than any other. And that what others call life is a series of belated acknowledgments of the places in which a blind, incomprehensible and endless erring deposits the eminent individuals who, in spite of themselves, develop systems that pretend to explain it, even as they are dragged down by it [G 81]).

10. W. Schelling, *Philosophy of* Art (Minneapolis: University of Minnesota Press, 1989), 251.

11. See Heidegger, *Being and Time*.

12. Emmanuel Levinas and Maurice Blanchot are the thinkers who have taken the implications of a deconstruction of the existential analytic of Heidegger's "Being to death" furthest. See Levinas's *La Mort et le temps* (Paris: L'Herne, 1991); Blanchot's *Le pas au-delà* (Paris: Gallimard, 1971) and *L'écriture du désastre* (Paris: Gallimard, 1980).

13. See Jean-Luc Nancy, *Le sens du monde* (Paris: Galilée, 1993) and *Être singulier pluriel* (Paris: Galilée, 1996).

14. For Gramuglio this is a central nucleus in Saer's fiction. See María T. Gramuglio, "El lugar de Saer," en *Juan José Saer por Juan José Saer* (Buenos Aires: Celtia, 1986).

15. I borrow the expression from Nicolás Rosa, *La lengua del ausente* (Buenos Aires: Biblos, 1997).

CHAPTER 5. *"REGIA VICTORIA"*: AFFECTS AND PERCEPTS

1. In *La narración-objeto* Saer states, "although I intentionally introduced some elements of the hard-boiled in several of my stories, approaching the detective genre head-on presented a series of problems because my deepest conviction is that the hard-boiled novel is a dead genre. The 'metaphysical detective fiction" that is announced by so many predictable back-covers is as much a stale genre as the modernist sonnet . . . I thought that going back to the *origins of the genre* could be an interesting solution not to parody it, but to rather take it as a point of departure and then go my own way" (159–60). However, Saer's treatment of the classical detective story ("its conscious and innovative use" [160]) authorizes us to include it in what has been called *anti-detective* fiction (see note 26 below). Morvan, the detective's name, can be easily related to the series of anti-detectives that, although inaugurated by Borges, has homophonic resonances with Beckett's Moran (*Molloy*) and Robbe-Grillet's Morgan. The figure of the detective that Pichón's story constructs combines features from the classical detective à la Dupin with those of the hard-boiled's private investigator. Morvan has the characteristics of the former: a singular way of life, an extreme austerity, loneliness, eccentricity, and superior analytical abilities ("His métier was not so much a job or a duty as a passion. He was the most upright officer . . . and the most punctilious as regards the law" [P 26–28]). Lautret condenses all the features of the private investigator: dubious methods that include the use of physical violence, a complete insertion in the realm of action, and the interaction with both the criminal underworld and legal channels. What characterizes Pichón's narration is its focalization on the inner sphere that, as in Simenon's "Maigrets" is what distinguishes the detective from other agents of the law.

2. G. Genette differentiates between external and internal narrators to the story. See Gérard Genette, *Figures III* (Paris: Éditions du Seuil, 1972), 176.

3. Alain Badiou, *Conditions* (Paris: Éditions du Seuil, 1991), 41.

4. The existence of a total text of detection is phantasmatic. The idea of a story able to propose a true enigma and the presentation of the rigorous deduction to its solution is structurally contradictory. As both Chandler and Simenon realized, in a detective story

the solution to the mystery is not the consequence of rigorous reasoning, but rather the result of the arbitrariness of the represented events (of the *narrative logic* that is problematic in itself). In "Casual Notes on the Mystery Novel," Chandler states, "it is the paradox of the mystery novel that while its structure will seldom if ever stand the close scrutiny of an analytical mind, it is precisely to that type of mind that it makes its greatest appeal," Tom Hiney and Frank MacShane, eds., *The Raymond Chandler Papers: Selected Letters and Non-fiction, 1909–1959* (New York: Atlantic Monthly Press, 2000).

5. Vallejo's verse is from "En las tiendas griegas" in *Los heraldos negros*.

6. See Ovid's *Metamorphosis*.

7. In River Plate slang "vieja" also means *mother.*

8. To which we must add the enigma of the narrative voice I mentioned above. The text stages the question of literature's *enigmatic* status by bringing together the signs of the literary transaction and those of everyday communication. The version of *literariness* that the text puts into scene falls upon the side of *conditionality*. For a distinction between constitutive and conditional poetics, see Gerard Genette, *Fiction et diction* (Paris: Éditions du Seuil, 1992), 3–5. Saer deals with this regime of *literariness* once again in *Las nubes*, a framed narrative in which Soldi ponders about the status of a manuscript he found in Santa Fé, that he transcribes and sends to Pichón with a letter in which *literariness* becomes the main issue: "We are very interested in your opinion because contrary to what I think, Tomatis affirms that we aren't dealing with an authentic historical document but with a fictional text. But I ask myself, what are the *Annals*, Lavoisier's *Memory on Calcination*, and the *Napoleonic Code*, the multitudes, the cities, the suns and the universe?" *Las Nubes* (Buenos Aires: Seix Barral, 1997),13.

9. Tzvetan Todorov, "The Typology of Detective Fiction," in *The Poetics of Prose* (Ithaca: Cornell University Press, 1977), 42–52.

10. See Robert Champigny, *What Will Have Happened: A Philosophical and Technical Essay on Mystery Stories* (Baltimore: John Hopkins University Press, 1980).

11. See Jacques Derrida, *La vérité en peinture* (Paris: Champs/ Flammarion, 1978).

12. Juan José Saer, *La narración-objeto. The Investigation* also rewrites sequences of *El río sin orillas, La mayor* ("A medio borrar"), and of early short stories.

13. See Yves Bonnefoy, *Mythologies, I* (Chicago: The University of Chicago Press, 1998), Pierre Grimal, *The Dictionary of Classical Mythology* (London: Blackwell, 1996); Françoise Létoublon, "Europe," in Pierre Brunel, ed., *Dictionnaire des Mythes Féminins* (Paris: Rocher, 2003), 698–706; and Pascale Alexandre-Bergues, "Hélène," in *Dictionnaire des Mythes Féminins*, 909–15.

14. The narrator establishes a chronological connection between Gato's disappearance and Julia's separation, the episode that allows for the discovery of *In the Greek Tents*: "Following the death of Washington Noriega, some eight years before, *at almost the same time, (casi en los mismos días)* as the disappearance of Gato, Pichón's twin Brother, his daughter Julia . . . separated from her husband and came to Rincón Norte to live in Washington's home (I 47/ P 51, my emphasis).

15. Pichón's story also begins *in media res* and with a phrase that seems to elide its antecedent: "There, however, in December, night comes on swiftly."

16. See Sigmund Freud, "Letter to Fliess, October 15, 1897" in *The Complete Letters of Sigmund Freud to Wilhem Fliess (1887–1904)*, trans. and ed. Jeffrey Moussaieff Masson (Cambridge, MA: Belknap Press, 1985); and The *Interpretation of Dreams*

(New York: Norton, 1965). For an interpretation of the "times" of the Oedipus complex, see Jacques Lacan, *Les formations de l'inconscient* (Paris: Seuil, 1998).

17. Julio Premat affirms that "one can read Saer's whole work as the progressive approach to the formulation of a destructive, sadic sexual drive whose roots are Oedipal . . . The phantasm that *The Investigation* puts into scene can be considered an essential phantasm that structures the whole work and . . . that it is therefore linked to the characteristic auto-thematism of Saer's writing." See *La dicha de Saturno. Escritura y melancolía en la obra de Juan José Saer* (Rosario, Arg.: Beatriz Viterbo, 2003),112.

18. As in Borges' "Ibn Hakkan-al Bojari, Dead in his Labyrinth," the mystery and its solution are also open to discussion and disagreement.

19. See Sigmund Freud, "Estudios sobre la histeria," in *Obras Completas, III* (Buenos Aires: Amorrortu, 1986); "Tres ensayos de teoría sexual," *Obras Completas, VII* (Buenos Aires: Amorrortu, 1986); "El delirio y los sueños en la 'Gradiva' de W. Jensen," in *Obras Completas, IX* (Buenos Aires: Amorrortu, 1988) "Se pega a un niño"; Roberto Harari, *Fantasma, ¿fin del análisis?* (Buenos Aires: Nueva Visión, 1998); Jacques-Alain Miller, *Dos estructuras clínicas: síntoma y fantasma* (Buenos Aires: Ediciones Manantial, 1989) Jean Laplanche and Jean-Bertrand Pontalis, "Fantasma originario, fantasmas de los orígenes, origen del fantasma," in *El (lo) inconsciente freudiano y el psicoanálisis francés contemporáneo* (Buenos Aires: Nueva Visión, 1969), 103–43; Roland Chemana, ed., *Diccionario actual de los significantes, conceptos y matemas del psicoanálisis* (Buenos Aires: Amorrortu, 1998).

20. In "Kant avec Sade" Lacan speaks of the "logic of the phantasm," given that the fundamental phantasm is a type of phrase that in logic is called axiom. Jacques-Alain Miller claims "the *fundamental fantasy or phantasm* is not an object of interpretation by the analyst, but rather the object of a *construction*. In 'A Child Is Beaten' the fundamental phantasm never appears as such in experience. It is a limit point of analysis that corresponds to the *Urverdrängung*, to what can never come to light in repression (Freud, *Inhibition, Symptom, Anxiety*)" (13). The phantasm is a formation that shields us from the anxiety caused by the Other's desire.

21. Roberto Harari employs the term in *Fantasma, ¿fin del análisis?* 8–9.

22. See Jacques Lacan, "Kant avec Sade," in *Le Séminaire Livre V. Les Formations de l'Inconscient* and *Le Séminaire Livre XVI, Logique du fantasme (1966–67)*, unpublished.

23. Claude Rabant, *Encyclopedia Universal.* "Œdipe" (Paris: PUF, 1986), 403.

24. The story of the lovers Moratí and Pitá, the witch Y Kuñapayé, and the deity Tupá. See Equipo NAyA, http://www.cuco.com.ar/.

25. See Cynthia Chase, "Oedipal Textuality: Reading Freud's Reading of Oedipus," *Decomposing Figures. Rhetorical Readings in the Romantic Tradition* (Baltimore: Johns Hopkins University Press, 1981), 175–95.

26. It would be possible to establish a homology between the positions of the detective and the criminal in both *The Investigation* and Borges's "Death and the Compass": Morvan is to Lonröt as Lautret is to Red Scharlach. If this is so, Pichón's detective story exhibits the law of the genre, from which it distances itself for two reasons. First, because it is recounted in terms of conventions closer to the hard-boiled or Simenon's "Maigrets," and second because it shares a series of features (the detective defeated by the criminal; the world, the city or text as labyrinth; the purloined letter; metanarration;

mise en abîme or object-narration; ambiguity, omnipresence, and lack of signification of clues) with so-called *anti-detective* fiction: "stories that evoke an impulse for 'detection' . . . only to violently frustrate it by refusing to solve the crime." See William Spanos, "The Detective and the Boundary," *Boundary 2*, no. 1.1 (1972): 147–68, and J. Ewert, "A Thousand and Other Mysteries," *New Literary History*, 56, no. 4 (1980): 263–78.

27. Alain Badiou, *Court traité d'ontologie transitoire* (Paris: Seuil, 1999), 23.

28. Ibid., 26.

29. Shoshana Felman reads *Oedipus King* as a protodetective fiction and argues that "the stroke of genius of the detective form in Sophocles . . . shows us in which sense one must understand Freud's suggestion according to which the structure of Oedipal suspense ressembles psychoanalysis: as in the process of analysis, detective fiction indeed consists in *narrating the displacement of the interpreter's blind spot*; in its being the narration of the interpretation's self-subversion." Felman calls the narrative that is founded in its own self-subversion (a reversal of the reader and detective's consciousness) an "analytic story." *The Investigation* stages an "analytic story," but *only* as *one* of its moments. See Shoshana Felman, "De Sophocle à Japrisot (via Freud), ou pourquoi le policier?" *Littérature* 49 (1983): 40–41.

30. Geraldine Penderson-Krag argues that the distinctive feature of detective fiction is the intense curiosity it arouses by suggesting to the reader the existence of a "secret fault between two people." The author links this feature to the interest we express in the "primal scene" (*Urszene*), and links the crime of the detective fiction to sexual intercourse, the victim to the paternal figure with whom the reader entertained negative feelings (oedipal) in childhood, and the criminal with the parental figure he associated with positive characteristics and that he imagines (unconsciously) to have been involved in a "secret crime," "Detective Stories and the Primal Scene," *Psychoanalytic Quarterly* 18 (1949): 207–14.

31. On the phantasm's passive regime (*pasivación*), see J-A Miller, "Dos estructuras clínicas," and Roberto Harari, *Fantasma ¿fin del análisis?*

32. "*Traversée du fantasme*" is the expression Lacan uses to define the analytical process. It is interesting to note that Harari thinks it is better to translate "*traversée*" by "going through" (*atravesamiento*) and not "crossing" (*travesía*), since the latter suggests the notion of a displacement along a surface (such as the crossing of a river [*travesía fluvial*] and if "we were to accept only the meaning of crossing (*travesía*), we would be suggesting a certain drifting which would not be totally inaccurate if we place it within its just limits. The drifting is situated in the realm of the Symbolic . . . What is truly localizable in the Real is the consequence of the *going through the phantasm* and not the phantasm itself" (16–17). We should keep this distinction in mind since it allows us to differentiate between the writing of the affects, localized in the real, and the phantasm, localized in the symbolic order.

Works Cited

JUAN JOSE SAER

En la zona. Santa Fé, Arg.: Castellví, 1960.

Responso. Buenos Aires: Jorge Alvarez, 1964.

Palo y hueso. Buenos Aires: Camarda Junior, 1965.

La vuelta completa. Buenos Aires: Biblioteca Popular C.C. Vigil, 1966.

Unidad de lugar. Buenos Aires: Galerna, 1967.

Cicatrices. Buenos Aires: Sudamericana, 1969; CEAL, 1983.

El limonero real. Buenos Aires: Planeta, 1974; CEAL, 1983.

La mayor. Buenos Aires: Planeta, 1976; CEAL, 1982.

El arte de narrar (1960–75). Caracas: Fundarte, 1977.

Nadie Nada Nunca. México City: Siglo XXI, 1980.

Glosa. Buenos Aires-Madrid: Alianza, 1986.

El entenado. Barcelona: Destino, 1988.

La ocasión. Barcelona: Destino, 1988.

Diálogo Piglia/Saer. Por un relato futuro. Santa Fé, Arg.: Centro de Publicaciones de la UNL, 1990.

The Witness. Translated by Margaret Jull Costa. London: Serpent's Tail, 1990.

El río sin orillas. Buenos Aires: Alianza Editorial, 1991.

Lo imborrable. Buenos Aires: Alianza, 1993.

Nobody Nothing Never. Translated by Helen Lane. London: Serpent's Tail, 1993.

The Investigation. Translated by Helen Lane. London: Serpent's Tail, 1994.

La pesquisa. Buenos Aires: Seix Barral, 1994.

The Event. Translated by Helen Lane. London: Serpent's Tail, 1995.

Las nubes, Buenos Aires: Seix Barral, 1997.

El concepto de ficción. Buenos Aires: Ariel, 1997.

La narración-objeto. Buenos Aires: Seix Barral, 1999.

El arte de narrar (1960–1987). Buenos Aires: Seix Barral, 2000.

Cuentos completos (1957–2000). Buenos Aires: Seix Barral, 2001.

La Grande. Buenos Aires: Seix Barral, 2005.

Criticism

Aira, César. "Zona peligrosa." In *El Porteño*. Buenos Aires, 1986: 185–87.

Albornoz, María Victoria. "Caníbales a la carta: mecanismos de incorporación del 'otro' en *El entenado* de Juan José Saer." *Chasqui,* 32, no. 1 (May 2003): 56–73.

Almazar, Marfa I. "De la escritura, la memoria y la percepción del mundo en *El entenado* de Juan José Saer." *Literatura y fines de siglo*, 2. Córdoba, Arg.: Comunic-Arte, 2000.

Amar Sanchez, Ana María, Mirta Stern, and Ana María Zubieta. "La narrativa entre 1960 y 1970. Saer, Puig y las últimas promociones." In *Capítulo. La historia de la literatura argentina*, V. Buenos Aires: CEAL, 1981: 651–60.

Andermann, Jens. "Antropofagia: testimonios y silencios." *Revista Iberoamericana*, 68, no. 198 (January–March 2002): 79–98.

Andrés, Beatriz. "El proceso de enunciación narrativa en *El entenado* de Juan José Saer." *Revista de Letras* 6 (1987): 97–108.

Astutti, Adriana. "Cicatrices." *Paradoxa*, 6, (1991): 62–67.

———. "Juan José Saer: 'La barrera de la identidad'." *Boletín del Centro de estudios de teoría y critica literaria* 7 (1999): 112–29.

Azubel, Ester. "Leer e interpretar desde la ficción." *Reflejos*, 8, (1999): 17–22.

Bastos, Maria Luisa. "Eficacias del verosímil no realista: dos novelas recientes de Juan José Saer." *La Torre* 4, no. 13, (1990): 1–20.

Basualdo, Ana. "Saer: el esplendor de la sintaxis." In *Juan José Saer, La ocasión*, 7–14. Barcelona: Círculo de Lectores, 1988.

Beceyro, Raul. "Sobre Saer y el cine." *Punto de vista*, 15, no. 43 (1992): 26–30.

Benitez Pezzolano, Hebert. "Encrucijadas de la objetividad." *Historia crítica de la literatura argentina*, 11, edited by Noé Jitrik, 143–59. Buenos Aires: Emecé, 2000.

Berg, Edgardo H. "Breves sobre *El arte de narrar* de Juan José Saer." *Celehis* 3, (1994): 153.

Bermudez Martínez, María. "Ficción y verdad en la literatura: continuación y redefinición de una tradición, Macedonio Fernández, Rodolfo Walsh, Juan José Saer, Ricardo Piglia." *Río de la Plata* 17–18 (1997): 111–28.

———. *La incertidumbre de lo real: bases de la narrativa de Juan José Saer*. Oviedo, Spain: Servicio de Publicaciones y Departamento de Filología Española, 2001.

———. "Líneas para un acercamiento a la narrativa de Juan José Saer." *Borradores* 6 (1998): 13–35.

———. "Sobre fatalidades y máscaras: tradición e identidad en la literatura argentina contemporánea." In *Actas del Congreso Internacional Literatura de las Americas 1898–1998*, II, edited by Juan Carlos Bohfo, 547–59. León, Spain: Universidad de León, 2000.

Boldori, Rosa. "Experimentación y apocalipsis en *Cicatrices* de Saer." AAVV. In *Narrativa argentina del litoral*, 157–200. Santa Fé, Arg.: Cuadernos Aletheia, 1981.

Bracamonte, Jorge. "Macedonio Fernández y Juan José Saer: la ficción crítica, proceso y gesto." In *Tramas para leer la literatura argentina*, I, 55–64. Córdoba, Arg.:1995.

———. "Lo autobiográfico en la reinvención territorial (sobre un texto 'menor' de Juan Jose Saer)." In *Desde la niebla. Sobre lo autobiográfico en la literatura argentina*, edited by Maria Elena Legaz, 85–107. Córdoba, Arg.: Alción, 2000.

Caisso, Claudia. "El torno a *El entenado*: circunloquios." *Revista de letras* 6 (1987): 109–14.

Capdevila, Analía. "Reflexión en dos tiempos." *Paradoxa* 6 (1991): 53–61.

Cariello Graciela. "La espacialización de *El entenado* de Juan José Saer." *Discusión* 1 (1989): 46–57.

Carrero Eras, Pedro. "Narrativa española e hispanoamericana: las novelas premiadas de Jose Manuel Caballero Bonald y Juan José Saer." In *Españoles y extranjeros: última narrativa (Estudios de crítica literaria)*, 140–42. Salamanca, Spain: Universidad de Salamanca, 1990.

Castro Perez, Pilar de. "Juan José Saer: en la incertidumbre de lo real." In *Encuentros hispanoamericanos. Realidad y ficción*, I (1990) y II, (1991), 287–91. Oviedo, Spain: Fundación Municipal de Cultura, 1992,

Cella, Susana Beatriz. "Una heterología por plenitud: acerca de *El entenado* de Juan José Saer y *1492. Vida y tiempos de Juan Cabezón de Castilla* de Homero Aridjis." *Literatura mexicana*, 2, no. 2 (1991): 455–61.

Chabado, Rubén. "Saer: la imagen del escritor." *Discusión* 1 (1989): 37–44.

Chejfec, Sergio. "Una gran obra sin preceptivas." *Babel* 1, no. 4 (1988): 4–5.

———. "La organización de las apariencias." *Hispamérica* 22, no. 67 (1994): 114–15.

Cittadini, Fernando. "La aventura del pensamiento y del lenguaje." *Espacios de crítica y producción* 13 (1993): 46–47.

Colautti, Sergio. "El limonero, el tiempo, la escritura (Una lectura de *El limonero real* de Juan José Saer)." In *Apuntes sobre la narrativa argentina actual. Borges, Piglia, Saer, Moyano, Castillo, Posse, Caparrós, Pauls*, 35–44. Rio Tercero, Arg.: IDAC Ediciones, 1992.

Contreras, Sandra. "*Glosa*, un atisbo de fiesta." *Paradoxa*, 6, no. 6 (1991): 43–52.

Corbatta, Jorgelina. "*En la zona*: germen de la praxis poética de Juan José Saer." *Revista Iberoamericana* 155–56 (1991): 557–68.

———. *Juan José Saer, arte poética y práctica literaria*. Buenos Aires: Corregidor, 2005.

———. "Juan José Saer: Narración versus Realidad." *Romance Languages Annual*, (1991): 153–73.

———. *Narrativas de la guerra sucia en Argentina*. Buenos Aires: Corregidor, 2000.

Corral, Wilfrido. "El canibalismo de la crónica colonial en la novela contemporánea: un ejemplo argentino." In *El texto latinoamericano*, 245–51. Madrid / Université de Poitiers, France: Fundamentos, 1994.

Croce, Marcela. "Las cicatrices repetitivas de la tradición: la narrativa de Juan José Saer." *Filología* 25, no. 1–2 (1990): 49–110.

Dalmaroni, Miguel y Margarita Merbilhaa. "'Un azar convertido en don'. Juan José Saer y el relato de la percepción." *Historia crítica de la literatura argentina*, 11, edited by Noé Jitrik, 321–43. Buenos Aires: Emecé, 2000.

Darre, María Celia. "Proust a través de un cuento de Juan José Saer." *Revista de literaturas modernas* 2 (1991).

De Grandis, Rita. "The first colonial encounter in *El entenado* by Juan José Saer: paratextuality and history in postmodern fiction." *Latin American Literary Review* 21, no. 41 (1993): 30–38.

Del Valle Guzmán, Raquel. "Regionalidad y textualidad." In *Crítica literaria*. Córdoba, Arg.: Editorial de la Municipalidad de Córdoba, 1992.

Díaz Quiñones, Arcadio. "*El entenado*: las palabras de la tribu." *Hispamérica*, 21, no. 63 (1992): 3–14. Reedited as *El arte de bregar*. San Juan, Puerto Rico: Ediciones Callejón, 2000, 105–123.

Ezquerro, Milagros, *Rencontre avec Juan José Saer*. Montpellier, France: CERS, 2002.

Fernandez, Nancy. *Narraciones viajeras: César Aira y Juan José Saer*. Buenos Aires: Biblos, 2000.

Foffani, Enrique and Adriana Mancini. "Mas allá del regionalismo: la transformación del paisaje." In *Historia crítica de la literatura argentina*, 11, edited by Noé Jitrik, 261–80. Buenos Aires: Emecé, 2000.

Frohlicher, Peter. "Testimonios de la irrealidad: *El entenado* de Juan Jose Saer." *Literaturas del Río de la Plata hoy. De las Utopías al desencanto*, edited by Karl Kohut. Frankfurt am Main: Verveurt, 1996.

Flirstenberger, Nathalie. "De pére en fils, le mythe de Laios dans *El limonero real*." *America* 19 (1997): 25–40.

Garramuño, Florencia. *Genealogías culturales. Argentina, Brasil y Uruguay en la novela contemporánea*. Rosario, Arg.: Beatriz Viterbo Editora, 1997.

Gasquet, Axel. *La literatura expatriada: conversaciones con escritores argentinos de Paris*. Santa Fé, Arg.: Secretaría de Extensión Universitaria, Universidad Nacional del Litoral, 2004.

Giordano, Alberto. *La experiencia narrativa. Juan José Saer, Felisberto Hernández, Manuel Puig*. Rosario, Arg.: Beatriz Viterbo Editora, 1992.

Girona, Nuria. "*El entenado* de Juan José Saer: la memoria de la escritura." *Modernismo y modernidad en el ámbito hispánico*, edited by Trinidad Barrera, 385–90. Seville: Universidad Internacional de Andalucía, 1988.

Gnutzmann, Rita. "El arte de narrar de Juan José Saer." *Cuadernos para la investigación de la literatura hispánica* 11 (1989): 183–86.

———. "Bibliografía de y sobre Juan José Saer." *Iris* (1996): 39–50.

———. "*El entenado* o la respuesta de Saer a las crónicas." *Iris* (1992): 23–36.

———. "Repetición y variación en *Lo imborrable* de Juan José Saer." *Iris* (1995): 107–21.

Goldberg, Florinda. "*La pesquisa* de Juan José Saer: alambradas de la ficción." *Hispamérica* 76–77, (1997): 89–100.

Gollnick, Brian. "El color justo de la patria: agencias discursivas en El entendado de Juan José Saer." *Revista de Crítica Literaria Latinoamericana* 29, no. 57 (2003): 107–24.

Gramuglio, María Teresa. "Las aventuras del orden. Juan José Saer, *Cicatrices*." *Los libros* 2, no. 3 (1969): 23–24.

———. "La filosofía en el relato." *Punto de vista* 20 (1984): 35–36.

———. "Juan José Saer: el arte de narrar." *Punto de vista* 7 (1979): 3–8.

———. et al. "Literatura, mercado, crítica. Un debate." *Punto de vista* 66 (2000): 1–9.

———. "El lugar de Saer." In *Juan José Saer por Juan José Saer*, 261–307. Buenos Aires: Editorial Celtia, 1986.

Heredia, Pablo. "Las referencias del discurso y el texto de la realidad. Un estudio de *El limonero real* y 'La mayor' de Juan José Saer." In *El texto literario y los discursos regionales*, 133–52. Córdoba, Arg.: Argos, 1994.

Iglesia, Cristina. "Cautivos y entenados (sobre *El entenado* de Juan José Saer)." In *Actas del XXIX Congreso del Instituto Internacional de Literatura Iberoamericana, III*, 339–44. Barcelona: PPU, 1994.

———. "La violencia del azar. Rituales y asesinatos en *Cicatrices* de Juan José Saer." *Quaderni del dipartimento di linguistica* 18 (1999): 135–142.

Jitrik, Noé. "Entre el corte y la continuidad. Hacia una escritura crítica." *Revista Iberoamericana* 102–103 (1978): 99–109.

———. "Lo vivido, lo teórico, la coincidencia." *Cuadernos americanos* 253 (1984): 89–99.

Kanzepolsky, Adriana and Marcela Zanin. "*El entenado*: un testimonio fallido." *Discusión* 1 (1989): 59–63.

Kohan, Martin. "Saer, Walsh: una discusión política en la literatura." *Nuevo texto crítico* 6, no. 12–13, (1994): 121–30.

Larranaga Machalski, Silvia. "Antonio Di Benedetto et Juan José Saer: périphérie et universalité." In *Relations entre identités culturelles: centre et périphérie*, edited by Agustín Redondo, 213–23. Paris: Presses de la Sorbonne Nouvelle, 1995.

———. "Argumentos de Juan José Saer: transgresión de géneros y estética de lo fragmentario." *America* 18–19, no. 1 (1997): 281–90.

———. "Juan José Saer: la locura de lo real." *Locos, excéntricos y marginales en las literaturas hispanoamericanas*, edited by Joaquín Manzi, 542–52. Poitiers, France: Centre de Recherches Latino-Americaines-Archivos-C.N.R.S.-Université de Poitiers, 1999.

———. "*La pesquisa*: el género policial a la manera de Juan José Saer." *Río de la Plata* 17–18 (1997): 60–77.

Linenberg Fressard, Raquel. "Lo borrable y Lo imborrable en la narrativa de Juan José Saer." *Construction des identités en Espagne et en Amerique Latine*, edited by Milagros Ezquerro, 273–82. Paris: L' Harmattan, 1996.

———. "Fiebre y geometría en *Glosa* de Juan Jose Saer." *Le roman hispano-americain des années 80. Les cahiers du CRIAR* 11, edited by Claude Cymerman, (1991): 103–8.

———. 1985 "*El limonero real* de Juan José Saer: essai d' interprétation onomastique." *Ibérica*, (1985): 83–90.

———. "'He weeps over Jim': l' intertextualité de langue anglaise dans la poésie de Juan José Saer." *Imprevue. Rio de 1a Plata* 1–1 (1995): 69–77.

———. "Titrologie et traduction: les titres dans les romans de Juan José Saer." *Paralleles—Cahiers de I' École de Traduction et d' Interprétation* 21 (1999): 59–68.

———. "Traduire et rapporter. Juan José Saer et les littératures non-hispaniques." *Colliers de litteratures et civilisations romanes*, 2, (1994): 119–25.

Link, Daniel."Medi(t)aciones de lo real en *El entenado*." In *La chancha en cadenas*, 68–70. Buenos Aires: Eclipse, 1994.

Luzzani, Telma. "Una estética del desamparo: ficción e historia durante la dictadura militar." *Río de la Plata* 11–12 (1991): 341–50.

Manzi, Joaquin. "Discurso de la locura y locura del discurso en la obra de Juan José Saer." *Locos, excéntricosy marginales en las literaturas hispanoamericanas*, edited by Joaquin Manzi, 553–63. Poitiers, France: Centre de Recherches Latino-Americaines-Archivos-C.N.R.S.-Universite de Poitiers, 1999.

———. "L' espace et la ville dans l'oeuvre de Juan José Saer." *La licorne* 34 (1995): 269–77.

————. "Formas de lo visible y lo invisible en Borges, Calvino y Saer." *Borges, Calvino, la literatura, II*, 265–80. Madrid: Fundamentos, 1996.

————. "Novela y crónica del descubrimiento en el Río de la Plata." *Historia y novela. La ficcionalización de la historia en la narrativa latinoamericana*, edited by Maryse Renaud y Fernando Moreno, 53–70. Poitiers, France: URA 2007-CNRS, 1996.

Montaldo, Graciela. *Juan José Saer. El limonero real*. Buenos Aires: Hachette, 1986.

————. *De pronto, el campo*. Rosario, Arg.: Beatriz Viterbo Editora, 1993.

Monteleone, Jorge. "Eclipse de sentido: de *Nadie Nada Nunca* a *El entenado*." *La novela argentina de los ochenta*, edited by Roland Spiller, 152–75. Frankfurt-am-Main: Verlag, 1991.

————. "Intromisiones: Juan José Saer, *El entenado*." *Sitio* 4–5 (1985): 42–43.

————. "La voz quemada. Sobre la poesía de Juan José Saer." *Revista de lengua y literatura* 7, no. 13 (1993), 25–37.

Pauls, Alan. "Juan José Saer: *La ocasión*." *Babel* (1988): 4–5.

Perera San Martín, Nicasio. "El imposible encuentro." *Río de la Plata* 15–16 (1996): 101–9.

Perrone, A. "Borrar fronteras. Entrevista a J. J. Saer." *La Opinión cultural*, Buenos Aires, Mayo 23, 1976.

Pons, María Cristina. *Memorias del olvido. Del Paso, García Márquez, Saer y la novela histórica del siglo XX*. Mexico: Siglo XXI, 1996.

Premat, Julio. "Antonio Di Benedetto et Juan José Saer: périphérie et universalité." *Relations entre identités culturelles: centre et périphérie*, edited by Agustín Redondo, 213–23. Paris: Presses de la Sorbonne Nouvelle, 1995.

————. "El cataclismo de los orígenes: la pampa histórica de Juan José Saer." *Río de la Plata* 17–18 (1997): 689–700.

————. "El crimen de la escritura. La novela policial según Juan José Saer." *Latin American Literary Review* 24–48 (1996): 19–38.

————. *La dicha de Saturno. Escritura y melancolía en la obra de Juan José Saer*. Rosario, Arg.: Beatriz Viterbo, 2003.

————. "El escritor no es nadie. La improbable autobiografía de Juan José Saer." *Río de la Plata* 20–21 (2000): 511–19.

————. "El eslabón perdido. *El entenado* en la obra de Juan José Saer." *Caravelle* (1996): 75–93.

————. "La imagen de los desaparecidos. Psicoanálisis, historia y literatura en *La pesquisa* de Juan José Saer." *Creación e historia: los poderes de la imagen*, edited by Jacqueline Covo, 323–30. Lille: Presses Universitaires du Septentrion, 1998.

————. "Juan José Saer y el relato regresivo. Una lectura de *Cicatrices* (1969)." *Revista Iberoamericana* 192 (2000): 501–10.

————. "*La pesquisa* de Juan José Saer: retrato del escritor en psicópata asesino." *Locos, excéntricos y marginales en las literaturas hispanoamericanas*, edited by Joaquin Manzi, 564–76. Poitiers, France: Centre de Recherches Latino-Americaines/Archivos C.N.R.S.-Universite de Poitiers, 1999.

————. "Quelques orgies argentines. Les fêtes indiennes, de *La cautiva* à *El entenado*." In *Les représentations de l' Autre dans l' espace ibérique et ibero-americain*, edited by Agustín Redondo, 137–46. Paris: Presses de la Sorbonne Nouvelle, 1993.

————. "La Zona anegada. Notas sobre 'A medio borrar' de Juan José Saer." *América* 18–19, no. 1, (1997): 269–79

Prieto, Martín. "La tradición modernista." *Revista de lengua y literatura* 13–14 (1993): 61–66.

————. "Escrituras de la 'zona'." *Historia crítica de la literatura argentina* 10, edited by Noé Jitrik, 343–57. Buenos Aires: Emece, 1999.

Pulgarín, Amalia. "El descubrimiento y la conquista de América en la nueva novela histórica: Posse, Saer y Merino." In *Actas del XXIX Congreso del Instituto Internacional de Literatura Iberoamericana,* 515–27. Barcelona: PPU, 1994.

Quintana, Isabel. *Figuras de la experiencia en el fin de siglo. Cristina Peri Rossi, Ricardo Piglia, Juan José Saer y Silviano Santiago.* Rosario, Arg.: Beatriz Viterbo Editora, 2001.

Rafaelli, Graciela. "La obra narrativa de Juan José Saer." In *Crítica literaria,* 77–121. Córdoba, Arg.: Editorial de la Municipalidad de Córdoba, 1992.

Raviolo Mascaro, Martha. "La zona fundante. Una elección estético/ideológica en Juan José Saer." In *Critica literaria,* 7–72. Córdoba, Arg.: Editorial de la Municipalidad de Córdoba, 1992.

Retamoso, Roberto. "'A medio borrar': las formas narrativas de lo inenarrable." *Revista de Letras* 6 (1987): 131–43.

Riera, Gabriel. "La ficción de Saer: ¿una antropología especulativa?" *MLN* 111, no. 2 (1996): 368–90.

————. "Fidelidad al acontecimiento—De la narración en Saer." *Revista de Crítica Literaria Latinoamericana* 19, no. 57 (2003): 91–106.

————. "Juan José Saer." In *Encyclopædia of the French Atlantic,* edited by Bill Marshall. Oxford: ABC-Clio, 2005.

————. "*Regia Victoria* o más acá del fantasma (Encuentros con lo real en *La pesquisa*). *Revista Iberoamericana,* 2006.

Romano, Evelia. "*El entenado*: relación contemporánea de las memorias de Francisco del Puerto." *Latin American Literary Review* 23–45 (1995): 43–62.

————. "La ocasión para narrar: historia, alegoría y realidad en un texto de Juan José Saer." NRFH (1999).

Saad, Gabriel. "Œdipe avec et sans complexe: la lettre, la castration, la mort." In *Littérature et pathologie,* edited by M. Milner, 265–29. Paris: Presses Universitaires de Vincennes, 1989.

Saavedra, Guillermo. "Juan José Saer. El arte de narrar la incertidumbre." In *La curiosidad impertinente. Entrevista con narradores argentinos.* Buenos Aires: Sudamericana, 1993.

————. "Juan José Saer: los márgenes de una escritura." *Vuelta* 14 (1987): 59–60.

Sarlo, Beatriz. "Aventuras de un médico filósofo. Sobre *Las nubes* de Juan José Saer." *Punto de vista* 59 (1997): 35–38.

————. "La condición mortal." *Punto de vista* 46 (1993): 28–31.

————. "Narrar la percepción." *Punto de vista* 10 (1980): 34–37.

Scavino, Dardo. "*La pesquisa* de Saer o la deconstrucción de los hechos." In *Literatura policial en la Argentina. Waleis, Borges, Saer.* edited by Nestor Ponce, Sergio Pastormerlo, Dardo Scavino, 45–62. La Plata, Arg.: Facultad de Humanidades y Ciencias de la Educación, 1997.

————. *Saer y los nombres.* Buenos Aires: El cielo por asalto, 2004.

Solotorevsky, Myrna. "La desocultación del artificio en 'Abenjacan el Bojarí, muerto en su laberinto' de Borges, *La pesquisa,* de Saer y *Citas de un* día de Jitrik." *Reflejos* 8 (1999): 7–11.

————. "*La mayor* de Juan José Saer y el efecto modelizador del *nouveau roman.*" *Neophilologus* 75, no. 3 (1991): 399–407.

————. *La relación mundo-escritura.* Gaithersburg, MD: Hispamérica, 1993.

Stern, Mirta. "El espacio intertextual en la narrativa de Juan José Saer: instancia productiva, referente y campo de teorización de la escritura." *Revista Iberoamericana,* 125, no. 10–11 (1983): 965–81.

————. "Juan José Saer, construcción y teoría de la ficción narrativa." *Hispamérica* 37 (1984): 15–30.

————. "Juan José Saer y la construcción de una teoría del relato." *Historia de la literatura argentina* 6, 656–60. Buenos Aires: CEAL, 1982.

————. "Prólogo." In Juan José Saer, *El limonero real,* I–XI. Buenos Aires: CEAL, 1981.

Stiu, María Elina. "*La ocasión* de Juan José Saer: el enigma de la racionalidad." In *Literatura argentina y nacionalisino (Gálvez, Fogwill, Saer, Aira),* edited by Miguel Dalmaroni, 79–89. La Plata, Arg.: Facultad de Humanidades y Ciencias de la Educación, 1995.

Sztrum, Marcelo. "Variación y fronteras lingüísticas en *El entenado* de Juan José Saer." *America* 8 (1991): 259–78.

Toloza, Fernando. "Perspectivas ambigüas: indicar, desviar, insistir (sobre *El limonero real*)." *Discusión* 1 (1989): 71–74.

Torre, María Elena. "Espacios públicos / Itinerarios privados: un recorrido por Puig y Saer." *Actual* 3, no. 33 (1996): 225–38.

————. "Juan José Saer en la zona crítica." *Las operaciones de la crítica,* edited by Alberto Giordano y María Celia Vázquez, 123–132. Rosario, Arg.: Beatriz Viterbo Editora, 1998.

Vezzeti, Hugo. "La nave de los locos de Juan José Saer." *Punto de vista,* 59, (1997): 39–41.

On Argentine and Latin American Literatures

Alonso, Carlos. *The Burden of Modernity. The Rhetoric of Cultural Discourse in Spanish America.* Oxford: Oxford University Press, 1998.

————. *The Spanish American Regional Novel, Modernity and Autochthony.* Cambridge: Cambridge University Press, 1990.

Altamirano, Carlos and Beatriz Sarlo, *Ensayos argentinos: De Sarmiento a la vanguardia.* Buenos Aires: CEAL, 1983.

Avelar, Idelber. *The Untimely Present: Postdictatorial Latin American Fiction and the Task of Morning.* Durham, NC: Duke University Press, 1999.

Balderston, Daniel et al. *Ficción y política. La narrativa argentina durante el Proceso militar.* Buenos Aires: Alianza, 1987

Barbero, Martín Jesús. *De los medios a las mediaciones. Comunicación, cultura y hegemonía.* 1987. Mexico City: Ediciones G. Gili, 1991.

Borges, Jorge Luis. *El idioma de los argentinos*. Buenos Aires: Seix Barral, 1994.

———. *Leopoldo Lugones*. Buenos Aires: Troquel, 1955.

———. *Obras Completas*. Vol. 1–3. Buenos Aires: Emecé, 1974.

———. *Obras Completas*. Vol. 4. Buenos Aires: Emecé , 1996.

Calveriro, Pilar. *Poder y desaparición*. Buenos Aires: Colihue, 2001.

Chiampi, Irlemar. *Barroco y modernidad*. Mexico City: FCE, 2000.

Di Benedetto, Antonio. *Zama*. Buenos Aires: Alianza, 1985.

de la Campa, Román. *Latin Americanism*. Minneapolis: University of Minnesota Press, 1999.

Gilman, Claudia. *Entre la pluma y el fusil*. Buenos Aires: Siglo XXI, 2003.

Giordano, Alberto. *La experiencia narrativa. Juan José Saer, Felisberto Hernández, Manuel Puig*. Rosario, Arg.: Beatriz Viterbo Editora, 1992.

González, Horacio. "El boom: rastros de un palabra en la narrativa y crítica argentina." *Historia crítica de la literatura argentina 11*, edited by Noé Jitrik, 405–30. Buenos Aires: Emece, 2000.

González Echevarría, Roberto. *Myth and Archive: A Theory of Latin American Narrative*. New York: Cambridge University Press, 1990.

———. *The Voice of the Masters. Writing and Authority in Modern Latin American Literature*. Austin: University of Texas Press, 1985.

Jitrik, Noé. "Prólogo" a Alberto Vanasco, *Sin embargo Juan vivía*. Buenos Aires: Sudamericana, 1967.

King, John. *Sur: A Study of the Argentinian Literary Journal and the Development of a Culture*. Cambridge: Cambridge University Press, 1986.

Kohut, Karl and Andrea Pagni, eds. *Literatura argentina hoy: de la dictadura a la democracia*. Frankfurt am Main: Verlag, 1989

Lafforgue, Jorge, ed. *Nueva Novela latinoamericana* (2 vol.). Buenos Aires: Paidós, 1969.

Libertella, Hector. *Las sagradas escrituras*. Buenos Aires: Editorial Sudamericana, 1993.

Ludmer, Josefina. *El género gauchesco. Un tratado sobre la patria*. Buenos Aires: Sudamericana, 1988.

Mangone, Carlos and Jorge A. Warley. "La modernización de la crítica. La revista *Contorno*." In *Historia de la literatura argentina, 5*. Buenos Aires: CEAL, 1982.

Masiello, Francine. *Las escuelas argentinas de vanguardia*. Buenos Aires: Hachette, 1986.

Moreiras, Alberto. *Tercer Espacio: literatura y duelo en América Latina*. Santiago, Chile: Universidad Arcis, 1999.

Panesi, Jorge. *Críticas*. Buenos Aires: Norma, 2000.

Portantiero, Juan Carlos. *Realismo y realidad en la narrativa argentina*. Buenos Aires: Procyón, 1961.

Prieto, Adolfo. *Literatura y subdesarrollo*. Rosario, Arg.: Editorial Biblioteca, 1968.

Rama, Angel. *La ciudad letrada*. Montevideo, Uruguay: Arca, 1998.

Ramos, Julio. *Desencuentros de la modernidad en América Latina. Literatura y política en el siglo XIX*. Mexico: FCE, 1989.

Reati, Fernando. *Nombrar lo innombrable. Violencia política y novela argentina: 1975–1985*. Buenos Aires: Editorial Legasa, 1992.

Romero, José Luis. *Latinoamérica: las ciudades y las ideas*. Mexico City: Siglo XXI, 1976.

Rosa, Nicolás. "Julio Cortázar," In *Historia de la literatura argentina, 5*, 97–120. Buenos Aires: CEAL, 1982.

———. *La lengua del ausente*. Buenos Aires: Biblos, 1997.

Rosman, Silvia. *Dislocaciones culturales: nación, sujeto y comunidad en América Latina*. Rosario, Arg.: Beatriz Viterbo, 2003.

Rubione, Alfredo E., ed. *En torno al criollismo. Textos y polémicas*. Buenos Aires: CEAL, 1983

Sábato, Ernesto. *El escritor y sus fantasmas*. Buenos Aires: Aguilar, 1963.

. *Tres aproximaciones a la literatura de nuestro tiempo: Robbe-Grillet, Borges, Sartre*. Buenos Aires: Editorial Alfa Argentina, 1974.

Sarlo, Beatriz. *Una modernidad periférica. Buenos Aires, 1920 y 1930*. Buenos Aires: Nueva Visión, 1988.

Sosnowski, Saúl, ed. *Represión y reconstrucción de una cultura: el caso argentino*. Buenos Aires: Eudeba, 1988.

Spiller, Roland, ed. *La novela argentina de los años 80*. Frankfurt am Main: Verlag, 1991.

Terán, Oscar. *Nuestros años sesenta. La formación de la nueva izquierda intelectual argentina.1956–1966*. Buenos Aires: Ed. El Cielo por Asalto, 1993.

Vezzetti, Hugo. *Pasado y presente. Guerra, dictadura y sociedad en la Argentina*. Buenos Aires: Siglo XXI, 2002.

Viñas, David. *Literatura argentina y política. De Lugones a Walsh*. Buenos Aires: Ed. Sudamericana, 1996.

Other Works

Agamben, Giorgio. *Language and Death. The Place of Negativity*. Translated by Karen Pinkus with Michael Hardt. Minneapolis: University of Minnesota Press, 1991.

———. *Stanzas. Word and Phantasm in Western Culture*. Translated by Ronald Martinez. Minneapolis: University of Minnesota Press, 1993.

Alexandre-Bergues, Pascale. "Hélène," In *Dictionnaire des Mythes Féminins*, edited by Pierre Brunel, 909–15. Paris: Éds. du Rocher, 2003.

Allemand, Roger-Michel. *Le nouveau roman*. Paris: Ellipses, 1996.

———. *Nouveau roman et archetypes*. Paris: Lettres Modernes, 1993.

———. *Le nouveau roman en questions*. Paris: Lettres Modernes Minard, 1992 .

Alter, Jean. "L'enquête policier dans le nouveau roman." In *Un Nouveau Roman?* edited by J. H. Matthews. Paris: Minard, 1964.

Badiou, Alain. "L' âge des poètes." *La politique des poètes. Pourquoi des poètes en temps de détresse?* edited by Jacques Ranciére, 21–38. Paris: Albin Michel, 1992.

———. *Conditions*. Paris: Éditions du Seuil, 1992.

———. *Court traité d'ontologie transitoire*. Paris: Éditions du Minuit, 1999.

———. *L'éthique. Essai sur la conscience du mal*. Paris: Hatier, 1993.

———. *L'être et l'événement*. Paris: Éditions du Seuil, 1976.

———. *Petit traité d'inesthétique*. Paris: Éditions du Minuit, 1999.

———. "Philosophie et poésie: au point de l'innomable." *Po&sie* 64, (1993): 1–18.

Bataille, Georges. *L'expérience intérieure*. Paris: Gallimard, 1954.

———. *La part maudite et La notion de dépense*. Paris: Éditions du Minuit, 1967.

Bellemin-Nöel, J. *Hacia el inconsciente del texto*. Buenos Aires: Hachette, 1982.

Benjamin, Walter. "The Storyteller." In *Illuminations*. New York: Shocken Books, 1969, 83–109.

Bessiére, Jean. *Enigmaticité de la literature*. Paris: PUF, 1993.

———. *Quel statut pour la littérature?* Paris: PUF, 2001.

Blanchot, Maurice. *L'écriture du désastre*. Paris: Gallimard, 1980.

———. *L'entretien infini*. Paris: Gallimard, 1969.

———. *L'espace littéraire*. Paris: Gallimard, 1970.

———. "La littérature et le droit à la mort." In *La part du feu*. Paris: Gallimard, 1949.

———. *Le livre à venir*. Paris: Gallimard, 1978.

———. "La parole vaine," In *L'amitié*, Paris: Gallimard, 1971.

———. *Le pas au-delà*. Paris: Gallimard, 1971.

Bonnefoy, Yves. *Mythologies, I*. Chicago: University of Chicago Press, 1998.

Boucher, Bernardette. *La sauvage aux seins pendants*. Paris: Hermann, 1977.

Brook, Peters. "Freud's Masterplot: Question of Narrative." *Literature and Psychoanalysis*, edited by Shoshana Felman. Baltimore: Johns Hopkins University Press, 1982.

Calle-Gruber, Mireille. *L'Effet-fiction. De l'illusion romanesque*. Paris: Nizet, 1989.

Célestin, Roger. *From Radical to Cannibals*. Minneapolis: University of Minnesota Press, 1996.

Chandler, Raymond. "Casual Notes on the Mystery Novel," in Tom Hiney and Frank Mac-Shane, (ed.). *The Raymond Chandler papers: selected letters and non-fiction, 1909–1959*. New York: Atlantic Monthly Press, 2000.

Charney, Hanna. "Oedipal Patterns in the Detective Novel," *Psychoanalytic Approaches to Literature and Film*, edited by Maurice Charney and Joseph Reppen, 238–48. Rutherford, NJ: Fairleigh Dickinson University Press, 1987.

———. "Pourquoi le 'Nouveau Roman policier'?" *The French Review* 46, no. 1 (1972): 17–23.

Chase, Cynthia. "Oedipal Textuality: Reading Freud's Reading of Oedipus," In *Decomposing Figures. Rhetorical Readings in the Romantic Tradition*, 175–95. Baltimore: Johns Hopkins University Press, 1981.

Chemana, Roland, ed. *Diccionario del psicoanálisis. Diccionario actual de los significantes, conceptos y matemas del psicoanálisis*. Buenos Aires: Amorrortu, 1998.

Clastres, Pierre. *Chroniques des indiens Guayakis*. Paris: Éditions du Seuil, 1984.

Combés, Dominique. *Poésie et récit. Une rhétorique des genres*. Paris: José Corti, 1989.

Combès, Isabelle. *La tragédie cannibale chez les anciens Tupi-Guarani*. Paris: PUF, 1992.

Corominas, J. *Diccionario Crítico Etimológico de la Lengua Castellana*. Madrid: Gredos, 1961: 54–57.

Couturier, Maurice. *La figure de l'auteur*. Paris: Éditions du Seuil, 1998.

Dällembach, Lucien. *Le récit spéculaire*. Paris: Éditions du Seuil, 1978.

Dastur, Françoise. *Heidegger and the Question of Time*. Atlantic Highlands, NJ: Humanity Press, 1998.

Debord, Guy. *La société de le spectacle*. Paris: Gallimard, 1972.

de Certeau, Michel. *Heterologies. Discourse on the Other*. Minneapolis: University of Minnesota Press, 1986.

———. *The Writing of History*. New York: Columbia University Press, 1988.

Deleuze, Gilles. *Difference and Repetition*. Translated by Paul Patton. New York: Columbia University Press, 1994.

———. *Francis Bacon. Logique de la sensation*. Paris: Éditions du Seuil, 2002.

Deleuze, Gilles and F. Guattari. *What is Philosophy?* New York: Columbia University Press, 1994.

Del Lungo, Andrea. *L'incipit romanesque*. Paris: Éditions du Seuil, 2003.

———. "Pour une poétique del incipit." *Poétique* 94 (1998): 131–52.

De Man, Paul. *Allegories of Reading*. New Haven, CT: Yale University Press, 1979.

Derrida, Jacques. *La Carte Postale*. Paris: Flammarion, 1980.

———. *Of Grammatology*. Translated by Gayatri C. Spivak. Baltimore: Johns Hopkins University Press, 1998.

———. *Psychè. Les inventions de l'autre*. Paris: Galilée, 1988.

———. *Writing and Difference*. Translated by Alan Bass. Chicago: University of Chicago Press, 1978.

———. *La vérité en peinture*. Paris: Champs/ Flammarion, 1978.

Dubrovsky, Serge. *La place de la Madeleine, écriture et fantasme chez Proust*. Paris: Mercure de France, 1974.

Dugastes-Portes, Francine. *Le nouveau roman: une césure dans l'histoire du récit*. Paris: Nathan, 2001.

Eisensweig, Uri. *Le récit impossible: forme et sens du roman policier*. Paris: Christian Bourgois, 1986.

Equipo NayA. *Diccionario de Mitos y Leyendas*. http://www.cuco.com.ar/.

Escoubas, Eliane. *Imago Mundi. Topographie de l'art*. Paris: Galilée: 1997.

Ewert, J. "A Thousand and Other Mysteries." *New Literary History* 56, no. 4 (1980): 263–78.

Felman, Shoshana. "De Sophocle à Japrisot (via Freud), ou pourquoi le policier?" *Littérature* 49 (1983): 23–42.

———. *Testimony. Crises in Literature, Psychoanalysis and History*. London: Routledge, 1992.

Fenves, Peter. *Chatter*. Baltimore: Johns Hopkins University Press, 1984

Foucault, Michel. *Language, Counter-Memory, Practice*. Edited by Donald Bouchard. Ithaca, NY: Cornell University Press, 1977.

———. *The Order of Things. An Archeology of the Human Sciences*. New York: Vintage, 1973.

———. "La pensée du dehors." In *Dits et écrits I*, 1954–1975, 546–67. Paris: Gallimard, 1994.

Frappier Mazur, Lucienne. *Sade et l'écriture de l'orgie*. Paris: Nathan, 1991.

Freud, Sigmund. *Collected Papers, III–IV*. London: Hogarth Press, 1952–53.

———. *The Complete Letters of Sigmund Freud to Wilhem Fliess (1887–1904)*. Translated and edited by Jeffrey Moussaieff Masson. Cambridge, MA: Belknap Press, 1985.

———. "El Delirio y los sueños en la 'Gradiva' de W. Jensen" y "El creador literario y el fantasma." In *Obras Completas, IX*. Buenos Aires: Amorrortu, 1981.

———. "Estudios sobre la histeria," *Obras Completas, III*. Buenos Aires: Amorrortu, 1981.

———. "Fragmento de análisis de un caso de histeria. Tres ensayos de teoría sexual y otras obras." In *Obras Completas, VII*. Buenos Aires: Amorrortu, 1981.

———. "La interpretación de los sueños." In *Obras Completas, IV–V*. Buenos Aires: Amorrortu, 1981.

Fusillo. Massimo. *Naissance du roman*. Paris: Éditions du Seuil, 2002.

García Düttmann, Alexander. *La Parole donnée. Mémoire et promesse*. Paris: Galilée, 1989.

Genette, Gérard. *Fiction et diction*. Paris: Éditions du Seuil, 1991.

———. *Figures III*. Paris: Éditions du Seuil, 1972.

———. *Introduction à l'architexte*. Paris: Éditions du Seuil, 1979.

———. *Métalepse*. Paris: Éditions du Seuil, 2004.

———. *Nouveau discours du récit*. Paris: Éditions du Seuil, 1983.

Gibson, Andrew. *Postmodernity, Ethics and the Novel: From Leavis to Lévinas*. London: Routledge, 1999.

Glaudes, Pierre. "Après coup." *Revue de Sciences Humaines* 50 (1995): 240–60.

Grimal, Pierre. *The Dictionary of Classical Mythology*. London: Blackwell, 1996.

Guerrero, Gustavo. *Poétique et poésie lyrique*. Paris: Éditions du Seuil, 2002.

Hamon, Philippe. *Introducción al análisis de lo descriptivo*. Buenos Aires: Hachette, 1988.

Harari, Roberto. *Fantasma, ¿fin del análisis?* Buenos Aires: Nueva Visión, 1998.

Hartog, François. *Le miroir d'Hérodote: Essais sur la representation de l'autre*. Paris: Gallimard, 1980.

Heidegger, Martin. *Being and Time*. Translated by John Macquarrie and Edward Robinson. New York: Harper & Row, 1962.

Holquist, Michael. "Whodunit and Other Questions: Metaphysical Detective Stories in Post-War Fiction." *New Literary History* 3 (1971–72): 135–56.

Hulmes, Peter. *Colonial Encounters. Europe and the Native Caribbean, 1492–1787*. London: Routledge, 1986.

Jakobson, Roman. *Essais de linguistique générale*. Paris: Éditions de Minuit, 1969.

Janvier, Ludovic. *Une parole exigeante: le nouveau roman*. Paris: Éditions de Minuit, 1964.

Kilito, Abdelfattah. *L'auteur et ses doubles*. Paris: Éditions du Seuil, 1984.

Kristeva, Julia. *Pouvoirs de l'horreur. Essai sur l'abjection*. Paris: Éditions du Seuil, 1980.

———. *La révolte intime. Pouvoirs et limites de la psychanalyse II*. Paris: Fayard, 1997.

Lacan, Jacques. *Autres écrits*. Paris: Éditions du Seuil, 2001, 11–22.

———. "Kant avec Sade," In *Écrits*. Paris: Éditions du Seuil, 1968.

———. *Le Séminaire de J. Lacan, Livre IV: La Relation d' objet*. Paris: Éditions du Seuil, 1995.

———. *Le Séminaire Livre V. Les Formations de l'inconscient*. Paris: Éditions du Seuil, 1998.

———. *Le Séminaire Livre VII. L'Ethique de la psychanalyse (1959–60)*. Paris: Éditions du Seuil, 1986.

———. Le Séminaire Livre XVI. Logique du fantasme (1966–67). Unpublished.

Lacoue-Labarthe, Philippe and Jean-Luc Nancy. *Le titre de la lettre*. Paris: Galilée, 1992.

Laplanche, Jean and Jean-Bertrand Pontalis. "Fantasma originario, fantasmas de los orígenes, orígen del fantasma." In *El (lo) inconsciente freudiano y el psicoanálisis francés contemporáneo*, 103–43. Buenos Aires: Nueva Visión, 1969.

Leclaire, Serge. *On tue un enfant: un essai sur le narcissisme primaire et la pulsion de mort*. Paris: Éditions du Seuil, 1975.

———. *Démasquer le réel*. Paris: Éditions du Seuil, 1990.

Le Galliot, Jean. *Psicoanálisis y lenguajes literarios. Teoría y práctica*. Buenos Aires: Hachette, 1977.

de Léry, Jean. *Histoire d' un Voyage faict en la terre du Bresil,* (1578). Paris: Libr. Générale Française, 1994.

Lestringant, Frank. *Le cannibale. Grandeur et décadence*. Paris: Perrin, 1994.

———. *L'Hugenot et le sauvage*. Paris: Flammarion, 1997.

———. "The Philosopher's Breviary: Jean de Léry in the Enlightenment" *Representations* 35 (1991): 120–37.

Létoublon, Françoise. "Europe." *Dictionnaire des Mythes Féminins*, edited by Pierre Brunel, 698–706. Paris: Editions du Rocher, 2003.

Levin, Samuel. *Linguistic Structures in Poetry*. The Hague: Mouton, 1972.

Lévinas, Emmanuel. *En Decouvrant l'existence avec Husserl et Heidegger*. Paris: Vrin, 1970.

———. *La mort et le temps*. Paris: L'Herne, 1991.

Lévi-Strauss, Claude. *Tristes tropiques*. Paris: Plon, 1955.

Lyotard, Jean-François. *La condición postmoderna*. Madrid: Cátedra, 1982.

———. *Dérive à partir de Marx et Freud*. Paris: 10/18, 1973.

———. *Discours Figure*. Paris: Klinksieck, 2002.

———. *L'Inhuman: Causeries sur le temps*. Paris: Galilée, 1988.

Maldiney, Henry. "L' Irreductible." *Epokhè* 3 (1993): 11–49.

Mallarmé, Stéphane. *Œuvres complètes*. Paris: Gallimard, Bibliothèque de La Pléiade, 1945.

Mannoni, Maud. *D'un impossible à l' autre*. Paris: Éditions du Seuil, 2000.

Merleau-Ponty, Maurice. *Phénoménologie de la perception*. Paris: Gallimard, 1945.

Mervalle, Patricia and Susan E. Sweeny. *Detecting Texts. The Metaphysical Detective Story From Poe To Postmodernism*. Philadelphia: University of Pennsylvania Press, 1999.

Miller, J. Hillis. *The Ethics of Reading*. New York: Columbia University Press, 1987.

————. *Reading Narrative*. Norman: University of Oklahoma Press, 1998.

Miller, Jacques-Alain. *Dos Dimensiones clínicas: síntoma y fantasma*. Buenos Aires: Ediciones Manantial, 1989.

Nancy, Jean-Luc. *Être Singulier Pluriel*. Paris: Galilée, 1996.

————. *Le sens du monde*. Paris: Galilée, 1993.

Nouvelle Revue de Psychanalyse. "*Destin du cannibalisme*." Paris: Gallimard, 1972.

Ovidio. *Metamorphoses*. Loeb Classical Library, Cambridge, MA: Harvard University Press, 1994.

Pederson-Krag, Geraldine. "Detective Stories and the Primal Scene." *Psychoanalytic Quarterly* 18, (1949): 207–14.

Platón. *Phaedrus*. Translated by Harold North Flower, Loeb Classical Library, Cambridge, MA: Harvard University Press, 1995.

————. *Symposium*. Translated by Harold North Flower, Loeb Classical Library, Cambridge, MA: Harvard University Press, 1993.

Prince, Gerard. *Narratology: The Form and Functioning of Narrative*. The Hague: Mouton, 1982.

Proust, Marcel. *A la recherche du temps perdu*. Paris: Gallimard, Bibliothèque de la Pléiade, 1996.

Rabant, Claude. "Œdipe," *Encyclopedia Universal*. Paris: PUF, 1998. 403.

Rabatel, Alain. *Une histoire du point de vue*. Paris: Klincksieck, 1997.

Rawson, Claude. "Cannibalism and Fiction,"*Genre* 10–11 (1977): 132–45.

————. "Indians and Irish: Montaigne, Swift and the Cannibal Question." *Modern Language Quarterly* 3 (1992): 43–76.

————. "Narrative and the Proscribed Act: Homer, Euripides and the Literature of Cannibalism," In *Literary Theory and Criticism. Festschrift in Honor of René Wellek, Part II*, edited by J. Strelka. Bern, Switz.: Peter Lang, 1985.

Real Academia Española de la Lengua. *Diccionario de la Real Academia Española*. Madrid: RAE, 1980.

Ricardou, Jean, ed. *Le nouveau roman*. Paris: Éditions du Seuil, Points, 1973.

————. *Nouveau roman, hier, ajourd'hui*. Paris: 10/18,1972.

————. *Pour une théorie du nouveau roman*. Paris: Éditions du Seuil, Tel Quel, 1971.

————. *Problemes du nouveau roman*. Paris: Éditions du Seuil, 1967.

————. *Nouveaux problèmes du roman*. Paris: Éditions du Seuil, 1978.

Ricoeur, Paul. *Time and Narrative*. Translated by Kathleen McLaughlin and David Pellauer. Chicago: Chicago University Press, 1983.

Riera, Gabriel. "Abyssal Grounds: Heidegger and Lacan on Truth." *Qui parle?* 9, no. 2, (1997): 70–97.

————. "For an 'Ethics of Mystery': Philosophy and the Poem." *Alain Badiou: Philosophy and Its Conditions*, edited by Gabriel Riera, 61–85. Albany: SUNY Press, 2005.

————. "*The Possibility of the Poetic Said*: Between Allusion and Commentary (*Ingratitude*, or Blanchot in Levinas, II)." *Angelaki: Journal in the Theoretical Humanities* 9, no.3 (December 2004): 121–35.

Rimbaud, Arthur. *Œuvres Complètes*. Paris: Gallimard, 1972.

Robbe-Grillet, Alain. *Pour un nouveau roman*. Paris: Éditions de Minuit, 1963.

Robert, Marthe. *Roman des origines et origines du roman*. Paris: Grasset, 1972.

Romano, Claude. *L'événement et le temps*. Paris: PUF, 1999.

Ruwet, Nicolas . *Langage, musique, poésie*. Paris: Éditions du Seuil, 1972.

Sartre, Jean-Paul. *L'être et le néant. Essaie d' ontologie phénomènologique*. Gallimard: Paris, 1943.

———. *L' imaginaire*. Paris: Gallimard, 1940.

———. *Qu'est-ce que la littérature?* Paris: Gallimard, 1948.

Scarpetta, Guy. *L'âge d'or du roman*. Paris: Grasset, 1996.

Schelling, W. *Philosophy of Art*. Minneapolis: University of Minnesota Press, 1989.

Sirvent, Michel. "Reader-Investigators in the Post-Nouveau Roman." *Romanic Review* 88, no. 2 (1997): 315–35.

Sophocles. *Oedipus, the King*. Translated and commentary by Thomas Gould. Englewood Cliffs: Prentice Hall, 1970.

Spanos, William. "The Detective and the Boundary: Some Notes on the Postmodern Literary Imagination." *Boundary 2*, no. 1.1 (1972): 147–68.

Staden, Hans. *The True History of its Captivity*. London: Routledge and Sons, 1928.

Szondi, Peter. *Versuch über das Tragische, Schriften*, I. Frankfurt am Main: Suhrkamp, 1978.

Taminiaux, Jacques. *Le théatre des philosophes*. Grenoble, France: Millon, 1995.

Todorov, Tzvetan. "The Typology of Detective Fiction." In *Poetics of Prose*, 42–52. Ithaca, NY: Cornell University Press, 1977.

Vallejo, Cesar. *Los heraldos negros*. Buenos Aires: Losada, 1976.

Vernant, Jean-Pierre and Pierre Vidal Naquet. *Œdipe et ses mythes*. Paris: Complexe, 2001.

Viveiros de Castro, Eduardo. *Arawaté: os Deuses Canibais*. Río de Janeiro: Zahar, 1986

Wolf, Nelly. *Une littérature sans histoire: essaie sur le nouveau roman*. Paris: Droz, 1995.

Index